huyukh

Sobeir
Basra

Mohammerah
Abadah
Bandar-i-Shahpur

Dahman
Sabukah
KUWAIT
Kuwait

BUBIAN I.
FELEJE I.
KARAGH I.

Shiraz

Bushire

Firuzabad

Lo

zafah

Maghris

PERSIAN

BU ALI I.

Mejmah
El Tueim

Qatif

Ras
Tannurah

Manama

Ras Reccan

GUL

KENN I.

Hoolah

Wab
Djuir
Meborraa

BAHREIN

WARDENS
Okai

QATAR

Doha

SATIEM I.

Bedaa

BIER AB

Sedus

HASA

Hofuf

yah
anfunah
urfah

Riyâdh

Dhalum

Naam

Hauta

Shaabar

EAST INDIA
COMPANY
IS.

Hajar

Ab

Katan

TRUCIAL

Tropic of Cancer

D

Laila

A

I   RUBA'   AL   KHA

(Great Sandy Desert)

Hammond World Atlas ~ 1937

Discovery!

The Search for Arabian Oil

Also by Wallace Stegner

Discovery!

The Search for Arabian Oil

Wallace Stegner

Selwa Press

Selwa Press
www.selwapress.com

First U.S. Edition
LCCN: 2006940912
ISBN: 978-0-9701157-4-4
Copyright © 2007 by Selwa Press.

Original edition published by
Middle East Export Press, Beirut, Lebanon, 1971
LCCN: 74-148026
All rights reserved.

Stegner, Wallace Earle, 1909-1993.
    Discovery! : the search for Arabian oil / Wallace
Stegner. — 1st hardcover ed.
    p. cm.
    Includes bibliographical references and index.
    Originally published in 1971.
    ISBN 978-0-9701157-4-4

    1. Arabian American Oil Company. 2. Petroleum
industry and trade—Saudi Arabia—History.   I. Title.
II. Title: Search for Arabian oil.

HD9576.S35A77 2007   338.2'7282'09538
                 QBI06-600345

Selwa Press 1101 Portola St. Vista, CA 92084
Printed in the United States of America
10   9   8   7   6   5   4   3   2   1

Arabia retains to an extraordinary degree
the power of conquering hearts.

Sir Arnold T. Wilson ~ *1931*

Contents

Foreword

Go out to your local library or bookstore and take down from
the shelf any of the renowned works of Wallace Stegner, one of
the most admired American writers of the 20th century. Before
the title page there will be a list of his books. There are the great
novels: *Big Rock Candy Mountain*, *Crossing to Safety*, and *Angle of
Repose*, for which he won the Pulitzer Prize. And there is
accomplished non-fiction, too, including his biographies of
Bernard de Voto and John Wesley Powell, and his late-life personal
testament, *Where the Bluebird Sings to the Lemonade Springs: Living
and Writing in the West*. What will not appear is any reference to
one of Stegner's most original and offbeat volumes, *Discovery!
The Search for Arabian Oil*. That is because this book has never
before been published in the United States and is unknown even
to many of Stegner's fans. A paperback version published in Beirut
in 1971 can be found in some libraries, but it is read mostly by
students of the early history of modern Saudi Arabia, a limited
circle of specialists.

The story of *Discovery!* and the peculiar fate of Stegner's
manuscript is a complicated and murky tale, almost as interesting
as the story recounted in its pages. But the book's odd history
does not detract from its merit as narrative. It is a brisk, muscular

and well-reported – if occasionally breathless – account of the creation and development of the oil industry in Saudi Arabia by American geologists and engineers in the 1930s and 1940s, one of the most important developments of modern Middle Eastern history.

Readers unfamiliar with the story of oil or the history of Saudi Arabia may not be aware of the grand and improbable drama that unfolded in the Arabian wasteland after the signing of the first oil exploration agreement in 1933. Stegner brings that drama to life with headlong prose and colorful characters, none of whom he had to invent. Even readers to whom that story might seem old news will find a wealth of new detail, crisply delivered. If nothing else, *Discovery!* is a tour de force of reporting, because Stegner spent only two weeks in the desert kingdom in 1955, yet through his interviews with oil company people and study of a substantial documentary record he produced a comprehensive narrative.

The country we know as Saudi Arabia was created in 1932 by Abdul Aziz ibn Saud, a warrior prince from a desert tribe who swept across the Arabian peninsula in the early years of the 20th century to establish the family rule of the House of Saud, which continues today. All kings who have followed Abdul Aziz have been his sons.

Abdul Aziz claimed a prize of seemingly dubious value. The country he created is vast but mostly barren, the terrain flinty and inhospitable. In the early 1930s it was one of the poorest and least developed countries on earth, its revenue sources meager, its people mostly illiterate and afflicted with diseases long ago brought under control elsewhere, the barren land uncrossed by roads or power lines. Its importance to the rest of the world lay entirely in its historic position as the homeland of Islam: the Prophet Muhammad's holy cities of Mecca and Medina were incorporated into Saudi Arabia during Abdul Aziz's decades of conquest, and pilgrims from around the Muslim world flocked to them each year.

A few adventurers believed, and the King hoped, that the unpromising landscape might contain reserves of oil, for the geology of the eastern region of the kingdom was similar to that of Bahrain, the small island offshore, where oil had been discovered a few years earlier. And so it was in 1933, in the depths of the Great Depression, that Saudi Arabia entered into an oil exploration contract with Standard Oil Company of California, a development that would change the modern world.

The task of mapping the geology of Arabia, finding likely sites to drill, sinking the wells, creating the tanks and pipes and separators and moving the oil to refineries – work performed in harsh conditions, under merciless sun, in a desolate landscape that provided no support, in a place where local workers knew nothing of electricity or machinery and every last nail and bolt and length of wire had to be imported – was carried out by California Arabian Standard Oil Company, or CASOC, a Standard subsidiary. Shortly before the end of World War II, three other major oil companies, Texaco, Exxon and Mobil, joined Chevron (previously Standard Oil Company of California) in a consortium known as the Arabian American Oil Company, or ARAMCO. In 1955 Aramco commissioned Stegner to write this history. By then the early days of geologists camping in tents and traveling by camel were well in Aramco's past; it was a large industrial enterprise based in an American-style company town, Dhahran, that it had created out of nothing in eastern Saudi Arabia.

Stegner (1909–1993) was by the mid-1950s well established on the faculty of Stanford University, where he ran the creative writing program, but it was a time when his books were not selling well and he needed extra money. Besides, the real-life story of Casoc appealed to Stegner, because it offered some of the favorite themes of his fiction – rugged men on the frontier, the allure of women in remote outposts, the impact on local people of what he calls "industrial civilization." He saw the oil industry in Saudi Arabia as comparable to the mines and railroads of the American

West. "Dhahran" substitutes easily for "Leadville" in this passage from *Angle of Repose:* "A camp that strikes it rich in the middle of a depression speaks as urgently to the well-trained as to the untrained. In Leadville, Harvard men mucked in prospect holes, graduates of MIT and Yale Sheffield Scientific School worked as paymasters and clerks and gunguards, every mine office was approached daily by some junior engineer with a diploma and a new mustache. . . . Leadville roared toward civilization like a runaway train."

He made the comparison explicit in evaluating the transformation this "industrial civilization" wrought on Arabia. "Industrial civilization made its way among the Indians of North America in the form of needles, awls, knives, axes, guns, woolen cloth," he wrote. A similar phenomenon developed in eastern Saudi Arabia when the oil men "began to tinker with the machines that made water and climate, and the smells that drove away the flies. And long before anyone knew the phrase, a revolution of rising expectations had begun. Saudi Arabia would never be the same."

Critics of the oil enterprise and of the way Casoc operated have tended to glamorize the pre-industrial way of life that oil swept away, as if it represented some kind of unspoiled purity, but in three decades of visiting Saudi Arabia I have never met anyone who believed the country was better off without the roads, electricity, running water and schools that oil brought. In all material ways, Stegner's belief that the discovery of the world's greatest reserves of crude oil was beneficial to Saudi Arabia is correct.

Stegner begins *Discovery!* with a description of Jiddah, the city on the Red Sea coast where the painstaking negotiations that led to the oil concession agreement took place. In 1933, Jiddah was a hot, smelly, ramshackle port town without electricity or running water, an environment quite alien to the oilmen, who swallowed their discomfort in pursuit of the prize. "Wearily the duelists fought it out," Stegner wrote, in bargaining that went on for more than three months, on one side frustrated Americans, on the other the King's representatives who were, as Stegner notes, "hardheaded, smart, patient, tenacious, wary . . . bargainers worthy of anyone's steel."

In those words Stegner shows his appreciation for one of the unlikely but inescapable truths about the early agreement between a giant corporation from the United States – the world's greatest industrial and economic power – and Saudi Arabia, which was at the opposite pole of human development. This was that the relationship was not so unequal as it might seem, because each side had something the other very much wanted: Saudi Arabia had the oil, the Americans had the capital and the technology required to produce it and get it to market. Different as they were culturally and materially, they needed each other. The Americans were not colonizers; they entered Saudi Arabia by invitation, not at gunpoint, and at any time they could be asked to leave.

Readers of *Discovery!* will find it populated by colorful characters who might have been sent by Central Casting: the bearded, rough-and-ready American geologists and engineers sweating and shouting as their cars sank in the sand, the shrewd Saudi finance minister Abdullah Suleiman, the impetuous Krug Henry and his whirlwind romance with a young Lebanese woman, the intrepid young guide known as Khamis, the spunky Anita Burleigh, the first American woman to travel across the country and meet the King. These characters appealed to Stegner's view of how frontier lands were brought into the modern era through the grit, determination, patience and courage of strong men and loyal women. And his account of Casoc's greatest moment of tragedy, the lethal explosion and fire that consumed Well No. 12 in 1939, makes a gripping narrative all by itself.

Stegner's account of how the relationship among these characters grew and prospered is largely favorable to the company, as would be expected in a commissioned work, but it does not ignore the disputes that inevitably arose between host and guest, or the dissatisfaction of the local workers. In the oil fields, Stegner observed, "the contact was man to man, and since each man was the product of a culture profoundly different from that which had formed the other there were inevitable incidents of misunderstanding, prejudice, conflicting notions of law and justice."

Commissioning Wallace Stegner to write an approved history of the oil venture's early days – a history that would accentuate the positive and show the oil company in a favorable light – was only one element of an extensive public relations effort that Aramco carried on for decades. The firm financed the production of a full-length pseudo-documentary film, *Arabia: Island of Allah*, that celebrated the feats of King Abdul Aziz and the material progress that came with oil. Fredric March was the narrator. A handbook for employees was expanded into a handsome coffee-table book, *Aramco and Its World*, and made available in the United States and Europe. It told the history of the oil patch, but it also celebrated Islamic history and culture. The company created a glossy magazine, *Aramco World*, to advance the same values.

Any serious business venture makes some investment in public relations, and Aramco's made sense in the context of the 1950s, when Aramco and its parent companies in the United States had ample reason to try to burnish the company's image, support the U.S.-Saudi alliance and present the American record in Saudi Arabia in the best light. Discontent over living conditions and wages was breeding agitation among the Arab workers. Iran, just across the Gulf, nationalized its oil industry in 1951, putting the idea of a state takeover in play throughout the region.

After the Egyptian revolution of 1952, the fiery Gamal Abdel Nasser, a secular populist, began denouncing Saudi Arabia and the House of Saud's arrangements with the oil company. Since Aramco could retain the concession only if the House of Saud remained in power and looked with favor upon the oil company,

Aramco's executives rightly viewed public relations as an important tool of corporate diplomacy.

And therein lay the root of their problem with Stegner's manuscript. He confronted the same difficulty faced by every artist who creates not because he is moved to do so but because some patron is paying him and will demand a suitable product. Stegner believed in the merits of the early oil men, believed in their energy, foresight and good will. He believed that the development of the oil industry was beneficial to Saudi Arabia and its people. But he also believed in his own honesty, and wished his narrative to be sufficiently credible and accurate to justify putting his name on it.

Writing at a furious pace, Stegner completed a draft manuscript within a few months after his visit to Saudi Arabia and sent it to Aramco's New York office in March 1956. That was a tumultuous year in the Middle East – Nasser nationalized the Suez Canal, and Israel, Britain and France went to war against Egypt – and the senior people at Aramco were preoccupied by those events and by King Saud's visit to the United States. Stegner heard nothing about his manuscript for the rest of the year. Inside Aramco, however, discomfort was brewing over what he had submitted.

Stegner felt that honesty compelled him to raise some issues that the company did not want ventilated in public. Company officials, who were paying for this project, understandably wanted to present a positive image that would please, or at least not offend, their Saudi hosts. Throughout 1957, Aramco executives haggled with Stegner over revisions to the manuscript. Stegner finally let his frustration spill over in a long letter to H. O. Thompson, an Aramco vice president, on January 24, 1958.

"This kind of book may be either of two things: It may be frankly a 'Company history,' written by Company employees according to Company specification and published with the Company's backing or at the Company's expense," he wrote.

"This makes it, essentially, a public relations job. Or it may be a book written by an outside observer, with more or less cooperation from the Company and with greater or less access to its records, but representing his interpretation of people and events and published under his name and at his responsibility. Done on this basis, its aim is the truth of history insofar as its author can attain it, and not the immediate and uncritical promotion of Company purposes and prestige.

"What we have been doing so far, I am afraid, is straddling two stools – having me, as a consultant on the Company's payroll, do a book that will represent my best understanding of Aramco's first ten years in Arabia, and that may be published under my name, but that at the same time will be satisfactory to the company and subject to its approval or disapproval." In the end, neither party ever got entirely what it wanted.

In March 1959, Thomas C. Barger, who began with Casoc as a geologist in the early days and rose to be chief executive of Aramco, wrote in a letter to another company official that while he had no problems with the manuscript upon a first reading, his unease had been growing for some time. He said he and another senior executive could not see how publication would advance Aramco's interests. "If you concur," he concluded, "we would both be well pleased if the manuscript were put into the files, to be looked at ten years from now."

Nothing more was heard of the manuscript until 1967, when it was unearthed by Paul Hoye, a young journalist who was just beginning a two-decade career as editor of *Aramco World*. With Stegner's assent, the manuscript – largely purged of material that had alarmed Aramco executives – was published in the magazine in fourteen installments.

Those became the fourteen chapters of a paperback book edition that was published in Beirut in 1971. That edition carried a notation that the text was "as abridged for *Aramco World* magazine," which was unnecessary because no other version had ever appeared, and this served only to alert readers that something might be missing.

The cover copy of the Beirut version said that Stegner was "an author, teacher, critic and conservationist. Born and raised amid the plains and hills of the American West – Iowa, North Dakota, Montana and Nevada – he drew from his experiences there the deep respect for and perceptive knowledge of nature, and people close to nature, explicit in such books as *The Big Rock Candy Mountain*, *All the Little Live Things*, and *The Sound of Mountain Water*."

Stegner not only assented to publication of this version, he also supplied a new introduction for the paperback edition. In it, he dismissed critics of the American role in Saudi Arabia as "hostile propagandists" and praised the "spirit of goodwill and generosity toward the Saudi Arabs as people" that he found among the Aramco personnel.

Aramco was nationalized in stages during the 1970s and has been fully state-owned for many years. Its senior executives are all Saudi Arabs, most of them products of the training programs that Aramco put in place half a century ago. The American oil companies that created Aramco still operate some facilities in the kingdom, such as refineries and lube oil plants, although they no longer have any concessionary status and must compete for contracts against all the other companies of the world. But Dhahran is still an American-style company town, the business climate there is entirely American, and the Saudi Arabs who run the enterprise tend to speak of their American mentors with respect and even affection. They concur with the verdict Stegner delivered in his introduction to the Beirut edition of *Discovery!* – that "American oil development in the Middle East has been, all things considered, responsible and fair."

Thomas W. Lippman
May 28th, 2006

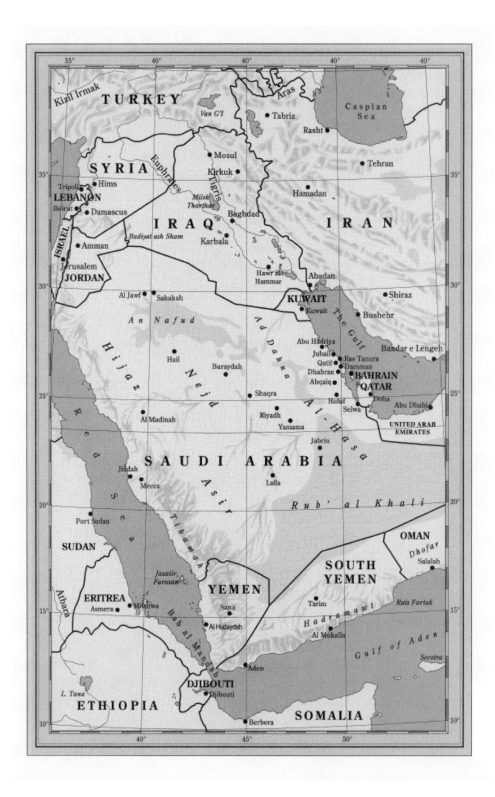

Introduction

The Arabian Peninsula, technically a part of the continent of Asia, is actually almost a separate entity. It lies like a boot-shaped plug between Africa and Asia, surrounded except on the north by water: westward is the Red Sea, southward the Gulf of Aden and the Arabian Sea, eastward the Gulf of Oman and the body of water most people call the Persian Gulf but which is firmly called the Arabian Gulf in Saudi Arabia. Its heel is almost within sight of the African coast where Ethiopia and French Somaliland come together; its horned toe, as if by a hard kick, has dented in the coast of Iran across the Strait of Hormuz.

Of this enormous boot, a subcontinent in size, the Kingdom of Saudi Arabia occupies all but the heel, the sole, and the toe. The heel is Yemen, the sole is South Yemen (formerly Aden) and Dhufar, the toe is Oman and the Trucial States up to and including the Shaikhdom of Qatar. Along the top of the boot Saudi Arabia is partially buffered from Iraq by a diamond-shaped neutral zone.

A similar zone which once separated the kingdom from Kuwait is still maintained as an area where oil wealth is shared but has been recently divided between the two countries as separate administrative areas. The rest of the way the northern boundary runs through stony deserts as far as Jordan, and then, in a series of angles, jogs southward and westward to a twelve-mile strip of Jordanian territory along the Gulf of Aqaba. This strip was part of a recent territorial swap with Saudi Arabia aimed at rectifying some of the more awkward borders and providing Jordan with more access to the sea than could be provided by the Port of Aqaba. Along much of its south and southeast borders, Saudi Arabia's boundaries remain politically imprecise and, in certain places, disputed.

Despite such imprecision, however, something may be learned from the maps. On one of the most recent, Saudi Arabia shows as four great geographical regions: the Hijaz and Asir along the Red Sea, Najd in the desert heart of the Peninsula, and the Eastern Province, or al-Hasa, along the Arabian Gulf.

You will not see on that map any of the customary blue patches that indicate bodies of water, and the blue lines that look like rivers are only wadis, dry watercourses that run, if ever, only during a rain. Except in the mountainous southern coastal regions, the Arabian Peninsula is one of the world's most barren lands – desert mountains, flint plains, salt flats, wildernesses of drifting sand. Throughout the land there is no river and no real lake; except in the Asir highlands the rainfall nowhere exceeds a few inches a year, and some of the uttermost deserts, such as the Rub' al-Khali, in the south, may see no rain for years on end.

Yet look for a moment at the Eastern Province, the region along the Gulf from Qatar to the Kuwait–Saudi Arabia Neutral Zone. It shows, in the density and variety of its map symbols, a quite surprising number of the installations peculiar to modern industrial civilization.

By comparison with the rest of the Peninsula, and by comparison with much of the Middle East, this northeast corner of Saudi Arabia is fairly densely netted with both secondary and primary roads, including a system of paved highways from Kuwait south as far as Selwa and another interior link toward Riyadh. The crossed line of the Saudi Government Railroad comes southwest from Dammam, on the coast, through Abqaiq and Hofuf and Haradh, where it turns due west toward al-Kharj and the national capital of Riyadh.

And not merely roads. Other symbols are packed into the map of this region: a red ship to show the marine terminal and major port at Ras Tanura; red arrows to indicate eleven airfields between Riyadh and Ras al-Mish'ab, just under the border of the Kuwait Neutral Zone; at Ras Tanura the red tower symbol of a refinery; in all the area from al-Mish'ab south, and especially in the area southwest from Ras Tanura, a web of red that indicates pipelines, and all along the web the red squares that show pump stations or gas-oil separator plants.

The place names, especially along the coast, mark real towns, not merely landmarks as so often is the case in this part of the country. Notice too the irregular pink splotches. There are relatively small ones such as Zuluf and Marjan, in the Gulf off Safaniya, other small ones on the shore at Abu Hadriya, Khursaniyah, Fadhili, Berri, Qatif, and Dammam, and a large one far inland at Khurais, in the belt of red desert known as the Dahna. There is a long oval one surrounding the town of Abqaiq, a small thin one at Fazran, and an enormous one, reaching across two degrees of latitude, between Fazran and Haradh. These are the Saudi Arab oil fields, the foundation on which so much of the Eastern Province and the nation itself is built, and one of the key elements in what, by 1970, had become a dangerously escalated Middle East situation. Check two of the larger ones against the mileage scale. The Abqaiq field is 33 miles long; the Ghawar, the biggest oil structure ever drilled anywhere, is 140 miles. As most of the world knows by now, one American company, the Arabian American Oil Company – ARAMCO – operates them all.

The red lines that indicate pipelines tie these fields to the major centers; to Abqaiq and Dhahran, the administrative center, to the refinery at Ras Tanura, and to the Bahrain Petroleum Company's refinery on the nearby island of Bahrain. From Qatif a red line reaches northwest to Qaisumah, just under the Saudi Arabian and Iraqi Neutral Zone. From Qaisumah a continuation, a long continuation, heads into the high northern desert on its way to the tank farm and marine terminal at Sidon, on the Levantine coast south of Beirut, 1,070 miles from the pipeline's beginning. This line marks the route of the Trans-Arabian Pipe Line – Tapline – an extension of the Aramco operation.

Tapline, which crosses turbulent Syria and Jordan and a patch of territory seized by Israel in the 1967 war, has had a shaky time since the war. Yet whatever happens, Tapline has already left an indelible mark on Arabia.

Since 1950, when the pipeline was completed, the life of those northern deserts has changed more than in the preceding thousand years. Its service road, now paved with asphalt, has become a new caravan route, radically altering the historic flow of trade, and used by trucks instead of camel trains. In its earliest days, wells drilled in connection with the construction and maintenance of the line changed, within a few months, the habits of Bedouins who in all the tribal memory had moved in certain directions at certain seasons, drawn by the gravitational pull of water.

Now they tended to cluster around the ample wells and watering tanks constructed by the company. One time at Ar'ar, near Tapline's Badanah pump station, there were concentrated 25,000 camels. That, to anyone who has heard even 10 camels in chorus, is a lot of camels. Since each camel, if water is available, will drink 50 gallons every three or four days, the demand on the tanks was of the order of 300,000 to 400,000 gallons a day, until the Saudi Arab government could arrange for some of the Bedouins to move off and ease the strain on water and forage – as well as lessen the work of the bulldozers assigned to periodically shove away the hills of dung from around the tanks.

By no means would or could all of the visitors move on, for within the first six years of its existence, Ar'arS – a town created entirely by the pipeline company and laid out by Tapline engineers

— had a population of 5,000 Arabs actively busy in turning from wanderers into townsmen. The other pump stations saw the same sort of growth. The closest parallel in history, probably, is what happened in western Canada when the Hudson's Bay Company, likewise a great company with a large concession in a mighty territory, established trading posts that quickly became the nucleus of Indian and Metis villages and that served as cores of European or Europeanized life within a radically different culture.

The pump stations themselves, a series of lonely, clean, prefabricated, air-conditioned suburban towns spaced 200 miles apart from Qaisumah to Turaif near the Jordan border, are a demonstration of how thoroughly industrial civilization overcomes the harsh natural conditions that would usually overwhelm a pastoral or agricultural people. Lacking water, Tapline's people produced it by drilling; lacking building materials and supplies of all kinds, they imported them by truck or airlift (their supply list at one point contained 26,000 items); finding the summer heat often unbearable, they conditioned their air; being located at remote outposts, they tied themselves to each other and to the world outside by HF voice radio and teletype. Three round trips a week at first (now down to one) by the "Milk Run" planes, DC-3s operated in conjunction with Aramco, brought mail, supplies, and passengers (and gave as well a regular visual check of the whole pipeline).

From Abqaiq, the center of Aramco's gathering system, through Qaisumah, Rafha, Badanah, and Turaif, to Sidon, is a geography unfamiliar to most Americans yet important to them. For as each of those towns and stations was built, it became an outpost of the West and of America, a demonstration not only of American skills but also of American culture. Even the most trivial contacts and the most unthinking acts were significant, for the Saudi Arabs were then quite poor but very proud, and the partnership with the West, and all the landslide of change that it has since brought, were still very new.

Thirty-five years ago there were few traces of westernization in Saudi Arabia anywhere outside of cities like Jiddah and Mecca, where pilgrims from outside the country had stimulated a relatively sophisticated mercantile class.

The shock that oil riches have brought to Iran, Iraq, Kuwait, Qatar, Abu Dhabi, and Libya was particularly strong in Saudi Arabia, for of all the Arab states Saudi Arabia, beyond the Hijaz, was for a longer period the most isolated.

Thirty-five years ago the network of roads that shows on today's map was nothing but a scrawl of caravan trails and wandering tracks that disappeared in the first sandstorm. Dhahran did not exist, Ras Tanura did not exist, Abqaiq did not exist, the pipelines and pump stations, the ports, the marine terminal did not exist. What existed, outside Jiddah, Riyadh, and Mecca, was the barren land alone, with its scattered palm gardens and its coastal pearling towns and its desert oases, its wandering tribes, its holy places, its religious zeal and its austerity and its suspicion of foreigners.

All that began to change when Aramco came to the Eastern Province. With that fantastic American energy and adaptability that in those days was the wonder of the world and would a few years later be its main defense against fascism, Aramco began to transform Arabia. With its miles of pipelines, its power plants and its paved roads, with its marine terminal, with its gas-injection plants, with its huge Ras Tanura refinery, with its gas-oil separator plants whose perispheres pop up out of the desert and sea like metallic mushrooms, and whose banks of flares are pillars of fire against the Arabian night – with all those things the men of Aramco began to change Arabia.

Collectively, or corporately, they performed prodigies with magical swiftness, so that the journalists who periodically wrote them up for the American press gave the impression they would be tongue-tied if they could not make references to "Aladdin's lamp."

It was magical. The applied skill and power as well as the

results are awesome in the mass, and the change that has come over Saudi Arabia, that dizzy and dangerous leap from "camels to Cadillacs," to use the tiresome cliche that to this day writers seem compelled to employ, is quite as impressive and probably every bit as important.

Every American, even if he could not place Saudi Arabia on the map, knows that Aramco is one of those "legendary institutions," in the words of James Morris, and it would be remarkable if the ordinary American with his love of bigness and his respect for practical know-how did not take some satisfaction in a corporation like this. It demonstrates us, in one direction, at our best. But it would be quite as remarkable if some did not see Aramco and its sister corporations as a sinister force embroiling us, for dirty dollars, in the power struggles of the Middle East.

This last characterization, which is the one proposed by emotional nationalists and the one consistently disseminated by hostile propagandists, reflects one aspect of the emergent unrest that has turned much of the Arab world away from the United States. It must be challenged, for unwilling as a democracy may be to take its own side in an argument, and meekly as it may believe the worst interpretations of its own motives, American oil development in the Middle East has been, all things considered, responsible and fair.

The companies will certainly be under continuing pressure to enlarge even today's sharing of the profits, especially as northern Europe's dependence on Middle East oil becomes increasingly apparent. But whatever the uncertainties of the future, Aramco can congratulate itself on a record that is a long way from being grossly exploitative or "imperialist." Its record probably contains both mistakes and inconsistencies, and it has indeed earned impressive profits, but in general its role and its intention have been to provide an alternative between willful foreign exploitation of the 19th-century kind, and willful nationalization such as has happened more recently.

Though the agreements and the policies of most of the Middle Eastern oil companies do not much differ these days, it was not always so; and it was almost inevitable that there should have existed in the beginning a certain competitive hostility between American and British oilmen, for they represented not only competing commercial interests but sharply differing philosophies of operation in underdeveloped countries. Their jockeying may have looked on some occasions like two western dogs quarreling over a Middle Eastern bone. Actually, it was both more and less than that.

Aramco has been the exponent, though not the sole exponent, of what David Finnie calls "involvement" as opposed to "isolation." Its concession agreement specifically prohibits it from political activity in Saudi Arabia, but it inevitably became deeply involved in the economic and social life of first the Eastern Province and then, as the impact spread, the country. Instead of living as an aloof enclave wielding great political power, as was the traditional and considered habit of the British, the Americans early on participated in local life, becoming teachers, advisers, and helpers, often getting stuck with responsibilities not properly theirs, often suffering from criticism that was emotional and unfair and badly aimed, giving generously and – by 1970 a familiar experience – often having their good intentions misunderstood and resented.

One consequence of having rigidly eschewed political influence was that Aramco lived a very jumpy life, considering its ponderous economic weight. It had to remind itself constantly that a concession is often no more stable than the regime that grants it, and ultimately than the people that support the regime, and that a concession must adapt to changing times and conditions. But it was the old British system, as applied in Iran in the 1950s, that got into trouble first, and as the old system saw the handwriting on the wall and brought itself to change, it changed in the direction that Aramco had already taken.

How long this approach will prove durable cannot be predicted now, obviously, but it would be shortsighted to discount it too soon. Despite important discoveries in Alaska and Norway, the West still needs Middle Eastern oil and still has the installations and the skills necessary to produce and market it. For their part, the oil-producing Arab states still need oil income to finance their ever-increasing development, and without foreign investment and foreign experts to practice and teach industrial skills, the pace of that development in most of these states would unquestionably be slowed.

To put it candidly, the only practical economic base for modernization of the Middle East now and in the foreseeable future is oil, and although some Middle Eastern statesmen have opted for nationalization or regionalization of the industry, the consequences can – as they did once in Iran – seriously damage the economy.

There is no guarantee, naturally, that leaders in producing states will see the risks plainly; nations and individuals have before this cut off their noses to spite their faces. But the history of Aramco demonstrates that with great patience on both sides, the partnership system can work to the satisfaction of both parties.

Unfortunately, not enough Americans know anything about this approach. That is one of the justifications of this book, which attempts nothing more elaborate than the story of the earliest contacts between Americans and Saudi Arabs, and the earliest formulations, by necessity, of the partnership idea. That was before Aramco was even Aramco, when it was still the California Arabian Standard Oil Company, or Casoc.

Aramco's stock, being held entirely by its parent companies, is not offered for sale on any exchange, and no casual stockholders see its annual reports. Its field of operations is remote, and to most Americans not quite real. For most of us, it lives a documentary or statistical or newsreel life, not an actual one; its name summons to the mind images not of flesh-and-blood

Americans and Arabs doing a job, but of pensive camels silhouetted beside a derrick, or the tracks of an exploration outfit across photogenic dunes.

Those who actually visit the country, however, get a quite different view, particularly after they have landed at the Dhahran field, driven off past a pale, utterly barren reach of scabby rock and sand, the knobby hills called Jabal Dhahran, and the starkly handsome, concrete shapes of the new petroleum college, and entered the huge gateway to Dhahran, a rather dated archway built for a visit from the King.

Inside the gate most visitors would feel as much at home as they would in any American bedroom suburb; it might as well be at one of the oil-discovery spots in the western United States – say Farmington, New Mexico – except that it is a great deal more attractive and has no motels. Bungalows, guesthouses, the dormitory-hotel called Steineke Hall, the plush quarters called Hamilton House reserved for royal visitors and high brass, would all be at home in the U.S.A. Nostalgia, with enormous effort, has created gardens, brought in soil to cover the nearly exposed limestone, blasted holes for the roots of oleanders and tamarisks, planted, watered, and nursed lawns and trees and hedges; and yards complete with Siamese cats and tricycles humanize every street. There is a community center with a swimming pool, tennis courts, terrace, library, movie theater.

An American town. And yet not quite. The style of the buildings is, without being uniform, consistent. The gardens and lawns are the product not merely of the after-work shirtsleeve puttering of householders but also of local gardeners. Company maintenance crews come to fix the refrigerator when it goes out, or to repair the screen door that the dog has broken through. There are no commercials to interrupt the music played over the company's station. The people you see are mostly company employees, unless they are company guests. The preoccupations are largely company preoccupations, the gossip largely company gossip. And although nearly a quarter of the kids in school are Arabs, and although to an American it looks faintly strange, so far as any Saudi Arab is concerned, this is America.

It is not customary in most circles to value over-highly, or beyond its pragmatic usefulness, the loyalty that corporations extract from their employees in return for wages, benefits, and whatever varieties of soma are necessary for enjoyment of the brave new world. I confess that I can personally conceive of higher objects of loyalty than the great industrial corporation, and higher ambitions than to be a "good company man." I doubt that I should like to live in Dhahran, or in any company town, and not simply because of Saudi Arab Prohibition, though that is unquestionably hard on American morale. For some tastes, the company town is too protected, too paternalistic, and ultimately too limiting. Yet in the early days there was a solid, pragmatic reason for developing Dhahran this way: to minimize the danger that individual peculiarity, irritability, or obtuseness would upset the delicate balance of mutual restraint.

Such considerations have steered Aramco through its whole development. As it grew it was forced by its susceptible position to adopt policies that were then, at least, industrially eccentric or advanced. It had to be concerned about the total well-being of its employees, both American and Arab, as well as about the well-being of the local Saudi population, which was its only available raw labor force and also its uneasy host.

On the edge of nowhere it had to provide the bulk of the housing, transportation, and entertainment for its employees, because American employees were hard to recruit, expensive to bring out, and difficult to hold, and Saudi employees had to be recruited from the coastal towns, some of them several days away by camel. Living by the sufferance only of a concession agreement, the company was hypersensitive to the terms of its survival. And the isolation of the country, the lack of contemporary skills and knowledge, made Aramco, whether it wanted to be or not, teacher, banker, surveyor, engineer, builder, scientific adviser, and general Big Brother to the Saudi Arabs.

To put it more directly, the range and frequent altruism of its activities made Aramco worthier of a man's loyalty than companies which could claim only the colder justification of profits. And the men who made Aramco, often thrown on their own resources, constantly tested by excruciating difficulties of terrain, climate, shortages, distances, and the handicaps of being the first strangers in a suspicious and stranger-shy country, developed quite without encouragement an unprecedented degree of loyalty. First of all, they had a loyalty to the job, a devotion to the very difficulties that threatened to break their backs. Beyond that, they found themselves spokesmen and carriers for a half-realized nexus of democratic ideas, and having themselves helped to build these notions into the company's program, they respected the company for what they had put into it.

A spirit of goodwill and generosity toward the Saudi Arabs as people, along with a sense of pride in this new sort of industrial relationship, is still surprisingly common at all levels of Aramco personnel in the field. And among the managerial people who are also veterans of the early difficult years in Arabia it is exceedingly strong: it has become with many the truest justification of their lives. Even Aramco's public relations men, who as skeptical and possibly cynical writers of company blurbs might be expected to doubt their own statements, have expressed this spirit.

Several years ago, for example, Michael Cheyney published the first book of personal reminiscence to come out of the Aramco experience, *Big Oil Man from Arabia*. In it Cheyney was flippant, irreverent, amused, and possessed of a sound sense of the ridiculous even when the ridiculous involved himself or his bosses. He understood that some Arabs, particularly the ones Aramco has helped to educate, found – and still find – the missionary spirit irritating. But he did not kid the company's intentions or minimize the potential virtue of its welfare and training program. For that, as a sound implementation of the partnership ideal, he had only applause, the more persuasive for being the expression of a skeptic who was not, in all the ways usually desired by the front office, an impeccably good "company man."

What the welfare and training program amounts to now – or at least what it amounts to in the optimum statements that make their way into four-color printing jobs – may be gathered from the 1969 Report of Operations. Much of what is reported are standard means of keeping the employees physically contented, but other items, like Aramco's training program, go deeper.

Aramco has had a training program of a fairly extensive kind ever since 1939, but its coherent and integrated plan began in 1950. Since installing job training in that year it has steadily increased the number of Saudi Arabs in skilled jobs, so that in 1969 in its three Industrial Training Centers in Ras Tanura, Abqaiq, and Dhahran, it gave training in specialized courses to more than 1,300 Saudis, it included 346 Saudis in a managerial "grid" program in which participants tackled complex managerial problems, and it had enrolled in the Saudi Development program 722 high-potential employees. In addition it sent 209 Saudis abroad for study, 58 of them in universities, the others in schools of accounting, finance, electronics, and so forth. Aramco, moreover, picks up the tab for numerous Saudis who are chosen by the Saudi government for higher education abroad.

This is one way to make a new world. And if some of these college-trained Saudis return to jobs with Aramco and find themselves dissatisfied, caught between traditional Arabia and the industrial West and fully at home in neither, that is the calculated risk any program of change must take, and at least the enlightened in Aramco's management are perfectly willing to take it; it will test the practicability of the "involvement" to which Aramco and by now most Middle Eastern oil companies have committed themselves.

Another way is to see to the health of the people. The Eastern Province is no health resort yet, but it is certainly better off today than it was thirty-five years ago. There is one of the best hospitals in the Middle East at Dhahran, and excellent clinics in Abqaiq and Ras Tanura. In 1969 doctors performed 242 operations on crippled children under a new specialized orthopedic service. For sixteen years Aramco has also helped sponsor a trachoma research project in partnership with the Harvard School of Public Health.

And add to the training and health programs things more specifically economic. Some of them, such as severance pay, retirement pay, and death and disability benefits paid to employees, are now common in the Middle East, but were wildly unorthodox when introduced.

Other benefits, such as the thrift plan that encourages employee saving by payroll deduction and gives solid cash rewards to the thrifty (worth $12 million in 1969), are manifestations of the long-term company hope – almost wistful at times and almost certainly doomed to disappointment – of getting out of social engineering and back in the business of producing oil. The Tapline official who kept a bottle of black crude oil on his desk to remind him what business he was in has counterparts on the Aramco management committee.

Through what they call the Local Industrial Development Department (LIDD), the company has tried hard to speed up its return to the oil business. This division had as a goal assisting Arab enterprise – a chore which both self-interest and necessity would have forced upon the company even if it had not had the slightest impulse to be Big Brother.

Its program recognized three stages. The first was employment of Arabs by the company, with company encouragement for savings and the accumulation of capital. The second was establishment of independent Arab contracting and merchandising to serve company needs – one of the standard instruments was a car or truck, contracted to the company for taxiing or hauling. The third stage was development of "home-grown" private industry, Arab-owned and Arab-operated.

In a way it was like Europe's Marshall Plan, and the results, in a smaller way, were not too dissimilar – as a look at the boomtown of al-Khobar would suggest.

Thirty-five years ago al-Khobar was nothing but a couple of palm-thatch fishermen's *barastis.* Now it is a solid half mile of glass-fronted, electric-eyed, mercury-vapor-lighted shops, bottling works, cement plants, garages, and whatnot. In al-Khobar nowadays Aramco housewives can buy, never at too ruinous prices and sometimes at bargains, things that a few years ago would have been available no nearer than Beirut, and perhaps London or New York. Shopkeepers who twenty years ago spoke no English and knew not the slightest thing about American habits will now provide French perfumes, Japanese cameras and tape recorders, Italian sports cars, Swiss watches, Danish furniture, television sets, and tranquilizers.

The men who achieved this transformation were not oilmen; they were hard-working Saudis, many of whom, fifteen to twenty-five years ago, were untrained boys in *gufiyas.* But LIDD was an important factor. By quietly encouraging businessmen to form stock companies to assemble capital, by bringing ambitious contractors in from small individual plants to larger plants, by offering engineering advice, purchasing advice, geological advice, stimulating the easily stimulated local imagination – by giving, in brief, the Province's economics a shot in the arm – LIDD led the Eastern Province into the American consumptive pattern and the productive patterns that supply it. Think of this as good or bad, as you will: it is what the Saudis themselves wanted – what, ultimately, they will not be denied.

The dislocations inherent in such change were, of course, enormous. According to Cheyney, the national average earnings for a Saudi Arab in the 1950s were less than $50 per year. Today, the average pay of a Saudi worker with Aramco is $3,349, and 98 percent of Aramco's nearly 11,000 Arab employees save part of that by the Thrift Plan. Already a small but solid middle class has been established with everything in the way of economic ambition and cultural change that the birth of such a class implies. By 1969 nearly 40 percent of Aramco's Saudi employees had reached supervisory and management positions. Add to these the eager entrepreneurs of al-Khobar, Dammam, Hofuf, and elsewhere who have built company wages into private businesses, and you have a total of many thousands who have been galvanized, or catapulted, into relative affluence and growing awareness.

This, whatever the intention was, has been one of Aramco's most significant results, and however things may look to the parent company stockholders, or to young nationalists impatient of delay, to a historian, Aramco's effect upon Saudi Arabia and its auguries for the future seem at least as significant as its annual production of crude or its annual distribution of dividends. It may even, as anthropologist Carleton Coon has predicted, "go on record as one of the outstanding jobs of social engineering in this phase of the history of the world."

With that much preliminary we may turn to the story of the men who began the process of imposing these new patterns of work and thought upon the blistered face of Arabia thirty-five years ago.

Wallace Stegner

Chapter One
~ *Contact!* ~

The Jiddah that T. E. Lawrence knew, "a dead city, so clean underfoot, and so quiet," its narrow streets overhung by houses "like crazy Elizabethan half-timber work . . . gone gimcrack to an incredible degree," has been transformed in the past thirty-five years into a modern city of many times its pre–World War I size, so changed from the old that a returning pilgrim would hardly recognize it as the same place. But in 1933 Jiddah still presented to the sea its ancient, unreal facade. Tightly concentrated, surprisingly tall, it sprang up on the barren shore, squared by the wall that Steve Bechtel's bulldozers would one day push down. Its four-or five-story buildings with their cut-out arches of windows and their ranks of ornate balconies might have been made of sticks and pasteboard; or it might have been a child's city of blocks knocked out of plumb. It looked, said one traveler, like a city that had slept on its feet for ages but had been prevented from lying down to sleep properly.

In the old town, in those days, the walls leaned together over alleys barely wide enough for two donkeys to pass; the warped, carved, weathered balconies all but touched. Minarets tilted dizzily and the whole town sagged and slouched on foundations gradually sinking into the unconsolidated coral sand. In its crooked enduring way it looked as ancient as Genesis, and some thought it was.

Around Jiddah the shore could only be Arabia – pale, seared, discharged of color, treeless, spotted with sparse shrubs. The land flows down from the distorted rim of mountains to the mirage-like margins of the Red Sea, where beaches grade imperceptibly into coral bottoms and barely covered reefs and the gradually deepening waters mottled in scallops and bays of tan, near-white, emerald, finally blue. Jiddah has been the official harbor of Mecca since the year 648, and this vision of a tall wobbly city on a naked shore before papier-mâché hills has been the first sight of the Holy Land for millions of the devout making the hajj to the birthplace of the Prophet, only forty miles to the east.

It looked no different to the pilgrims who approached its shallow and difficult harbor in the Khedivial steamer *Talodi* on February 15, 1933. But these were pilgrims of an unprecedented kind. None of the faithful in all the thirteen-hundred years of the pilgrimage, and no invader in the city's total history, had brought such a potential for change. Not even Aelius Gallus, during his invasion of Yemen in 24 BC, had touched it, really. Rome reeled back from the inhospitable Arabian Peninsula and left Jiddah on its timeless shore. The Portuguese who attacked the city in 1541, and the British who shelled it in 1858, had knocked down a few buildings, but changed nothing.

And even 'Abd al-'Aziz ibn 'Abd al-Rahman Al Faisal Al Sa'ud, commonly known to the West as Abdul Aziz Ibn Saud, completing his conquest of the Hijaz in December 1925, had intended to make few changes except in the ruling family. He was concerned to establish order, reassure the leaders of Muslim countries worried about the safety of the pilgrimage, and win recognition from foreign powers. Jiddah's tiny foreign colony was allowed to go on in its old way, the only enclave of non-Muslims in all the lands that Ibn Saud now controlled and that in 1932 would be named Saudi Arabia. It had adjusted itself to Arabian ways and to the prohibitions of the Wahhabi government; and where it could not comfortably adjust, it somehow managed to achieve certain western pleasures, keeping its cameras out of sight, playing its hidden radios and phonographs softly and in secret, smoking only in the legations, getting a drink as it could.

The Committee for the Commendation of Virtue and the Condemnation of Vice, though zealous to clean up corruption, granted in Jiddah a sort of diplomatic immunity: the need for foreign recognition was more potent than the patriotism of Ibn Saud's Ikhwan armies. In return for the consideration shown it, the foreign colony was discreet; no one of the group there, which was dominated by the British and the Dutch, wanted to overturn any applecarts. Foreign-colony Jiddah seemed as little interested in innovations as Arabia itself.

But now change entered in a suit of wrinkled whites and a sun helmet – change in the person of a smooth-faced American businessman of forty named Lloyd N. Hamilton.

Accompanied by his wife and by another American couple acting as his advisers and assistants, Mr. Hamilton was to bring the nervous needs of the 20th century into contact with the undeveloped possibilities of a land older than Abraham. Into a country whose energy had been supplied for millennia by donkeys and camels he came to discuss the more explosive energy of oil.

Lloyd Hamilton was a lawyer and land-lease expert of the Standard Oil Company of California, known in cablese and abbreviated business talk as "Socal." His wife Airy was along for the ride. They were accompanied by Karl and Nona Twitchell, two of the very few Americans who in 1933 knew anything whatever about the Arabian Peninsula. Standing on the *Talodi*'s pitching deck, all a little queasy from the stiff *shamal* they had bucked on the way across from Port Sudan, and sick of the steamer after sixteen rough hours, they watched the city spring up before them as the harbor opened. They passed the half-sunken hulk of the ship *Asia* tilted on her reef, they began to be surrounded by the slant sails of dhows. Ahead of them the dark keyhole arches of the quarantine dock emptied robed figures onto the quay. Launches started out toward them.

The four went below to get their bags ready. They were, without knowing it, social and economic revolution arriving innocently and by invitation, but with implications more potent than if their suitcases had been loaded with bombs.

No event in history is without antecedents — antecedents that reach back indefinitely into the past. In all recorded history there is no such thing as a true beginning. If we wished to trace the development of Middle Eastern oil, we could find the fact of oil's existence and the human knowledge of its uses far back in the twilight where history and legend blur. Bitumen from oil seeps waterproofed the ware of potters in Ur of the Chaldees; Noah smeared his ark, within and without, with the same pitch.

But this story does not pretend to deal with the development of Middle Eastern oil. It pretends only to be a part of the human record of some of the men who lived some of the actions — the story of the pioneers of one company in one country for a limited number of years. And so it is necessary to go back only far enough to understand the circumstances that sent Lloyd Hamilton to Jiddah, and to touch for a moment on the difficult and awkward situation into which he stepped.

The difficulties were religious and political as well as commercial, for Hamilton was not merely industrial civilization meeting an ancient culture of patriarchal shepherds and oasis townsmen. He was also the outsider aspiring to do business with the most fundamentalist sect of Islam. Further, he was American business trying to get a solid foothold in a country which the United States had officially recognized only two years before, and in an area into which American enterprise had thus far never penetrated.

As time would show, he was more. He was the spokesman of a kind of foreign development prepared to operate strictly as a business, and that in itself was revolutionary. Political domination, restrictive treaties, government partnerships, "designated instruments" were not hiding behind him. Absent, also, was the imperial conviction that commerce was possible in undeveloped countries only when tied to colonial administration.

The United States government was so far from being involved in Hamilton's business that it didn't even have a representative in Saudi Arabia. American missionaries had been so little concerned – and so little able – to make converts to Christianity that their efforts had been confined to the periphery of the Peninsula – Kuwait, Aden, and Muscat. According to a traditional formula, the flag followed the missionaries, and trade followed the flag. Here, trade came first, and came alone.

For generations the British Empire had maintained political and commercial primacy in both the Red Sea and the Persian Gulf (in Arabic usage, the Arabian Gulf). All around the Arabian Peninsula's southern and eastern shores, along the seaboard from which once the dhows of pirates had burst forth to raid ships plowing the lanes of empire, the British Navy had established dominance, and British political agents had enforced treaties. There had been no other way of maintaining order and keeping the trade routes open.

The treaties left the little shaikhdoms around the coast (none of which was ever consolidated into Ibn Saud's kingdom) technically independent in domestic matters, but delegated management of their international relations to Great Britain. The shaikhs of Kuwait, Bahrain, and Qatar, and the lesser shaikhs and chiefs of the Trucial Coast, refrained from piracy as requested, drew their annual bounty money, and did pretty much what the British political agents told them to do.

The paper signed by Zaid ibn Khalifa, chief of Abu Dhabi, in 1892, was a representative treaty: he bound himself, his heirs, and his successors never to enter into any agreement or correspondence with any foreign power other than Britain; never to permit, without specific British consent, the residence in his territory of any foreign representative or agent other than British; and never to sell, cede, mortgage, or otherwise grant rights to any of his territory without the British blessing. That pretty effectively shut the door in the faces of foreigners snooping for commercial advantages in the British-protected domain of Abu Dhabi.

Ibn Saud, however, proved too big for British policy to control. After his Ikhwan armies chased Sharif Hussain of the Hijaz clear off the Peninsula and into exile on Cyprus, he held a position of unassailable strength, and gained full British recognition of his sovereignty by the Treaty of Jiddah in 1927. With respect to oil and Mr. Hamilton's mission, this was to be an important exception.

Long before Ibn Saud solidified his control over Arabia, British power sat solidly in what were then the two important oil nations of the Middle East: Iran and Iraq. The Anglo-Persian Oil Company at Abadan was not merely under contract to supply fuel to the Royal Navy; it was more than half owned by His Majesty's government, and had been ever since 1914.

There was thus more than the usual cooperation between British business and British foreign policy: the two were virtually identical, and Anglo-Persian operated not simply as a "designated instrument" but as an owned and operated, overt instrument of British policy.

A collection of companies owned the Iraq Petroleum Company in 1933. The Near East Development Corporation, originally owned by five American companies, three of which sold out in the early '30s, held 23.75 percent of the IPC stock. British-Dutch and British interests, including Anglo-Persian, held twice as much. British influence was enhanced by the fact that the company operated under the eye and protection and with the active cooperation of the High Commissioner and his representatives in Baghdad, Mosul, and Basra.

The owner companies of IPC, in 1928, had bound themselves, by the so-called "Red Line Agreement," not to explore or develop independently any region which lay inside the boundaries of the old Ottoman Empire. Outside competitors unwelcome to the IPC and Anglo-Persian group were excluded by England's treaties with the shaikhs, and by her political domination throughout much of the area. Only Saudi Arabia, in fact, lay outside the sphere of effective British control.

There was a third oil area, not merely potential but already producing, where American enterprise *had* won a concession from the British. This was the island of Bahrain, twelve miles off the Arabian mainland in the Gulf. Though the Shaikh of Bahrain, like the coastal shaikhs, was tied by treaties with Britain, a combination of circumstances and the energy of a few men had allowed him to make commercial agreements with an American company. The story of the opening of Bahrain is so necessary a preliminary to the negotiations for which Hamilton came to Jiddah that we must go back eleven years before Hamilton's arrival, to the year 1922. We can confine our attention to a ruddy, genial, hearty, energetic, undiscourageable New Zealand adventurer named Major Frank Holmes.

Holmes was one of those who, as Bernard De Voto once said, awake alertly in the night, hear history's clock strike at a critical time – but count the strokes wrong. He was on the trail of a big idea very early, but as it happened, arrived just a little too early and in not quite the right way. During World War I, after active service which included the Gallipoli campaign, Major Holmes had worked for a time in the Admiralty, where access to petroleum maps left him thoughtful. At the beginning of the 1920s he showed up in Bahrain to work on the water system, and he was such an agreeable fellow, so uniformly good-natured and so full of bustle and steam, that he made many friends among both British and Arabs. When a group of London financiers formed the Eastern and General Syndicate to promote profitable enterprises in the Arabian Gulf area, Holmes was their natural choice as the company's Bahrain agent.

The Eastern and General Syndicate was interested in oil, but it was not an oil company. It proposed either to act as negotiator for oil companies which wanted concessions but lacked contacts for making them, or to obtain the concessions first and then sell them to companies which would explore and develop them.

Obviously the Anglo-Persian and Iraq Petroleum people were going to keep their eye on Holmes' activities. Obviously, too, the best chance for Eastern and General would lie at some place outside British political influence – Saudi Arabia, for instance. A land almost cut off from modern history, nearly untraveled by Europeans, it had been in times past a byword for the fabulous. As a nation, it was bounded on the east by Bahrain's pearls, on the west by King Solomon's mines, on the south by frankincense and myrrh. Oil under it? Why not?

Holmes almost made the dream come true. In the boiling heat of the Arabian summer of 1922 he rode across deserts only a handful of Europeans had ever seen, and talked with Ibn Saud in his fortress capital of Riyadh. Again in November he intercepted the King (then called the Sultan of Najd and Its Dependencies) at Hofuf, in the al-Hasa oasis. He followed him to al-'Uqair, where the King was holding a conference with Sir Percy Cox, the British High Commissioner in Iraq.

Sir Percy, with the interests of Anglo-Persian in mind, turned an understandably cool eye upon Holmes' efforts and advised the King that concessions for the exploration of al-Hasa were premature at that time. Premature or not, Holmes pursued the King back to Hofuf and in the teeth of Sir Percy's plainly indicated objections obtained a concession to explore for oil over 60,000 square miles of al-Hasa, Arabia's eastern province.

But then, disappointment. The task of trying to find and develop oil fields in a country which lacked most of the elements necessary to support such an industry – good roads and communications, skilled labor, transport, supply centers – and which few foreigners entered except during the pilgrimage season, did not appeal to any of the oil companies, European and American, to which the syndicate offered its concession.

After several years, during which some Belgian geologists tried without success to discover what was under al-Hasa's dunes and gravel plains, the syndicate defaulted on its annual rental payment and let the concession lapse. It thereby gave up one of the greatest oil reserves in the entire world – it had heard the clock strike, but counted the strokes wrong. But there was after all no way for the concessionaires to know what they were relinquishing. Moreover, by the time they let al-Hasa go, they had a more promising prospect going on Bahrain.

The Bahrain concession was granted to Holmes by the Shaikh of Bahrain, with British approval, in 1925, and was renewed in 1927, the year in which the Iraq Petroleum Company brought in the big Kirkuk field. At the end of November 1927, the syndicate sold an option on the Bahrain concession to Eastern Gulf Oil, and Gulf sent out a geologist, Ralph Rhoades, to explore and map the island.

Rhoades found on Bahrain a perfect structure, a textbook dome, but he had no way of knowing, without drilling, whether there was oil in it. And Eastern Gulf, having bought something it liked the looks of, now found itself unable to go ahead. It was reminded that it was a subsidiary of Gulf Oil, and that Gulf was a part of the Near East Development Corporation, which was in turn a part owner of the Iraq Petroleum Company and a signatory to the recent Red Line Agreement. Eastern Gulf then offered its Bahrain option to the IPC, which decided against it because its geologists reported the Oligocene-Miocene formations, oil-producing in Iran and Iraq, to be missing from Bahrain. So Eastern Gulf sold its option to Standard of California, a complete newcomer in the Middle East.

Socal too had its difficulties, this time with the British Colonial Office and the Political Agent on Bahrain. Nearly two years of negotiations and compromises were needed to produce an agreement. It stipulated that the company developing Bahrain must be a British company, registered in Canada, and must establish an office in Great Britain, in the charge of a British subject, for maintaining communications with His Majesty's government; one director must be a British subject, persona grata to the British government; as many of the company's employees as was consistent with efficient operation must be British or Bahrainis; and the company must maintain on Bahrain Island a "chief local representative" whose appointment must be approved by the British government and who must, in all his dealings with the Shaikh of Bahrain, work through the British Political Agent.

Thus, with one hand tied behind it in political restrictions and red tape, the first wholly American-owned oil company came into the Middle East. The Eastern and General Syndicate signed a final agreement with the Shaikh of Bahrain on June 12, 1930, and on August 1 it formally assigned the concession to Socal's new Canadian subsidiary, Bahrain Petroleum Company, or Bapco, whose first chief local representative was Major Frank Holmes.

The home office of Socal at 225 Bush Street, San Francisco, was separated from Bahrain Island by half the globe, and in 1930 by an almost complete lack of dependable information, as well as by a certain reluctance on the part of more conservative members of the board of directors. The search for new foreign reserves, necessarily both speculative and expensive, was no new experience for Socal.

It had spent millions of dollars, without success, on exploration and drilling in Mexico, Venezuela, Colombia, Ecuador, Argentina, the Philippines, and Alaska. But by the time the Bahrain agreement was concluded, the world was deep in the Great Depression. Oil was in oversupply, and the price had dropped to a dime a barrel in Texas. As a result, only a few men in the company were advocating the Middle East venture. These were mostly from the producing department: producing men always have felt that the time to look for oil is when there is already plenty of it. That is when concessions and leases are easiest and least expensive to get, and that is when you must find oil if you want to have your share for the future.

One of the most persistent, enthusiastic, and effective of the directors was Maurice Lombardi. He was supported by William H. Berg, another director, who later became president of the company; by Reginald Stoner, manager of the producing department; and by the two chief geologists, Clark Gester and "Doc" Nomland. And Lombardi had an able and industrious aide in Francis B. Loomis, once Under-Secretary of State for Theodore Roosevelt and now a consultant on foreign affairs for Socal.

These men were all enthusiastic about Rhoades' Bahrain report; they had all recommended the purchase of Gulf's option. But Lombardi was not content to wait while long-drawn-out negotiations were carried through. He had Loomis do some cabling for permission, and on May 14, Fred A. Davies, a geologist, and William F. Taylor, general superintendent of the foreign division, stepped ashore on Bahrain from a British-India boat and were welcomed by Major Holmes.

It took them no long time to determine that Bahrain should be drilled, though Davies warned that it could not be considered a first-class wildcat prospect. Davies "spotted" the well, choosing a site that the drillers later swore was the one place on the whole island that never had a breeze, and then he and Taylor turned their eyes across the gumdrop-green water to the pale shore of Arabia, where the light at sunrise and sunset picked out a cluster of hills. It was Davies' conclusion that anyone who developed Bahrain ought to try to get a look at al-Hasa as well, thus corroborating hunches that Lombardi, Loomis, and Nomland had had without ever seeing the country at all.

But Holmes, it turned out, could not or would not get them over there or arrange an audience with Ibn Saud. He had many excuses, he stalled, he warned them about being seen talking to Anglo-Persian people, for fear Ibn Saud should get suspicious of political motives and refuse to deal for concessions. Cables went back and forth, to and from London and San Francisco, and Davies waited, and waited some more, on through the time of *shamals* and into the time of the soaking hot winds from the southeast. The little lost island adrift in the steamy Gulf began to be a prison; across the channel the tantalizing Arabian shore swam in and out of haze and fog and heat waves.

By the end of June, Taylor had gone home, and Davies, never quite sure that he wouldn't be called back to inspect Arabia, left Bahrain and went on up to Baghdad. Still no word from Holmes, who was supposed to be busy arranging permissions. Davies poked on into northern Iraq, telling no one where he was going or what he was doing, which was inspecting geological sections in order to have a better notion of what might lie under the crust of Bahrain and Arabia.

An amiable and distinguished-looking tourist, he took a look at a good part of Iraq before a horse persuaded him to go home. The horse was skittish, the stirrups were short, and Davies had very long legs. He was humped up in the saddle like a folded katydid, and every time he bounced, the prospector's pick in his belt pecked the horse on the haunch. Eventually the horse bolted, piling Davies onto some rocks. Davies broke a blood vessel above his right hip. His car and driver got him back to Mosul, where he lay in the hospital for a month. Still no word from Holmes. Davies hired another car and took an inspection trip into Iran and returned. Still no word.

On September 17, after four strenuous months in the area, Davies sailed for home without ever having had that look at Arabia which had been one of his principal reasons for coming. But the little he had seen, and the inferences he had been able to draw, had made it certain that if and when opportunity presented itself, Socal would be at least as interested in Arabia as in Bahrain. Also, Davies need not have lamented his lost chances in al-Hasa. As it turned out, he would spend a good part of his life there.

On August 7, 1930, a week after the Bahrain concession was formally assigned to Socal by the Eastern and General Syndicate, a quite different but likewise important event took place on the other side of Arabia: Harry St. John B. Philby embraced Islam.

Philby, late of the British Colonial Office, once of the Indian civil service, once a colleague of Sir Percy Cox in India and Mesopotamia, one of the great explorers of the Arabian Peninsula and a great Arabist, was now selling Ford cars in Jiddah. He had been a friend and on occasion an adviser of Ibn Saud since they first met in Riyadh in 1917, when Philby crossed over from al-'Uqair to persuade Ibn Saud to keep the peace with Sharif Hussain, Britain's ally, and harry the Rashidis, allies of the Turks and Ibn Saud's mortal enemies.

Philby had broken with the Colonial Office and had been allowed to resign for his outspokenness in criticizing certain British policies. He had lived in Jiddah since 1925. Since 1929, when the first Model A Fords gave his business a smart fillip, his home had been the Bait Baghdadi, a huge, century-old pile built on land reclaimed from the sea and once the residence of the Turkish Wali of the Hijaz. In it, though by no means wealthy, Philby lived the life of an influential shaikh, intimate with the great of the kingdom.

When he finally made the decision to accept Islam he telephoned some of his friends and then drove to Hadda, where he was met by the Deputy Foreign Minister, Fuad Hamza, and by the Minister of Finance, Shaikh Abdullah Sulaiman. They helped him perform the proper ablutions and purifications and drove him to Mecca, where he went through the rituals of the Lesser Pilgrimage under the tutelage of Shaikh Abdullah's secretary. The next day they all drove to Taif, in the hills, to receive King Ibn Saud's congratulations.

Philby's embracing of Islam would seem important only to himself. But the conversion was important to others as well, and to the development of Middle Eastern oil. It brought Philby even

13

closer to Ibn Saud than he had been, and confirmed him as a confidential and trusted adviser on matters of international relations and international trade. And Philby was not only strongly sympathetic to Arabs and their country and their way of life; he was also outspokenly critical of British colonial policy.

It was sometime after Philby's conversion, during one of their intimate talks, that the King expressed his concern about the poverty of his kingdom, then almost entirely dependent for cash on the fees charged pilgrims. Philby told him Arabia was like a man sleeping on top of buried treasure: why didn't he take steps to develop the country's mineral resources? The King retorted that for a million pounds he would give mineral or oil concessions to anyone – had already, with disappointing results, given a concession to Holmes.

If the King had only known it, Fred Davies had recently gone back to the States after a frustrating four months of trying to make contact and talk about precisely these same mineral possibilities. But out of Philby's talk with Ibn Saud came at least one definite result: Philby reminded the King that Charles R. Crane, a member of the American plumbing-manufacturing family and a philanthropist extraordinary, had landed briefly at Jiddah a few years before. Ibn Saud had not given him an audience. Yet somebody like Crane, philanthropic and American rather than political and British, might hold the key to Arabia's future.

The King agreed, Philby communicated, and in 1931 came Charles Crane, eager to help in any way he could. An ardent friend of the entire Middle East ever since, in 1919, he had helped write for Woodrow Wilson an ill-fated and disregarded report recommending the self-determination of people in the area, Crane had already, in 1926, loaned the services of Karl Twitchell, a mining engineer, to the Imam of Yemen. He would be happy to make the same loan to Ibn Saud, to have Twitchell prospect for water, oil, and minerals, and make a report that could be used as a basis for later development.

Thus came Twitchell, a Vermont Yankee with an Irish-born wife, and he prospected up into the northern Hijaz, and into the mountains northeastward which some thought the Land of Midian and the place of King Solomon's mines. He also went clear across the mountains, across the Tuwaiq Escarpment and the Dahna sands, and on to the *sabkhas* and dunes of the Gulf coast, so that he was the first American engineer to visit the shore which Fred Davies had eyed wistfully from across the channel in the summer of 1930.

It was not the fault of Socal officials, especially Loomis and Lombardi, that Twitchell was the first to examine al-Hasa. Communication (or the failure to establish it) was such that Socal for some time had no notion of Twitchell's activity, and they had no real assurance that Holmes had told Ibn Saud of their own eagerness to set up talks. While they groped blindly for contacts in the forbidden kingdom, Karl Twitchell went up and down Arabia sniffing for oil seeps and quartz outcrops, and a wildcat crew spudded in the first well on Bahrain, Jabal Dukhan No. 1, on October 16, 1931.

Twitchell's reports in 1932, after he had visited the well being drilled on Bahrain, so encouraged Ibn Saud about oil and gold prospects that he commissioned Twitchell to communicate to oil or mining companies in the United States, Arabia's willingness to discuss concessions.

In March 1932, Lombardi wrote Holmes reminding him that it was a long time, and he hadn't yet made his promised visit to the King. On April 2, Ed Skinner, manager of Bapco on Bahrain, wired Taylor that Holmes expected to see the King in Jiddah at the end of that month, and that a new element had come in by reason of Gulf Oil's interest in an Arabian concession. Apprehensive about being frozen out, Socal immediately sent Loomis and Lloyd Hamilton to London to see what could be done from there, and arranged for a geologist, Robert P. Miller, to go on to Bahrain to watch the first well, and to select a second well location.

For a year and a half they had jockeyed and corresponded and guessed in the dark. Then on June 1, 1932, Jabal Dukhan No. 1 came in with a heavy flow of oil from the Cretaceous, thus confounding the geologists of Anglo-Persian, who did not think oil would be found in formations older than the Asmari limestone. Holmes, who had made excuses for not going to Jiddah in April, said in June that he was prevented by the King's grief over the death of his favorite wife. Tied to the syndicate by the Bahrain deal, but growing more and more restless with the delays, Socal explored other possibilities. Philby told Loomis about Twitchell and Twitchell's reports, and for the first time Socal learned that the King himself had been trying to make contacts.

By August 26, the delays had begun to seem so meaningless and fantastic that Loomis gave the syndicate an ultimatum: if nothing were done by November 1, Socal would consider itself free to try independent negotiations with Ibn Saud. The next week Loomis cabled Philby, who had returned to Jiddah, to see if he would be available as a contact man. It seemed that the only way to make sure some competitor did not slip into Arabia ahead of them was to give Ibn Saud a direct word about Socal's interest.

Loomis would be cabling Philby for a long time, for Philby and his wife were driving to Jiddah by way of Belgium, Holland, Germany, Austria, Hungary, the Balkans, and Istanbul, and thence going by ship to Alexandria and by land to Suez to catch the Khedivial mail boat home. They were many weeks on the road, while uncertainty mounted in London and elsewhere.

By the time Philby got back to Jiddah and cabled his willingness to serve and Ibn Saud's willingness to negotiate, Loomis had met Twitchell in Washington and signed him too as a contact man. So in the end, Socal wound up with both Twitchell and Philby as advisers, though the agreement with Philby was not completed until after Hamilton reached Jiddah. With the way finally cleared for discussion, the Hamiltons and Twitchells left London for Marseilles and a January 28 sailing on the Henderson

Line ship *Burmah*. Shortly afterward, Lombardi also left London, on his way via Istanbul and Basra to Bahrain. He not only wanted to look into the new oil field there, where the second well was now being drilled, but he wanted to be reasonably close to back up Hamilton in the negotiations.

Thus it was – after years of guessing, negotiation, and just plain luck – that Lloyd Hamilton sailed into Jiddah harbor that February day in 1933 to begin the long months of negotiations that would one day send Arabian oil out to the western world and bring the western world to Saudi Arabia.

Chapter Two
~ The Crucial Corner ~

However unsteady the profile of Jiddah had been from the sea, the quay was as solid as a knock on the head. The docks were crowded with the curious; the smells of the city smote the newcomers. Karl Twitchell's assurance that they would be admitted with only a cursory customs examination proved unreliable. Some officer had missed his signals, and Airy Hamilton watched – and so did about a thousand interested spectators – as every intimate article of her clothing was pulled out and shaken and stuffed back in again.

Then the streets of Jiddah, the flavor of a forbidding land: sand-floored alleys, sun-smitten squares, and the shadows, almost impenetrable by contrast but shot with beams and slants of light, under the tin and board and palm-frond roof of the *suq*; the loom of the city's mud and coral wall, glimpses of tiny shops crammed with rugs, copper, strange foods. This world startled them with contrasts – white teeth flashing from a black beard, eyes of an incredible aliveness in a dark face under a turban or framed by a *ghutra*; an occasional woman in sepulchral black, only the hint of eyes showing behind the mask's square holes, the robed figure as nervous as a runaway child.

And the Grand Hotel, balconied at all three stories, ornamented along its roof with merlons and crenels of plaster. They were its first guests. Twenty or thirty workmen had been busy on it for several weeks, renovating it not only for the Americans but for future use as a first-class hotel for wealthy pilgrims accustomed to western comforts. In all the 1,300 years of the hajj there had been no such public accommodations in Jiddah, and the Americans approached it with interest and entered with curiosity.

On the whole, the government had done well by them. By the standards of that time their quarters on the top floor were lavish — two great high-ceilinged bedrooms with brass beds and washbowl sets; a dining room big enough for banquets and furnished with table and chairs; a well-furnished living room the size of a basketball court, divided into two sections which they christened the coffee shop and the lounge. And two bathrooms.

The Twitchells, old Arabian hands, were very well pleased, but Airy Hamilton called her husband in and showed him the facilities with raised eyebrows. There was no running water. Bathing was evidently to be performed by standing in a tin pan and pouring water over oneself. Fair enough.

Of servants there seemed to be dozens, whose principal duty seemed to be to rise respectfully when anyone came in or out. They were the friendliest and most smiling of mortals, a mixture of Arabs and Somalis, and as curious as the crowds on the dock. It was not unreasonable that they should be, for these four were the only Americans in Arabia, and there hadn't been enough of their tribe there before them to make them a familiar sight.

Within hours of their arrival the foreign colony of Jiddah began to pay calls. All knew what they were there for; there were no leading questions. Invitations were issued and accepted; they began to feel their way into the city's mysteries.

Then on the fourth day came driving from Mecca the most influential man, next to the King, in Saudi Arabia. This was Shaikh Abdullah Sulaiman, the Minister of Finance, small, polite, acutely intelligent, capable of instant and bold decisions and of long and shrewd maneuvering. The ladies had put on their best dresses and covered their arms; the gentlemen had brushed their hair and donned coats. The Arabian delegation came in single file, according to rank. Thank God, thought the Hamiltons, for the Twitchells, who spoke some Arabic, and for the servants, who seemed to know what to do.

They introduced themselves and they sat around the walls and had tea and cakes, and they talked politely of banal things, through a suave interpreter named Najib Salha, who had worked for British firms in the Sudan and Egypt and was now Abdullah Sulaiman's private secretary. Then came coffee, poured ceremoniously from a beaked pot into small handleless cups, a sip or two to each cup. Everything was very deftly done. The spectacle of their own formal hospitality astonished them; they felt that it had been a picturesque and instructive hour when the Minister of Finance, through Najib, begged leave to go.

It was only then that they found Shaikh Abdullah's capacity for single-minded attention to business. This had been purely a social call, but Shaikh Abdullah understood that they had come to talk about oil, and he wanted to know what time suited them. He himself suggested eight that evening. A little startled, for they had an invitation to dine at the British Legation, Hamilton said that eight would be perfect. It was a good sign that Shaikh Abdullah was so eager.

Later, when everyone had gone, Hamilton went out in the late afternoon onto their balcony. Across the rooftops, on the perilously slanting shelf of a minaret, he saw the white figure of the muezzin, and heard the high wavering cry. In the streets passersby and shopkeepers prepared themselves, and down below him his own servants were aligning themselves in prayer, bending and rising with their faces all turned toward the east. The crooked alleys of Jiddah were half filled with dusk; from the *suq* he heard the complaining snarl of a camel, and then for a moment in the stillness, the perhaps imaginary mutter of a whole city's prayers.

For all the promptness with which Abdullah Sulaiman got down to business, American industry was not destined to make fruitful contact with Arabia in one ceremonial coffee visit and an evening's conversation. It would be three and a half months of hard, hot, discouraging work before Hamilton and the King's ministers would succeed in hammering out an agreement.

The men with whom Hamilton dealt most frequently were Shaikh Abdullah, a Najdi by birth; Fuad Hamza, the Deputy Foreign Minister; and the King's confidential secretary Yusef Yassin. Hardheaded, smart, patient, tenacious, wary, they were bargainers worthy of anyone's steel, and Hamilton was handicapped in his negotiating by his ignorance of Arabic and of the Arab character and culture.

British political opposition, too, made itself almost immediately apparent in the hospitably hostile attitude of Sir Andrew Ryan, the British Minister. It was likewise clear that Socal would not have a clear field, but would have to compete for a concession with at least the Iraq Petroleum Company and perhaps others.

Most complicating of all was the fact that in Iran and Iraq, on the strength of enormous potential production and enormous proved reserves, new agreements profitable to the local governments had recently been made; and on Bahrain oil had been struck with the first well. It was these agreements and discoveries that the Saudi ministers were using as a basis for judging the value of their own concession. There was a fair possibility that the combination of hard bargainers, outside political and economic competition, and excessive expectations on the part of the Saudi Arabs would result in a higher price than a very speculative wildcat was worth.

To counter these difficulties, Hamilton had certain advantages. He was as shrewd a bargainer as even Shaikh Abdullah, and his ignorance of Arabic and Arab customs was partly offset by the presence of Twitchell and Philby. Philby particularly, from his station in Mecca, was in a position to forward information on government attitudes almost as soon as they crystallized.

The IPC, whose representative Stephen Longrigg turned up on March 12, was a definite threat to Socal's chances, but Longrigg very shortly gave indications that his principals were less interested in developing Arabian oil than in preventing others from doing so and that their purse strings were by no means wide open. It looked as if IPC could be outbid. And Saudi Arabia, as Hamilton well knew, was deeply in debt, hard hit by the worldwide depression, and desperate for cash to meet its new, growing responsibilities.

How desperate, the Hamiltons very soon saw, for the pilgrim ships began to unload their passengers through the quarantine dock, and the damp-sand streets of Jiddah began to fill with pilgrims of all colors and nationalities. A few appeared in the Grand Hotel; the alleys below the Hamiltons' balconies were spotted with moving black umbrellas, camels, cars, donkeys, people. But not enough, not nearly enough. The hajj which only a few years before had drawn 235,000 pilgrims would this year draw not more than 50,000. The state, which under Ibn Saud had suddenly begun to require vastly greater services and incur vastly greater expenses, saw its revenues dwindling to a trickle. Abdullah Sulaiman, in Philby's words, had for two or three years been trying to "get a quart out of a pint bottle."

Yet the negotiations for an oil concession were as difficult as if the ministers had not a fiscal care in the world. They played Longrigg's presence against Hamilton's, and vice versa, and played offer against offer. No sooner had Hamilton got what he thought were outrageous demands down to something reasonable and got San Francisco's approval of an offer, than the ministers made new demands as extravagant as the old ones.

Hamilton at one time went up to Cairo to confer with Lombardi, who had come over from Bahrain, and there encountered Major Holmes, also over from Bahrain, with some proposals he wanted to make Ibn Saud on the oil rights to the Saudi Arabia–Kuwait Neutral Zone, which were shared half-and-half between Ibn Saud and the Shaikh of Kuwait. Holmes' proposals, however, later fizzled out when he got to Jiddah.

The story of the three and a half months during which Lloyd Hamilton worked out his concession agreement with Ibn Saud's ministers has been told several times: by Philby in his *Arabian Days* and *Arabian Jubilee*, by Twitchell in *Saudi Arabia*, by Longrigg in *Oil in the Middle East*, by Benjamin Schwadran in *The Middle East, Oil, and the Great Powers*, by Marquis Childs in an article in the old *Collier's* magazine. But it has never been quite fully or quite accurately told, even by the people who participated in it.

For one thing, not even Twitchell knew that Philby was acting as a consultant for Socal, and Longrigg, who had served with Philby in Mesopotamia, tried at one point to turn over his job as IPC negotiator to him, so that Longrigg could get back to his pipeline job at Haifa.

Sometime some historian, working from Hamilton's and Lombardi's letters, will relate the episode in detail, but even if incomplete the negotiations suggest the way in which men, corporations, and governments, moving almost as if by some ineluctable force, turn the crucial corners of history.

The concession for which Longrigg and the IPC unsuccessfully bid and which Hamilton won would insure – or compel – Saudi Arabia's entrance into the modern world. It would also mark a step in the decline of British power in the Middle East, and the second step – a huge one – in the entrance of America into the region. For Great Britain the painful politics of relinquishment of power; for Saudi Arabia the unsettling effects of sudden wealth and abrupt cultural change; for America, though it came here without political intention, the inevitable political responsibilities of massive involvement – they were all implicit in the drama of demand and offer, stipulation and concession, in which Hamilton and the ministers were engaged.

On April 20, Hamilton gave Shaikh Abdullah the company's last offer, the one on which he advised the company to stand. It called, among other things, for an advance loan of £30,000 gold to Saudi Arabia, with a second loan of £20,000 eighteen months later; for the beginning of exploratory geological work within three months; for drilling within three years at the latest; for a guaranteed royalty somewhat less than the ministers had persistently asked; and for development as fast as was consistent with good oil-field practice.

There was every reason to believe that the ministers would accept these terms. Hamilton expected it; he was, in fact, assured of it, because one of these mornings Shaikh Abdullah called on him at the Grand Hotel, informed him that the King was briefly in Jiddah and would like to see him, and escorted him and Twitchell to the palace a mile or two outside Jiddah's walls.

A few minutes in that monumental and kingly presence compensated for weeks of shadowboxing with the negotiators. Sitting in the great *majlis*, surrounded by fierce-looking guards and servants who wore pistols when they brought coffee, Hamilton, as he said later to his wife, was almost scared to move. But he was greatly impressed by Ibn Saud, by his size (the King was over six feet four), by his dignity, by his grasp of the issues at stake. And he was greatly heartened by what Ibn Saud said. The King liked the speed with which the Americans had developed Bahrain, and the methods they had used there. Though if he could suit himself he would prefer to develop the country's resources alone, without the help or the intrusion of foreigners, if he had to deal with western companies he liked the Americans better because geographically they were so far away. And so with regard to these latest terms, the King believed Hamilton could rest easy.

After that interview, about which he told no one, Hamilton was perfectly assured that if anyone got the concession it would be Socal; he did not need Philby's letter from Mecca which said that the King had been putting pressure on the ministers and that things looked propitious.

But on the day when Hamilton submitted his final terms, something happened that threw the whole tangled negotiations into a snarl again. April 20, 1933, was the day on which the United States announced an embargo on gold. Within a few days Lombardi was cabling from London to hold everything, and the Netherlands Bank in Jiddah had raised the value of the gold pound from $4.87 to $5.60. Within another few days it climbed to above $6.00 — carrying with it the whole price of Hamilton's carefully negotiated agreements. It was not clear, from Jiddah, exactly what the embargo meant, apart from a perhaps temporary devaluation of the dollar. At worst, it might mean complete abandonment of the gold standard, with fatal consequences for the concession, since Saudi Arabia insisted on being paid in gold.

Initially Hamilton was not seriously alarmed, and he did not pass on to the government San Francisco's proposal that all concession payments be pegged at a value of $5 to the gold pound. In London, Lombardi went on trying to find out how gold might be secured, since it could not be shipped from the United States; he investigated the importation of sovereigns from India at a three-shilling premium, and the purchase of bullion in the London and Amsterdam financial markets at the present premium value of gold, without liking either alternative.

The ministers, still hopeful of playing one bidder against the other, asked Hamilton for a revised statement of the April 20 terms, and got it finally on May 3, Hamilton having delayed because he knew the IPC, through Longrigg and Sir Andrew Ryan, was trying hard to discover the Socal terms in order to make up its mind about a topping offer. (It made up its mind on May 5 that it did not want to compete further, and thus left Socal alone in the running.)

The summer heat grew in Jiddah's streets and in the fanless and iceless Grand Hotel. The tension in Jiddah's social life grew too. The more remote tensions of the world's financial collapse seemed, in the circumstances, less critical than they were, but they were critical enough to make Socal seriously consider pulling out of the negotiations, and to cause Hamilton days and nights of strain. Even when he was convinced he was winning, or about to win, delays and snags blocked a final approval. In Mecca Philby, after attending a meeting of the ministers on May 8 in which the draft of Hamilton's final offer was debated point by point, wrote jubilantly that the thing was in the bag.

And yet the conferences and arguments went on – May 14, May 16, May 18, May 23 – with the tough bargainers Shaikh Abdullah, Fuad Hamza, sometimes Yusef Yassin, always the interpreter Najib Salha. The government steadfastly clung to its wish to be paid in gold and its insistence that the initial loan be repayable out of only 10 percent of royalties. Socal, though it consented to make the initial payment in gold, insisted that it must be protected from having to buy further gold at premium prices in case the gold embargo persisted, and that the first loan must be repayable more promptly than 10 percent of the purely hypothetical royalties would do it.

Hamilton had already had a hard time instructing the ministers in what he meant by a loan – money that must be repaid, even if there never were any royalties – and had already made a major concession by designating the loan as interest-free in deference to the Muslim law against usury.

Wearily the duelists fought it out until, on May 29, Shaikh Abdullah signed the Concession Agreement at Kazma Palace on the outskirts of Jiddah. It became effective on July 14 by publication in the official government journal. The terms were far below those which the Saudi Arab government had first proposed, but well above what Socal considered justifiable for a mere look at a wildcat prospect. The Saudi Arab government was to receive an initial loan of £30,000 gold and another loan of £20,000 in eighteen months. The first annual rental of £5,000 was also to be in gold, but the second loan and all subsequent rental or royalty payments could at Socal's option be made in other currencies on the basis of a flexible exchange formula.

26

The company would begin exploration within three months and keep at it until it started drilling or gave up the concession. It would start drilling no later than three years from the effective date of the concession and drill until it gave up or developed commercial production, which was defined as 2,000 tons of oil per day. On the announcement of commercial production, it would pay the Saudi government a royalty advance of £50,000, and a year later it would pay £50,000 more. The agreement was good for 60 years; it covered the whole of eastern Saudi Arabia, from the Gulf to the western edge of the Dahna sands, and from the northern to the southern boundaries – both ill-defined – of the country.

In a separate and private agreement, Socal acquired preferential rights in other areas reaching west from the Dahna; it could, by matching any offer made in good faith by any other company, acquire the right to explore and develop in this additional territory. As for the Neutral Zone, the Private Agreement specified that the company could acquire rights there too, by matching any terms obtained by the Shaikh of Kuwait for his share.

What Hamilton had thought might take a few weeks had taken three and a half months. After he had signed the agreement with Shaikh Abdullah, the Hamiltons left Twitchell to look after details (Philby had already gone on to Cairo on a business trip) and took several weeks' vacation in southern Europe, winding up in London about the first day of July.

While they were traveling, six copies of an "impressive piece of paper," in both English and Arabic, went back and forth across the ocean and received the signatures of many people. By the end of July, Hamilton had it in his hands to forward to W. F. Vane, head of the land-lease division, in San Francisco. It contained then the signature of Amir Faisal, Foreign Minister of Saudi Arabia, on behalf of his father Ibn Saud. The Amir's signature was authenticated by the Dutch Vice-Consul in Jiddah. Hamilton jokingly doubted the necessity of having the Vice-Consul's signature authenticated by the Minister of Foreign Affairs at The Hague, and the signature of the Minister of Foreign Affairs validated by the American Minister to the Netherlands. And yet the weight of this impressive piece of paper warranted the most gingerly and reverential treatment: such documents as this, stemming from the work of such people as humorous, boy-faced Lloyd Hamilton, make the future of nations and alter the economic equilibrium of the world.

Now there were only loose ends to be tied. Hamilton tied them from London, where he set up a small permanent office for the company. He arranged with Twitchell, still looking after the company's affairs in Arabia, to take two cars and two light trucks, with drivers and mechanics, across to the Arabian Gulf coast as soon as arrangements could be made; there he would help start two geological teams on the first explorations. He began stirring up San Francisco about possible use of a plane in Arabia, as permitted by a clause in the Private Agreement. And he made a deal with Philby for the lease of Philby's old, delightfully dilapidated palace, the Bait Baghdadi, as a Jiddah headquarters.

Philby, now that he had the government monopoly to sell Ford cars, was moving outside the walls to an old building known as the Green Palace, given to him by the government to house his expanded operations. Philby would leave furniture and equipment, including an electric-generating plant, behind him for the use of the junior land-lease man who would shortly be sent out to represent the company.

As for the gold sovereigns for which the Saudi ministers had so tenaciously dickered, they were a little delayed. Socal's unoptimistic application for a permit to export the sum of $170,327.50 in gold received no reply from the United States Treasury Department, and on July 26, within a few days of the due date, Hamilton made an emergency arrangement to have 35,000 gold sovereigns shipped to Jiddah by the Guaranty Trust

Company of London. The move proved wise when Dean Acheson, then Under-Secretary of the Treasury, denied the export permit on July 28. The boxes of gold went out from London on a P & O steamer on August 4, and on August 25 Twitchell cabled that he had counted them out on the tables of the Netherlands Bank in Jiddah under the eyes of Shaikh Abdullah Sulaiman, and had Shaikh Abdullah's receipt.

That was the first-act curtain. The second act would follow after a brief intermission.

Chapter Three
~ The Beachhead ~

From the point of view of the men who made the beachhead, what they came to do was a job like other jobs. From the perspective of history and with the map in mind, it was an assignment to challenge the most rash; seen in retrospect, it has the nostalgic, almost mythic quality of an action from the age of giants.

The job was the exploration, above ground and below, of some 320,000 square miles of desert, most of it barely known, most of it casually mapped, some of it visited by westerners only two or three times in all its history, some of it so arid that the Bedouin tribesmen who wandered across it on their annual migrations went for weeks without water, living on the milk of camels which in turn could drink the brackish water of the few wells.

And they were to do the job in the face of enormous difficulties: a transportation system consisting of only a handful of cars supplemented by camels and donkeys; roads, when they found any roads at all, that were braiding caravan trails across the gravel plains and among the dunes. They were, furthermore, half a world away from their base of supplies, and with hardly a shop or store or warehouse where they could buy so much as a nail or a pair of pliers, much less the complex spare parts of a mechanized civilization. They would be many hundred miles from the Arabian center of authority, the Jiddah-Mecca-Taif-Riyadh axis, and yet have available to them only the beginnings of a modern communications system. Ibn Saud had conquered his Wahhabi followers' distrust of the telephone by having passages of the Koran read over it, but the telephone so far linked only the cities of the Hijaz.

By 1931, intent upon holding his territories together, and knowing the necessity for good communications, the King had established a rudimentary net of wireless stations. When the American geologists started work at Jubail in the fall of 1933, there were stations in that town, in Qatif down the coast, in Hofuf some forty miles inland from al-'Uqair, and in Riyadh, capital of the Najd. Communication with Jiddah or the United States, however, involved several relays, and for a long time no message could be sent directly to Bahrain, only twelve miles away. Even internal messages, transmitted as they were in a language unfamiliar to the operators, often in code, and by relatively inexperienced men, could emerge at the far end as pure gibberish.

Not the least of the difficulties was the uncompromising nature of the country itself. Their base map was the 1:1,000,000 British War Office map of the Arabian Peninsula. From that, from Arab informants, from Twitchell and Philby, and from the few books available to them (Lawrence's *Revolt in the Desert*, Bertram Thomas' *Arabia Felix*, a few others), they could know the general conformation of the peninsula that thrust like the head and lower shaft of a putter down into the Arabian Sea. They knew that along the west, above the Red Sea coastal plain, the crystalline basement rocks were exposed as worn mountains rising in altitude to the south on the border of Yemen.

They knew that to the east of these mountains was a long curve of westward-facing cliffs and escarpments not unlike the persistent cliff-lines in Utah and Arizona, though less grand, and that the roof strata forming these escarpments dipped almost imperceptibly to the east. They knew that along the eastern side of the 1,000-mile crescent of the escarpments lay the belt of dunes called the Dahna, connecting the two great sand deserts: on the north the Great Nafud and on the south the Rub' al-Khali – this last an immense, lonely, nearly waterless waste crossed only by Thomas and Philby among Westerners, the great Empty Quarter of Arabia.

East of the narrow Dahna sands lay the Summan Plateau, broken limestone country that faded on the north into the flint desert along the Kuwait and Iraq borders, and on the south into another gravel plain, the Abu Bahr, "the father of the sea." They knew that below Jubail, on the Gulf, a belt of moving dunes blew southward across the salt flats of the coastal region, and widening as it went, melted into the Jafura sands which in turn melted into the northern Rub' al-Khali.

They knew a few words by which the Arabs described the topographical features of their country: *sabkha*, salt flat; *dikaka*, sand plains held down by sparse shrubs; *dibdiba*, the flint desert; *jabal*, a hill; *wadi*, a watercourse; *'ain*, a well or tank.

The concession area took in the whole eastern portion of Saudi Arabia, from the Gulf to the Dahna and from the Wadi al-'Ubayyid on the Iraq border to the mountainous southern edge of the Rub' al-Khali – an area larger than all Texas. These things, the men who made the beachhead knew in a general way; the particulars, including what lay underneath the often featureless desert, were all to be learned.

To start the job there were at first two men. A little later a third would come to open a government relations office in Jiddah. And over a period of weeks and months a few others would dribble into al-Hasa by ones and twos, handpicked for pioneering work and bringing with them elements of the absolutely indispensable equipment. When they had their full complement there would be, in al-Hasa itself, a total of ten. Theirs was a landing touched with wonder, imminent with consequences. They came like discoverers, and if they did not often stare at each other with a wild surmise, being practical men with a job to do, they could not be insensible to the things around them, and their capacity for wonder would not go totally untested.

When Robert P. (Bert) Miller and Schuyler B. (Krug) Henry crossed the channel from Bahrain to Jubail in Saudi Arabia, they brought with them a combined total of two and half years' experience on Bahrain, a smattering of Arabic, and a determination to get to work right away. But as the Saudi Arab customs launch slipped past the careened dhows on the mudflats inside the breakwater, they and Karl Twitchell, who had crossed the Peninsula to help them get started, saw that getting down to business was going to be a little harder than they had expected.

On shore were gathered robed throngs of people, throngs who obviously represented more than the normal population of the town. As they stepped out to be greeted by the local amir and the soldiers who were to form their compulsory escort, they learned that several dignitaries from Jubail and Qatif, the big oasis down the coast, had come to greet them too, as well as many Bedouins from the hinterlands. All apparently were planning a big celebration of welcome.

Miller and Henry, however, had other plans, and after paying the proper courtesy calls and drinking the appropriate number of cups of coffee, they spotted a *jabal* to the south and, learning that it was called Jabal al-Berri, piled into the two touring cars that Twitchell had rented from the government in Jiddah and driven across country for their use. If they had hoped to discourage the holiday spirit of the crowds they were disappointed. Everyone climbed aboard camels and white al-Hasa donkeys, and streamed after them.

For part of the seven miles to Jabal al-Berri the cars served them; then the going got sandy and rough, and amid much laughter they accepted a lift from the camels that the soldiers had forehandedly brought along. They looked over Jabal al-Berri without finding anything to excite them, came down again, mounted the camels and started back across the great *sabkha*. Suddenly the solid earth veered before their eyes, the intense light flawed and changed, and unknown Arabia grinned at them — a sudden distorted grin — as the ring of the horizon boiled and floated with mirages.

Around its edge, dunes and runty palmettos were stretched and warped until they looked like cliffs or forested headlands. Camels and their riders came over the rim as tall as towers. The cars parked on the flats loomed like grain elevators on the Nebraska plains, and the pearling town of Jubail, which they knew had only a thousand or so people, threw up a skyline like New York's, a vision of cloud-capped towers and gorgeous palaces.

The geologists, a little dazed, clung to the camel saddles, tried their best to adjust comfortably to the camel's rocking ride, and headed back to the town. Beyond the jut of rocks and the careened dhows, out between the muddied waves slapping the beach and the bank of dark blue sea that underlined the horizon, they could see the Gulf's own images of persistent unreality.

The waves ran quartering, and along the meeting line of green water and blue, a *jalbout* beating up the coast seemed to drive at a tremendous clip. They saw it racing past, but looked again in a few minutes and found it still there, and looked in an hour and found it still there, painted against its backdrop of sea and sky, entranced in its mirage of motion. They observed it curiously, not knowing then that during their Arabian experience, on the occasions when they had a minute or an hour to observe and think, they would feel as entranced and frozen in unreal motion as that *jalbout* beating up the coast.

One of the first decisions Miller and Henry had to make was where to set up headquarters. It was the opinion of Muhammad 'Ali Tawil, the local customs officer and government representative, and other Saudi Arabs that Hofuf, in the great al-Hasa oasis, would make the best headquarters location. Miller and Henry had their doubts, and they could be satisfied only by a look.

Within the first week, accompanied by their guards, cooks, interpreters, drivers, mechanics, and hangers-on, and carrying shovels to help them get the cars through, they explored westward as far as al-Hinnat and southward to Qatif and its great palm gardens and flowing wells. They spent a day on Tarut Island.

Five days after their landing, on September 28, they were walking around among the limestone hills called Jabal Dhahran which they and Davies had seen from Bahrain. Reasonably sure that the structure had good closure, they marked this area as one worth detailed study, and named it the Dammam Dome.

By the last day of the month they were down at Hofuf, where they set up a kind of office in a house rented from the great merchant family of the Gosaibis, Bahrain agents of King Ibn Saud. A few days later they drove north to al-Hinnat and closed the traverse of their first Arabian reconnaissance.

By the end of those first hot, disorganized days, more things were clear than that the humpy *jabals* near Dammam warranted closer study. It had been made abundantly clear that al-Hasa simply wouldn't do. The flies were maddening, the palm gardens were cut by canals that bred far too many anopheles mosquitoes, and the canals had very inadequate bridges for motor traffic.

Miller chose instead Jubail, the place of their landing. It was, by comparison with Qatif and Hofuf, a cool and breezy town, and it had a fair port for the landing of supplies from Bahrain. So he kept as a branch office the Hofuf house the Gosaibis had provided, and had the Gosaibis engage him another in Jubail.

It could have been much worse — an enclosed court 300 feet square, with rooms built against the inside of the wall and only one great arched gate. There was plenty of locked space for storing equipment. The roof was open; they found early that it was a good place to sleep. All the house needed were a few modern improvements, and all the two pioneers needed were reinforcement and supplies.

Reinforcement came first to Jiddah, where Bill Lenahan, a baby-faced young University of California graduate with six years of South American experience, a marvelously persuasive and mellow speaking voice, and a temper like a wildcat, arrived on October 18. His arrival caused no ripple in the lives of the party in al-Hasa, for he was 750 air miles away, an indefinite time by the Saudi telegraph, seven to ten racking days by car, more than two weeks by the fastest racing camel.

But the al-Hasa pioneers felt solidly strengthened by the arrival at al-'Uqair on October 22 of a geologist named J. W. (Soak) Hoover, with a mechanic, a helper, two drivers, and three Ford touring cars. Still reacting as if he had only a few days before al-Hasa would sink into the sea, Miller wasted not an hour on indoctrination or acclimatizing: he got Hoover unloaded and brought him straight to the Dammam Dome, where he and Henry set up a camp nine miles south of the village of Dammam to start the detailed study of the *jabal* area. They had with them two cars, not too mobile in the dune sand, and a driver and mechanic whose information on the high-compression engine was somewhat indefinite.

As soon as the reinforcements arrived Twitchell took the two government cars and the remains of his Hijaz retinue and made his fourth and final trip across Arabia. The man whose explorations and recommendations had guided the King's decision to talk to Socal (which on November 8 created a subsidiary named California Arabian Standard Oil Company – Casoc) would end his connection with the company at the close of the month, after he had helped Bill Lenahan get established in the Bait Baghdadi in Jiddah.

Immediately after Twitchell's departure, as if to emphasize both the need of good government relations and the difficulty of maintaining them, Muhammad 'Ali Tawil, the local customs officer, got it into his head that he was obligated to collect duty on the food and supplies Miller had shipped in. Until then Tawil and the Americans had got on very well: obviously Tawil and the local amir had strict instructions to be friendly, agreeable and helpful; as for the Americans, they were determinedly being the pleasantest people the Arabs had ever known. But on the duty problem Tawil was adamant. He read his orders that way. Miller, knowing that such duties were specifically forbidden in the Concession Agreement, refused to pay them. Away went a long, tangled, coded message to Lenahan asking him to straighten out the matter and have the Minister of Finance send the proper instructions to Tawil.

In Jubail, Tawil regularly came with his dignified white beard and requested payment of the duties. The geologists steadfastly refused. The quarters in the compound remained almost as bare as the tent camp at Dammam, without plumbing or electricity, refrigeration or fans or Flit. They ate rice and boiled sheep and dates, dates and boiled sheep and rice, and ate them with the less patience for thinking about the stateside luxuries that lay piled up on Tawil's docks.

Only the weather treated them well. Though at midday the temperatures were still in the 90's, and though they sometimes felt that they could wring water out of the air simply by closing their fists, the nights were cooler, and the *shamals*, which inland would be loaded with sand, came in at them in gusty rushes from the Gulf. This was what would one day be called "executive weather," the pleasantest time for visits of inspection by big brass from the States. The pioneers waited for Lenahan's reply, and ate their rice and sheep and dates, and got along.

On November 10 the beachhead expanded again. Art Brown and Tom Koch came into al-'Uqair with two 2 ¾-ton rear-wheel-drive trucks equipped with dual high-pressure tires. They brought also four Hijazi drivers whom Twitchell had taken to Bahrain for training in the Bapco shops. Then on the 21st Hugh Burchfiel arrived, fussy, finicky, able, bald as a cue ball. He had come out from the States with a mechanic named Felix Dreyfus, but Dreyfus had burned his hand and had stayed behind on Bahrain for treatment.

Early in December an engineer, Allen White, came ashore with three pickup trucks, an interpreter, and a cook. All were welcome, especially White, whose seasoning in foreign oil work had begun in Venezuela, and who had been one of the Bapco pioneers on Bahrain. He had surveyed that entire concession, and was the only real Arabic scholar in Casoc's early days in Saudi Arabia. The interpreter, then only a boy, was 'Ajab Khan, who had come originally from Peshawar, now in Pakistan, and who over the ensuing years was of great service to the company.

Meanwhile, the disagreement with Muhammad Tawil continued. Tawil came around regularly to collect the duty; Miller continued to refuse it; the canned goods and dehydrated foods that they coveted piled up in the Jubail and al-'Uqair customs houses. Finally, it came to a head when Tawil, demanding the duty which it was his job to collect, lost his temper and rose to stamp out of the room. But before he could reach the door he met a messenger, part of the Saudi telegraph system, bearing the word of Abdullah Sulaiman that the food for the geological parties was to be admitted free. The embattled geologists praised the name of Lenahan and the institution of the Jiddah office and radically altered their diet.

By Christmastime, when Miller went over to Bahrain to meet Doc Nomland, chief geologist from Socal headquarters, the landing party had had its period of trial and discovered some of its errors. The location of their headquarters at Jubail was confirmed when Nomland, coming back with Miller and the new mechanic, Dreyfus, took one look at Qatif's picturesque, inadequately bridged, and wriggler-filled ditches. At that time Hoover, Henry, and Burchfiel were working out of Jubail, and Koch and Brown in the country out from Hofuf, where Allen White had charge of the sub-office. They had begun to cover ground among them, and had learned a few things.

38

They had discovered that the trucks, with their hard dual tires, were worthless in sand, though they could use one for limited service in Hofuf. The other was left for a while at al-'Uqair and then with some difficulty got up to Jubail after the winter rains. The usefulness of these trucks was more inspirational than practical. The experience of digging and brushing and pushing them out of sand and *sabkha* was good for the character; it was also good for the imagination. It demonstrated comprehensively and at once the need for all-wheel drive and low-pressure tires in this country where all work for a good many years would be off-road work.

This was a challenge that would beget a response, a necessity that would be the mother of invention, and some of the pioneers in al-Hasa would be pioneers also in the development of low-pressure flotation of heavy equipment. For the moment, they cursed their trucks and found little use for them. The touring cars did get around, though they were often stuck and though they showed a pernicious habit of breaking springs and front cross-members.

As for Arab-American relations, diplomats might have learned from either side. Except for the difficulty with Tawil about the duty on food, there had been nothing approximating an incident. The Americans were energetic and enthusiastic, knew their geology, and went about their work as if they were in Colorado. The Amir of Jubail, the qadi, the guides, the soldiers were friendly. Cautiously, visitors and residents explored each other's peculiarities. It was surprising to both sides to find that Arabs and Americans laughed in the same places; it was at first a possible irritation and later a basis for respect when the Americans found Saudi Arabs tough, independent, and disinclined to give in in an argument, and the Saudis found Americans more willing to fraternize than the British.

Still, there were minor sources of friction. The soldiers supplied by the Amir of al-Hasa, Abdullah ibn Jiluwi, Ibn Saud's first cousin once removed and old battle companion, were well-behaved enough, but there were sixteen of them to each field party, far too many, the Americans thought, simply to demonstrate to the Bedouins that the foreigners traveled under the protection of Ibn Saud.

Their supplies and gear burdened a dozen camels, and the flocks of animals that were necessary for their support seemed to draw after them all the flies in Arabia.

Since the trucks had proved useless in cross-country work, all camp luggage had to come by camel, and though a good pack camel could take 400 pounds, it required many such camels to keep two geologists and their keepers and protectors in the field. The result was they were all but immobilized by the size of their supporting parties, and the amount of work done was very much less than the geologists, left to themselves, could have done alone.

There was, however, no apparent way of cutting down, for not only did the government insist that the soldiers were necessary for their protection, but the Arabs were constitutionally and culturally inhibited from combining jobs. A driver drove, a mechanic repaired, a camel driver tended the camels, a cook would not be caught dead doing a houseboy's job of serving, a houseboy would quit before he would remove a cook's kettle from the fire. As a result, whenever any two geologists took off into the desert, there went with them an interpreter, a cook, a cook's helper, a houseboy, a mechanic, a mechanic's helper, a driver, anywhere from fifteen to thirty soldiers, and four camel drivers.

Their equipment would include a Ford touring car, a half-ton pickup, a minimum of twenty riding camels, and a dozen big baggage camels. On these last would be piled three 10 x 20 tents of goat hair, with grass matting for the floors, a 10 x 12 silk tent, collapsible tables, chairs, cots, food, cooking utensils, gasoline stoves and lamps, and (if it hadn't already been sent out on a supplementary camel train) gasoline in five-gallon cans.

Also aboard somewhere or set up for use en route would be a chronometer, a transit, sketchboards of a type designed by Miller, allowing use of continuous rolls of sketching paper, three Brunton compasses, drafting equipment, four one-gallon water cans, six *ghurbas* or waterskins holding from six to ten gallons each, four oversized waterbags, and an assortment of tools and spare motor parts and spare tires and spare front springs. No radios; those didn't come along until the spring of 1934. No geological party went into any area without first notifying the government representative, who notified the Ministry of Finance, which then issued permission and assigned guards and soldiers. To get such an outfit going was like starting a military offensive.

Nevertheless they were beginning to know their job – then the preliminary job of geological reconnaissance – and were beginning to get it done. They were incomparably better desert drivers than in the beginning; they knew their way around the coastal area, and Brown and Koch were beginning a two-month camp at 'Uray'irah, 60 miles southwest of Jubail. But they had hardly made a dent in the 320,000 square miles, and they yearned for the airplane that rumor said was on its way to them.

The plane was absolutely essential for understanding the country's structure, for there were few commanding points from which to get a broad view. Dips in outcrops were low and often ambiguous, and in many areas, as at Qatif, where some of the palm gardens and wells themselves were going under, the surface of the country was buried under moving dunes.

Nomland looked all this over for more than a month, gave it his blessing, and started across country in a touring car. His way was made treacherous by rainstorms, which hardened the dunes and made them passable but turned the *sabkhas* into crusted sinks likely at any time to let a car down to the running boards.

The car gave out before they reached Jiddah; a party of rescuers dispatched by Lenahan and the government brought Nomland in. He was needed at that moment, because the IPC was dickering for a concession in western Arabia, and there was a question whether or not Socal would choose to compete. Nomland took a quick look over the northern Hijaz, found the rock all igneous except for a strip near the coast, and recommended that Socal forget it.

Arabia on both coasts settled back into its apparent catalepsy. The foreign colony in Jiddah continued to go on Sunday evenings to the receptions of Sir Andrew and Lady Ryan, or they shot rabbits from cars out on the gravel plains, or swam in the protected waters inside the reefs.

Bill Lenahan, looking disgustedly around the enormous barrenness of the Bait Baghdadi, put up with Philby's iron cots and decrepit furniture because he had to, but he did not delay long in finding a newly built and better house, next to the Saudi Foreign Ministry, and putting workmen to renovating it as the Bait Americani. When he was told that it would have water closets, Sir Andrew Ryan poffed and poshed; the British Legation had sand buckets, like all the rest of Jiddah. Sir Andrew was of the opinion that water closets would not work in Jiddah.

Across Arabia – doggedly, by car and camel – the job went on. Hoover and Henry, who had been detailing the Dammam Dome, had gone over to join Burchfiel, mapping the country west of Jubail as far as al-Lihabah, and down the coast to Qatif. Brown and Koch were still working out of their camp at 'Uray'irah, between Hofuf and Hinnat. Allen White was still in the Hofuf office, keeping Brown and Koch in touch with the rest of the parties, and sending them the things they needed in the way of supplies.

If the men who made the beachhead had thought to add up the hours they worked, they would have found themselves doing time and a half or double time, but they seldom thought of the hours. If the weather was good, they worked, lining themselves out across the low sand ridges and the dunes; and with Brunton compass and speedometer they made great traverses, mapping as they went and checking the traverses with Brunton triangulation and occasional astronomical fixes. It wasn't exactly mapping of a geodetic accuracy, but it was far and away the most accurate mapping that had ever been done in Arabia, and for their immediate purposes it was quite accurate enough.

In bad weather, when *shamals* blew the whole world into a gritty red-brown darkness, or heat waves jiggled the *jabals* and clanged in the brainpan like gongs, or when, as it did in December and January, the wind grew raw and icy, they stayed in their tents, inked in the field pencil work on the maps, and slept.

Once in a while they took part of a day and went gazelle hunting with the soldiers. But most days they were in the field all day and at their drafting boards half the night, and up at five for another run; and slowly the unrelieved and featureless country began to take shape on their rolls of sketch paper, more real there than it sometimes seemed in the heat dance of noon or with the shadowless dusk of a sandstorm sweeping across it.

In spite of constant and acute discomforts, this was a contented group of men by and large. They grew mighty beards, competitively, and horsed around and tried their muscles as young men will, and mourned, without complete conviction, the lost company of ladies and the drink that used to cheer a glum time of day.

They watched carefully to avoid friction with their Arab helpers, and did their level best to be charitable when some Arab customs jarred their sense of logic. They practiced their Arabic on children and soldiers and houseboys and visitors from the towns, drank pots of sweet tea and cardamom-flavored coffee, and learned not to use the left hand in eating. Finding Arabs like other people elsewhere, they learned to like some of them better than others, and they made some progress toward knowing themselves and the country in which they worked.

These were the days, it seemed later, when Saudi Arabia's astonishing push toward modernization began, the days when a revolution of *things* began in eastern Saudi Arabia. For whatever they may think of the nations which produce and possess them, whatever distaste they have for their beliefs, their dress, and their politics, no people in history has been able to resist for half an hour the *things* that people like this small contingent of geologists bring with them. The Saudis were no different. However odd they found these newcomers among them, the things this crowd of tinkerers, mechanics, and gadgeteers brought with them, imported later or ingeniously improvised, were irresistible.

Shortly after the first supplies began to arrive, a boy who had been hired to supply the Casoc compound with water ran into a very odd situation. He emptied the usual number of *ghurbas* of water into a 55-gallon drum at the side of the house, only to see it vanish. He inspected the drum for a leak, shook his head, and brought more water. Again he looked in. Again it had vanished. It wasn't until he had spent two hours pouring water in that the level of water reached the top of the drum, at which point he wrapped his *ghutra* across the lower part of his face and hastened uneasily away. What he didn't know was that the tinkerers and gadgeteers society had spent an hour or two installing a huge indoor tank and hooking it up to the drum outside.

Such improvisation was just the beginning. When, in the spring of 1934, a shipload of tools, nuts, bolts, wrenches, dies, pipes, fittings, wire, insulators, and other industrial bric-a-brac cascaded off a supply ship, the tinkerers and gadgeteers society really went to work. They installed showers fed by gravity from the roof, modernized the mud-brick privy with a combination of lime and Flit guns, and, with a hundred yards of fabric screen that some foresighted individual had ordered, screened off their building from the ever-present swarms of flies.

One of the major improvements in their lives came about with the construction of a still that could produce several gallons of distilled water a day. That innovation, some of them insisted later, saved at least the sanity and possibly the lives of the hypochondriacs who tasted water the way the Borgias tasted wine. And if they feared, as some did, that distilled water would not replace the minerals they lost by evaporation, they could judiciously mix it with well water until the flavor and saline content suited them. They had as many formulas for drinking water as Americans at home have for martinis.

For many Arabs the most fascinating innovations were the two 32-volt, 3,000-watt Kohler generators. Many Saudis had seen electricity on Bahrain, of course, but the less sophisticated were quite startled when the little glass balls hanging from the ceilings suddenly lighted up one night. A few may have suspected the work of jinns, but most noticed that the wires from the little balls led into the walls and out to a power panel of brass knobs and handles of black wood and on to the gasoline engines in the compound. They noticed too that along with the light bulbs there appeared on window sills in the dining room and at various spots in the living quarters, and even up on the roof where the Americans were sleeping, certain small instruments with spinning blades inside a wire frame. At a signal they began to turn with a humming noise, then disappeared in a blur. It didn't take them long to learn that it was dangerous to poke their fingers behind the wire and that it was pleasant to sit in front of the current of cool air on a hot day.

For the tinkerers society the photo lab was a major challenge. The aerial films that would be used when the company's airplane arrived were 10 inches wide and 100 feet long; there were no trained helpers; the water came in lukewarm even from the oversized waterbags where they cooled it by evaporation. And the lab was very dark and hot and oppressive. After a time, in the outside wall of the darkroom there appeared a loop of six-inch pipe like a loop of gut from a sheep's opened belly, and this fitted into two five-gallon gasoline tins, one on top of another, which had been stuffed with wool made from fibers of glass. Somewhere within these cans or inside the loop of pipe or inside the lab was a fan, and those who worked in the darkroom after that reported that even in a sandstorm the air which blew from the end of the pipe was clean and almost cool.

All this made an impression in the Eastern Province of Saudi Arabia. For when they had turned on the fans, shot down the flies with their Flit guns, screened the windows, turned on the lights, and spread oilcloth across their tables, they began to entertain. And when the Amir came and the *ra'is al-baladiyah* or mayor came, and the *qadi*, and dignitaries such as Muhammad Tawil, Muhammad Gosaibi of the great merchant family, and Arif Effendi, chief of the local Saudi police, it was not long before they remarked on the value of these comforts and casually inquired where they might obtain some of the same.

The products of the tinkerers and gadgeteers society become absolutely indispensable as soon as they are known. There is no resisting them. Industrial civilization made its way among the Indians of North America in the form of needles, awls, knives, axes, guns, woolen cloth. It is legitimate to believe that something of the kind began in eastern Saudi Arabia long before any oil was found there, when the men of the beachhead in Jubail began to tinker with the machines that made water and climate, and the smells that drove away the flies. And long before anyone knew the phrase, a revolution of rising expectations had begun. Saudi Arabia would never be the same.

Chapter Four
~ The Plane ~

Among the agreements worked out between Standard Oil's negotiator Lloyd Hamilton and the representatives of King Ibn Saud, one of the most important was the company's right to use airplanes in its exploration work. The agreement was subject to strict but unspecified limitations, but the merest look at the map of the concession area told Socal officials that they would need to use the right.

In September 1933, about the time Miller and Henry were establishing the beachhead at Jubail, Clark Gester, Socal's chief geologist, called in a former employee, an ex-Navy pilot then conducting an air mapping business in Los Angeles. Gester knew Dick Kerr from a long time back, and knew him as a man peculiarly qualified for jobs demanding ingenuity, versatility, and imagination. Kerr was a graduate geologist from the University of California; he was a pilot and a mechanic; he was an excellent photographer; he boiled over with energies and enthusiasms. And if on a job he ran into something that he didn't know, he was the kind who would go without sleep for three nights in a row and come up knowing it. If you had tied his elbows he could not have talked.

Gester wanted him to frame a proposal to make an aerial geological reconnaissance on a contract basis, do the necessary aerial photography, and provide air support for ground parties in Arabia. Kerr looked up Arabia in the atlas, obtained the general impression that it was covered with high sand dunes, and decided that a small plane would work better than one of the latest Douglas models.

He and his partner, Walter English, submitted a proposal, Gester and Doc Nomland approved it, and Socal ordered a special Fairchild 71 from the Kreider-Reisoner plant at Hagerstown, Maryland.

It would have a hole in the bottom for taking vertical photographs, a removable window on each side for taking obliques, and in deference to the expected sand it would have the biggest tires they could find: 36 x 18s.

Charley Rocheville, who would be Kerr's co-pilot and mechanic, designed an extra gas tank, which left seating space for only four people but increased the cruising radius to a safe 350 miles. Kerr bought all the equipment and supplies he thought necessary (including 5,000 gallons of aviation gasoline in five-gallon cans), shipped them direct to Bahrain on the Socal tanker *El Segundo*, and headed for Maryland to give the makers of their plane some pointers.

In the midst of that the firecrackerish Kerr somehow found two weeks to tackle a major problem: how to get film that could stand up to Saudi Arabia's heat. He went to Rochester, New York, and there conducted a series of tests with the Eastman Kodak plant for the developing of aerial films in warm water, since, rumor said, even the drinking water in Arabia never got cooler than a slow boil.

Between them, he and the Eastman research division found a process of hardening the film with potassium chrome alum, and succeeded in developing film at water temperatures as high as 120 degrees. By the end of the month, Kerr had his photographic supplies taken care of and was in New York buying electrical parts and water distillation equipment for his desert darkroom.

Kerr had arranged for the plane, due to be completed on February 1, 1934, to go as deck cargo on the S. S. *Exochorda* of the American Export Lines, sailing February 6, but it was not until the day before the *Exochorda* was to sail that the plane was delivered. Hastily, Charley Rocheville took it for a half-hour test flight to see if it flew – it did – and then, with Kerr, headed for North Beach, Flushing, now the site of La Guardia Airport, where they had to land it on a foot of new snow.

Next morning a crane set it, with its wings folded locust-fashion, on a barge, and an hour before sailing time the barge bumped alongside the *Exochorda*. The captain, a man named Reyerson, was not pleased, and was not going to accept any airplane this late in the game. But Dick Kerr was a hard person to refuse; if he couldn't talk you down he grinned you down. At four that afternoon the *Exochorda* put out to sea with the Fairchild 71 parked on its afterdeck and Kerr and Rocheville frantically lashing it down and getting canvas covers over it.

Twenty-three days out of New York they pulled into the harbor at Alexandria, unloaded it from the deck, and watched anxiously as it was ignominiously hauled six miles through the city with its tail skid on a donkey cart and about a hundred Egyptians helping to pull and push. North of the city, at a small private airport called ar-Ramlah (meaning "the sand"), they tested the Fairchild thoroughly, and made friends with Royal Air Force officers, who gave them copies of the RAF flight maps to all the places they would stop en route to Saudi Arabia: Cairo, Gaza, Rutbah Wells, Baghdad, Basra, Kuwait, and Bahrain.

When at last they were ready to take off and fly the last leg, however, they found that they could not leave Egypt without a *triptyque*, a *carnet de passage*, and God knew what else. That meant explanations, forms, the posting of bond, little journeys from official to official, the discovery that they would have to move the airplane to Cairo to get clearance, long arguments with customs about the precise purpose of all the miscellaneous cargo aboard the craft. After two weeks of it they were about convinced that they would spend the rest of their lives in Cairo, but the RAF people did them favors and got them their permit.

If it occurred to them that they would need permission not only to leave Egypt but to land in Saudi Arabia, they did not let the thought bother them; with their Egyptian papers finally in their hands they went to the airport and looked aloft. A sandstorm was blowing, the visibility was about a hundred yards, their eyes and teeth were full of grit. But they had been in Egypt all they wanted to be; they climbed in and took off for Gaza.

Visibility upstairs was no better than down below; within a short time they had completely lost sight of the ground, except those parts of it which were flying in small fragments in the air. Acknowledging that they couldn't possibly find Gaza in the murk, Kerr turned back – and found that he couldn't find Cairo.

Eventually he did find the Nile Delta, whose agricultural development held down the sand and permitted some low contact flying back up the river. With wheels practically scraping the housetops they located the airport and came down. There some displeased officials informed them that since they had now used up their permit to leave Egypt, they would have to obtain a second one.

That took most of another week. This time, when they took off, they waited for clear weather. Their friends the RAF escorted them to Ismailia in two fighter planes, partly out of friendship and partly to see that they crossed the Suez Canal at that particular spot and no other.

Gaza held them overnight. In the morning they left for Baghdad, with a planned fuel stop at Rutbah Wells, but they arrived at Rutbah Wells on the bumper of a brisk tail wind, and having plenty of fuel, decided to go straight on to Baghdad. Over the Euphrates they met another sandstorm that reduced visibility and had them hedgehopping across the bald, barren desert. Expecting the region between the Tigris and Euphrates to be a Garden of Eden, they went straight over the mud town of Ramadi on the Euphrates, recognizing the river but not the town.

The country was so much more barren than their expectations that they thought they were lost. They decided to hold speed and course for one hour; then, if they had not found Baghdad, they would turn back to the Euphrates and hunt a landing place. They were about to turn to the river when they found themselves flying over a big town that turned out to be Baghdad. They were surprised. So were the airport officials, who chided them for not keeping to their announced schedule, pronounced *shedule*.

Again the Royal Air Force was friendly, entertained them, sent them on next day to Basra to yet another RAF mess and more entertainment. But the Basra RAF was emphatic about two things: under no circumstances should they fly over the Shaikhdom of Kuwait, and under absolutely no circumstances, no matter who told them it was permissible, should they try to land in Saudi Arabia.

They should go to Bahrain and let the RAF there try to get them permission to cross over. To the RAF pilots, who had perhaps listened to too many exaggerated and fanciful stories about Bedouins, coming down in Saudi Arabia sounded, rightly or wrongly, like finding yourself afoot at night in leopard country.

It did no good for Kerr and Rocheville to protest that their outfit at Jubail had all the necessary permission and had already laid out a landing strip. The RAF could not be convinced, and insisted that the two should accept as a present a pair of .45 automatics. The thought that perhaps he had better cable Bahrain, and try to get a message to Jubail that they were arriving, entered Kerr's head, but it seemed a lot of trouble. And anyway, the plane could get there long before any message.

They did follow the advice about not flying over Kuwait, staying out to sea south from Basra until they were well past the shaikhdom. Then they turned in to the Saudi Arab coast and flew down along it, rubbernecking at the occasional black patches of Bedouin tents, the improbable-looking palm gardens, the shoreline colored like changeable silk, with arrowy fishtraps pointing out toward deep water and an occasional dhow leaning across the wind and the cormorants thronging on bare coral islands.

Finding Jubail gave them no difficulty. They made one pass over it and saw an airstrip (Burchfiel and Dreyfus had dragged it the week before), and they saw people standing whose mixture of clothing said that they were not quite Arabs. Rocheville was flying the plane. He circled and brought her in, and because he was up in the nose he insisted later that he was definitely the ninth Casoc man to arrive in Arabia. Kerr, who was out of the plane first, disputed his claim. But Kerr achieved another distinction by his rush to put his feet on Arabian soil: he was immediately arrested by the Amir of Jubail for landing without permission.

The Amir was greatly agitated. Though he had heard from Miller, who had heard from Lenahan, that the plane was on the way, he had received no orders about it from his government. When he saw the Fairchild coming in, he rushed a detachment of soldiers to the field to protect it from the crowd. The crowd, hearing the plane and then seeing the scramble of the soldiers, rushed after. When the Fairchild came in, touched its wheels and bounced and rolled to a stop, and the door opened and Dick Kerr burst out to greet al-Hasa, the joy of the crowd could not be contained.

They surged forward to meet him, the soldiers set upon the crowd with canes and camel sticks and scattered them over the desert, and the Amir, trembling with outrage, arrested Kerr and Rocheville and ordered the plane taxied to the compound and padlocked. No one was to either fly it or work on it. Two days later he said it should be taken to Tarut Island and there impounded under the protection of the Amir of Qatif until the government sent some sort of instructions about it.

Miller, naturally, did not want the delay and nuisance of taking the plane to Tarut Island and leaving it there, possibly exposed to the fingers of the curious. He stalled by demanding that the pilots first be allowed to inspect the landing field on Tarut, to see if it was safe, and he had Burchfiel arrange donkeys to take them from the boat to the field, some distance inland.

Kerr, though somewhat crestfallen at the effect he had created by his dramatic arrival, was not so crestfallen he was going to ride any donkey. He could make better time walking. So he suffered a second humiliation. The white donkey, its forelegs and ears stained with henna, took off and left him as if he were standing still: al-Hasa donkeys, he discovered, can out-walk, out-trot, and out-gallop a man.

The Tarut field they found short, bumpy, and dangerous, with the shells of old planes scattered over it. Happily, they reported to the Amir that they could not possibly set the Fairchild down there. Unhappily, the Amir insisted; Miller said he would not order the plane to be moved: if the Amir wanted to have somebody take it over there, that was his responsibility.

In Jiddah, meanwhile, Lenahan was finding the airplane problem more difficult than the problem of customs duties. The King and Abdullah Sulaiman were both extremely angry about the unauthorized landing of a foreign plane on Saudi Arab soil, and half-inclined to rescind the temporary general permission contained in the Private Agreement. There was a short, almost savage flurry of irritability: impetuousness of the Dick Kerr variety, innocent though the Saudi government finally understood it to be, could be dangerous.

Suspicion communicated itself downward, too. The government radio operator, during all the excitement, was sitting one day in the padlocked plane with the radio turned on, and heard the signal of Bushire, across the Arabian Gulf in Iran. Convinced that the oil men had been sending messages to Iran, he rushed to report, and neither he nor his superiors could be placated until it was demonstrated to them that the plane's sending apparatus was hopelessly broken down, and that no one could have sent a message if he had wanted to.

Eventually everyone *was* placated, and eventually it came out that Ibn Saud had two very good reasons for being upset at the unauthorized landing: he was having trouble with the Imam of Yemen (trouble that was to break out into war the following May); and he was afraid that if they flew too low or too far in toward the Najd, the Bedouins might be tempted to try out their shooting eyes. Kerr and Rocheville kept discreetly to themselves the unheeded warnings of the RAF in Basra.

For those reasons the King insisted they use no radio, fly high, and stay out of the interior. The prohibitions reduced the usefulness of the plane, but it was still better and faster than the car-and-camel caravans for reconnaissance.

While Lenahan worked to get the restrictions lessened or removed, Kerr and Rocheville prepared the Fairchild, and on March 30, quite a while after they had leaped out to embrace the sands of Arabia and the Amir of Jubail, they made their first tentative air explorations of the concession. The first flight took them down the coast as far as Selwa, at the foot of the Qatar Peninsula, the second over the Ras Tanura sandspit, Tarut Island, and the Dammam Dome.

To achieve the most within the limitations imposed upon them, Miller proposed, and Kerr agreed to, a plan of flying straight parallel courses six miles apart, over any area to be studied, while geologists with drafting boards mounted by the windows sketched everything in the three-mile strip on each side. They noted everything – settlements, 'ains, palm gardens, physiographic details, caravan routes – and if they saw anything that looked particularly interesting they photographed it. The most interesting thing they had so far found, the Dammam Dome, they photographed very thoroughly from the highest altitude they could get the Fairchild to reach.

But it was aerial surveying against difficulties and it strained their capacities for adaptation. For one thing, on top of the limitations imposed by the Saudi government, Kerr discovered that he had a mild personnel problem. Felix Dreyfus, technically a mechanic, had come out to Arabia expecting to have something to do with airplane work, and his expectation was not unnatural. Back in Sausalito he had once built himself a homemade plane and got it to fly. Later he had been a pilot and mechanic for the Loening Amphibian Ferry Service across San Francisco Bay, and when Socal drilled a wildcat on Santa Rosa Island off Santa Barbara, he had flown the company plane back and forth across the channel there.

Now here were Kerr and Rocheville taking over the whole air operation, and Dreyfus was disappointed. But his first disgruntled suspicion could not persist in the face of Kerr's good nature, and in the face of the fact that Kerr was not a company employee, but an independent contractor. Dreyfus eventually shrugged away his disappointment, and when Lenahan got the ban lifted against flights to the interior, and a little later got the restriction removed against use of the radio, Dreyfus turned his ingenious and multiple talents to the task of keeping the radio communications system running. He made no pretense of being a radio technician, but they had little out-of-order time.

With radio permitted, the field parties acquired ears, though not yet a voice. The only voice was that of the plane's transmitter, kept constantly busy sending messages and time signals to the ground camps, and reporting its position every half hour to Jubail. It had a good many positions to report, for now they were systematically coordinating air and ground work and getting Arabia onto paper.

They established a carefully checked east-west baseline clear across the concession, from Jubail to the Dahna sands, and a north-south line from Jubail to Selwa. From these they worked out a net of aerial triangulation and tied it in with the map data, the ground traverses, and the astronomical stations of the ground crews. As fast as they got something new, Allen White transferred it onto his base grids.

Almost at once they found themselves correcting the existing maps, which were based primarily upon the data of a few explorers and upon camel traverses. Camels did not have odometers, and explorers in Arabia had not had the advantage either of radio time signals or of chronometers that worked.

All of the explorers, of whom Philby turned out to be the most dependable, had managed to get a reasonably good latitude fix by an observation on Polaris at upper and lower culmination without knowing the time, but establishing longitude required either accurate chronometer time or a radio time signal. Now, equipped with both, the Casoc parties found some points on the map of al-Hasa off by as much as twenty-five miles.

Through the good flying weather of April they were able to be in the air three or four days of each week. When they had photographed the coastal area they gave Henry, Hoover, Koch, and Brown a helping hand by flying them over the regions they had been working with no higher point of vantage than the top of a dune, a truck, or a camel. Toward the end of April the plane established Henry and Hoover in a camp 160 miles west of Jubail, farther out in the desert than they had yet dared to go, and used that camp with its camel-supplied gasoline dump as a base from which to cover previously unstudied country.

It was fair country to fly in except when the sand blew, and after their experience in Egypt they watched the barometer very closely indeed. Landing was not the problem Kerr had feared. The large soft tires of the Fairchild, though they had a tendency to make the plane unstable and cut its speed by fifteen miles an hour, permitted them to come down even in soft sand, and they could taxi across sand that the touring cars could not traverse.

Most of the time they were within gliding distance of gravel plains or the coastal *sabkhas*, on which they could have landed even with hard tires. The *dikaka* was the only kind of country that gave them bad dreams. Across these sandy plains, sometimes level, sometimes rolling, always closely set with tough runty shrubs hardly two feet high, the prevailing north wind had built little washboard ridges on the leeward side of every bush. *Dikaka* was no place to try to land an airplane.

Quite apart from the terrain, they worried some during that first season about what might happen to them if they had to make a forced landing out in the empty desert. Even assuming that the Bedouins were well-disposed, how would they manage to survive heat, thirst, sandstorms, serpents in a region without a tree or a settlement, with no human habitation except the occasional black tents of the tribes of Ishmael? Experience taught them that they need not fear.

The Bedouins had a habit of seeing everything that went on; even in a region apparently empty of humanity, they had the knack that some of the Americans had observed among the Navajo. Beside a broken car or a stranger afoot or mounted, they could appear out of the ground. And the "Bedouin telegraph" worked magically: along its human transmission line messages moved swiftly and directly to Ibn Saud. If they had ever been forced down, the Bedouins would probably have picked them up within hours, taken hospitable care of them, and turned them over as soon as possible to the nearest government officials.

They learned ways of making use of the bareness of the terrain. When a field crew, depending on the plane for supplies, wanted to move to another location and, not yet equipped with radio transmitter, could not inform headquarters, they simply wrote their instructions on the earth.

Sometimes they drove a car or pickup around and around until they had worn a plain circle into the ground, and then across this they drove a directional arrow pointing toward their new camp. Above it they wrote in the ground with shovels the compass reading, and below it the number of miles to the new camp. Then they sprinkled the whole sign with gasoline and set it afire and burned it black against the face of the desert. It could be read from the air miles away.

With the plane, spare parts could be flown out on a day's notice, and the danger of car trouble or breakdown in the desert was reduced to practically nothing. What was more important, the infrequent mail that trickled in by launch or dhow from Bahrain could be delivered quickly. They might still be at the utter end of the world, but they were not out of touch either with the world or with each other. That, as the first year in the field wore on, would make a difference. . . .

Chapter Five
~ *The Pioneers* ~

In later seasons, and at a geometrical rate of acceleration, life in the coastal regions of al-Hasa would be transformed. Though for a number of years field trips would let recruits taste Arabia almost undiluted and unaltered, the coastal region was a frontier that changed with a magical swiftness once the Americans began to impose upon it the full range of their control over physical nature. The life the first ten men lived in their first season or two has already, after hardly more than thirty years, a remote and half-legendary look, and some of the towns they knew are now unrecognizable.

How was it? Later recruits always asked that as they tried to imagine their way back to a time when no Dhahran existed, and no Abqaiq, no Ras Tanura, no al-Khobar; when there was no place where you could buy spearfishing equipment or color film or a sports car; when there were no roads, no pipelines, no airfields, no U.S. consular officials, no international air transport, no piers, no air conditioning, lawns, swimming pools, golf courses, tennis courts, or clubs; no American women and children; no intricate corporate divisions and delegations of work and authority and loyalty. How was it when the few Americans wore not only the *agaal* and *ghutra*, but the *thaub*; when, except in the field, they walked around in sandals of ornamented camel hide? How did it feel to be thrown so completely on their own resources and their own decisions? How did they get along?

Not one of them, apparently, kept a diary for posterity, and they wrote few letters. (*Nothing new here. I'll write you a good long letter when we get back from our next desert tour. All well except for prickly heat.*) But being gadgeteers, they had camera bugs among them, and a good many of them are still around with memories not only unimpaired by time, but enhanced. From such sources came the answers to the question: How was it?

"I wonder who it will be?" Krug Henry had said to Bert Miller before they left Bahrain for the mainland. "In every outfit there's always one S.O.B. I wonder who it will be this time." But as their numbers grew to the final ten, and their weeks and months of frontier service lengthened, they found no S.O.B. among them.

For a while, after the arrival of the plane, it looked as if there might be coolness between Kerr and Felix Dreyfus; but Kerr was an overflowing spring of enthusiasm and good nature and horseplay, and an eager prier into everything that interested him (everything did); and Dreyfus was an exceptionally decent and intelligent young man. Coolness could not last. Within days they had forgotten everything but the competitive growth of their beards, and in that item Dreyfus, with a magnificent curling black Biblical set of facial hair, made them all look like boys.

They did not lack personal oddities, to be sure, and they were not in incurable good health. Miller worried too much. He was a terrier, a nibbler; he had a feeling that somehow they should be suffering considerably more hardships and making greater sacrifices. He seemed to vacillate between the opinion that desert duty, if properly organized, was the pleasantest of all kinds of foreign work, and the opinion that it was not quite normal to organize it *too* well and make it *too* comfortable.

Burchfiel and Hoover assured him a little sourly that they were making all the requisite sacrifices. Hypochondriacs, they swore they could taste camel urine in the water, their stomachs turned inside out at some of the food, and they listened anxiously at their own doors for the knockings of liver flukes, amoebas, roundworms, and other specimens of what was in those days still a lavish variety of intestinal parasites.

Dreyfus too worried about himself, but with more cause: he was what a later generation would have called accident-prone. His entry into Arabia had been delayed for weeks by a badly burned hand, and there was never a time in all his period of service when he was free of scabs, bruises, bumps. Likewise, he was pathologically difficult to awaken in the morning. When the rest of them struggled out from under the mosquito nets, and stood on the roof yawning and stretching and blinking into the intense flat morning light, there lay Dreyfus, stunned and paralyzed with sleep. They could shake him, yell at him, kick him, roll him out on the bare roof, set his bedclothes afire, blow him up – he slept on.

Their clothes, at first purely Arab, underwent progressive hybridizings, but they never adopted the sun helmets that were standard among the British on Bahrain. The *ghutra* they found most useful, both as costume, to match their beards, and as a protection against flies, wind, sand, and sun. It could be wrapped around the mouth or around the throat and used to wipe sand out of an eye. It shaded the back of the neck as well as the face. Because they all wore it, they blended more quickly and completely with the Arab population, and they felt themselves different, in dress and attitude, from the British: when they saw a Bahrain Englishman in his pukka sahib sun helmet, they referred to him among themselves as a lion tamer.

In most ways they were probably as far from giving up their own habits as the British, but they adapted in external ways, and an outsider seeing them robed and sun-blackened would have had trouble telling them from Arabs. Bert Miller, his face blurred by thin whiskers that flattened and widened his mouth, and with his eyes hidden behind round smudged glasses, might have been an exchanger of money in the Damascus *suq*. Krug Henry had a Christ-like beard that gentled and etherealized his face. He and Burchfiel could have been cast as two of the milder apostles. Dreyfus gleamed dark and reckless through his beautiful Phoenician mat, and Rocheville acquired a wise and self-contained look like Ibn Saud's. Hoover was the least Arab-looking of the lot: he had an incorrigibly blond Viking growth. It was a fact, which they might not have recognized or granted, that they were handsomer in Arab dress, bearded and with the *ghutra* framing and accenting the eyes, than they were in the clothing of their own country.

Even in a country with none of the artificial entertainment, they found recreation. They swam. They fished – with troll lines borrowed from dhow crews – and if they caught a *hamur* or a *shanad* and could get him to the table quickly, they ate him. It was the Gulf that gave them the most. The Gulf offered, as a matter of fact, excursions of considerable interest. Mikimoto's cultured pearls had not yet, in 1933 and 1934, nearly destroyed the Gulf pearl fisheries. They all managed at some time or other to visit the pearling dhows and watch the nose-clipped divers come shooting out of the green water as fast as barracuda with their oysters in the baskets.

Everybody too went to watch the curious spectacle of the dhows filling their water tanks from fresh undersea springs. With the dhow anchored directly over the spring (located by some skill that the Americans could not name), a diver went overboard carrying a rolled camelskin *ghurba*. Down on the bottom, distorted and wriggling, he opened the roll and placed the neck over the flowing fresh mouth of the spring. When he had been down about a minute a second diver went down, took over the *ghurba*, and let the first one rise for a breather. After three or four exchanges the skin would be fully distended. With a twist of the neckskin the diver floated it to the surface, the crew hoisted it aboard and dumped it in the tanks, and the divers started over.

Sometimes when the Portuguese man-of-war were around in force, the divers put on black cotton suits like long underwear. They did not fear at all the deadly five-foot sea snakes, fast enough to catch fish on the run, but they were extremely respectful of the jellyfish. At first the geologists thought this one of the positive cultural differences between an Arab and an American: an American, coming up from a dive and meeting a red-brown water snake nose to nose, was likely to tear the Gulf apart getting ashore or onto the boat, but meeting a little innocuous two-inch jellyfish with delicate trailing feelers, he had at first no such feelings of alarm. He acquired them, just as he acquired the Arab's disregard of the snakes. For the snakes never seemed to cause any trouble, but a jellyfish that laid his feelers ever so gently across a swimmer's chest left him burning as if he had been whipped with nettles dusted with red pepper.

As the season wore into May, however, no diversions could ease the growing strains. Desert temperatures had begun to lift above 110. The Bedouins had begun to gather in great camps around the wells; at waterholes the windlasses creaked almost the clock around and the donkeys pattered back and forth in their runways, drawing up in camelskin *ghurbas* the water for hundreds of impatient animals. From the north the dry *shamals* had begun to come down, filling the air with red-brown dust, grounding the air operations, driving grit through and into everything, and sandpapering the nerves. To make it worse, most of them, spongy with sweat all day and most of the night, bloomed all over their bodies with the red, intolerable rash of prickly heat.

Arab-American relations too began to show the strain. All season long Miller had had to deal only with the local government representatives, all of them concerned lest they make an error, most of them without authority to decide anything major. He had seen nothing, not a trace, of any higher officials, not even the redoubtable Ibn Jiluwi, the Amir of al-Hasa province. Far from their own base, they had been trying, often with difficulty, to establish or compromise matters of high policy with Muhammad Tawil, as isolated from his own base as they were. It was just as well the season was about over. The record of good relations might have eventually blown up if there had been many incidents such as a minor one at Dammam Dome. Going back there to finish the detailing of the structure, Henry and Hoover had found all their survey stakes pulled up, perhaps for firewood, perhaps out of curiosity, by the Bedouins.

Miller and Henry, the oldest among them in point of service, had been on rugged duty without a rest for more than eight months; the least seasoned, Kerr and Rocheville, were ripe for a change and a vacation after only two. Since the Concession Agreement specifically allowed field work to be suspended in favor of office work during the hot season, they closed up the Hofuf office on June 7, and brought up to take charge of the Jubail compound poor Allen White, who had already had the lonesome assignment at Hofuf. That was what he got for being their best Arabist. Dreyfus, unwell as he was, would have to stay behind with White to supervise the Arab mechanics in the job of bringing the transportation back into working order and modifying the cars and pickups to meet conditions in Arabia. Dreyfus would get his vacation of a few weeks in late June and July, White would finally get away in August.

The plane, with its wings folded, crept into its *barasti* hangar to sleep the summer through. Those who were going prepared joyfully to shake the sand of Arabia from their feet. But the one who shook it first shook it in a manner that distressed them all. Charley Rocheville, already sick, was hurt on a rough drive while looking for a site for a landing field near Jabal Dhahran, and had to be shipped to Bahrain on the first of June. The missionary hospital there, unable to do as well by him as it wanted to, advised him to go to London by an Imperial Airways Hannibal. From London he went on back to the Mayo Clinic in Minnesota, the first casualty of the Arabian campaign. He did not recover for several months, and even when he left Arabia, it was clear that he would not be coming back.

On June 6, 1934, as one of their last acts of the initial field season, they completed the detailing of the Dammam Dome. Kerr came down from Jubail and took a lot of horizontal pictures with the airplane camera. They piled up a cairn of stones to mark what they hoped would be the first Arabian oil well, Dammam No. 1. Its location would be visited again later in the month by Hoover and two Bapco engineers, and on the basis of their report on water, harbor, and road possibilities the company would decide whether or not to go ahead with plans for drilling.

If they did decide to drill, they would be two years ahead of the time enforced upon them by the Concession Agreement. Political and competitive reasons for promptness were persuasive; they wanted to show Ibn Saud that they could be as swiftly successful as Bapco had been on Bahrain. And two of the reasons why they were able to complete the preliminaries well ahead of schedule were the geological acuteness of Miller and Henry, who had in the first week discovered Jabal Dhahran to be a structure, and the industry and devotion of the original ten during the first hard months.

Lebanon, where the seven geologists were gathered by mid-July, first elevated them to beatitude and then let them sag into a mental and physical collapse. No sooner had they arrived in the cool mountain climate of Dhour el-Choueir, where Miller had booked them all *en pension* at the Medower Palace Hotel, than the uncertain ailments of Hoover and Burchfiel turned into colds and bronchitis. Those who escaped the germs were afflicted by a great lassitude, an unwillingness to stir except in the rediscovery of diversions and pleasures that they had almost forgotten existed.

In the Medower Palace dining room they ate well and largely, became connoisseurs of the wines of Lebanon. They kept their own table, invited many guests, and every Thursday listened with flattering attention to an orchestra of Russian refugees. There were women around, too: wives and daughters of Lebanese and Egyptians, and Jewish families from Haifa. It was all most pleasant, and thoroughly unproductive.

By the second Thursday of their stay, however, they had begun to recover. And since Burchfiel and Hoover were recuperating, and Miller was getting ready to go on to London and spend a month arranging supplies and conferring with Hamilton, they all decided to have lunch together. They sat down, looked over the menu and the wine card, listened vaguely to the refugee Russians who were tuning up. And then the dining room door opened to admit a woman and a girl.

Krug Henry was facing the door. His eyes followed the pair to their table, stayed on them as they sat down, did not even look away when the girl, petite, dark-eyed, and pretty, glanced across at him. She blushed. Henry did not hear the ribald and witty words of his companions. If the girl had carried a charge of 6,600 volts he could not have been more paralyzed. But he did not waste a moment. He was an extremely direct man, and in this instance he knew his own mind completely.

Within minutes he had bribed the headwaiter to arrange an introduction through the girl's mother, had overpowered the mother's objections, and had brought the two to the geological table. Only when he had them there did he begin investigating the possibilities of conversation. He himself spoke English, some Arabic, and Spanish with a Venezuelan accent. He discovered that Mlle. Annette Rabil, Lebanese-French and the daughter of an engineer who had helped build the Suez Canal, spoke French, Arabic, and Italian. It wasn't the best combination, but it would do. And she was an excellent listener.

By the time Bert Miller left for London, Madame Rabil was scared to death. She had never experienced such an approach. For assistance she called in Annette's two sisters, but they quickly melted before Henry's advances and became his allies. The Egyptian women in the hotel were agog and aghast. Did he mean to marry her? If not, how did he dare take her photograph? Why would he spend every spare minute in her company? They sympathized with Madame's troubles and were so delighted they could hardly talk about anything else. The geological table was an uproar of festivity every night.

Unfortunately, and unwelcome as it was, there was also work. Hoover and Henry, who in their first report had recommended drilling the Dammam Dome, were now working on their second. It concerned an "area in Hasa" and they had concluded that though surface geology revealed no clear indications of oil-accumulating structures, geophysical methods to learn more about it would be justified.

While they worked on this, Burchfiel was preparing a general report called *Arabian Geology, al-Hasa Concession* (in which he was pointing out that the only place that justified test drilling was the Dammam Dome), and Koch and Brown, who had covered more territory than any of them, were also recommending, in a report on central Hasa, further exploration by geophysical methods. When this was done, they said cautiously, enough would be known to permit the company to decide whether it should retain or relinquish the concession.

In the meantime Henry's romance proceeded apace, and sometime in August, Bert Miller, then in London, received a cable. It said that Krug Henry had married Annette Rabil and needed 50 pounds.

Hugh Burchfiel had gone into Beirut with Henry to pick out the diamond. Since they did not fully trust the jewelers of the gold *suq*, and since they themselves were experts on rocks, the diamond was subjected, said Dick Kerr later, to every mineralogical test known to man before it finally wound up on Mlle. Annette's finger. The two were married in the Rabil home in Beirut with many geological attendants and Tom Koch for best man, and the foundation was laid for another revolutionary innovation in Arabia. In 1937, Annette Henry would be one of the first two wives to arrive at the company's primitive outpost at Jabal Dhahran.

Nothing else in the summer of 1934 quite equaled for interest Krug Henry's whirlwind courtship, but other things were happening nonetheless, some of them important. Casoc, after some pondering, decided to take the recommendations of its geologists and drill the Dammam Dome. It was time to go back to work.

The work, of course, had never really stopped; it had just been upstaged by the events in Beirut. Even there it had never quite come to a halt, and in places like Bahrain, where Fred Davies was working out the logistics of a drilling operation, and in places like London, Cairo, and Jiddah, it had gone along at a pace fast enough to suit even the man who was expecting al-Hasa to sink into the sea tomorrow: Bert Miller.

Miller was having a busy summer. In London he had discussed the problems of the past year and the plans for the next with Lloyd Hamilton and he was now in Cairo to do the same with Bill Lenahan, up from Jiddah where he had paid over Casoc's second £20,000 loan to Saudi Arabia, opened negotiations for land in Ras Tanura, and ironed out some more problems about the plane. There was much to discuss, but the paramount problem was relations with stubborn local officials. Lenahan said that everyone from the King on down was anxious to help, and Miller, relieved, went on to Beirut to collect his geologists and lead them back to Saudi Arabia.

In Lebanon, there were also problems. Burchfiel was in the hospital and Felix Dreyfus, who had been left in Arabia, was shortly to join him. An infected appendix, they learned later, had sent him off to Bahrain for surgery, after which his doctor told him to take a vacation. Allen White and the head Saudi mechanic, Nasser, were left to hold the fort at Jubail, though that meant a heroic unbroken sticking-out of the hot season. Dreyfus set out for the Kashmir in India, suffered an attack that he was certain

Houston Public Library
Check Out Summary

Title: Discovery! : the search for Arabian oil
Call number: 338.2728209 S817
Item ID: 33477456533995
Date due: 8/18/2015,23:59

Title: Zondervan essential atlas of the Bible
Call number: 220.910223 R225
Item ID: 33477483442720
Date due: 8/18/2015,23:59

Title: Bible code III : saving the world
Call number: 220.68 D787
Item ID: 33477460123809
Date due: 8/18/2015,23:59

Title: The biblical world : an illustrated atlas
Call number: 220.910223 I76
Item ID: 33477456136078
Date due: 8/18/2015,23:59

meant heart failure, and decided he had better go to Lebanon. With his fingers on his own pulse he did so – by way of the Kashmir, a return trip to and up the Gulf, and an overland trip across Iraq and Syria. In a hospital in Lebanon he and Burchfiel comforted one another for a month before they felt strong enough for a second go at al-Hasa. They arrived in Jubail on October 20.

That was just about a month after the star Canopus was first seen on the southern horizon, the signal for the Bedouins to break up their great camps around the wells and start the season of wandering. Canopus was a corner around which the seasons turned; after it appeared, the weather felt cooler, whether it really was or not; from then on there could be rain, and hence grass. The desert after that might be found, as the Arabs said, "alive," and what was a good signal for the Bedouins was a good signal for geologists. The 1934–35 field season had been going for nearly a month when Burchfiel and Dreyfus arrived.

Unexpectedly, returning to Jubail was for the geologists a little like returning home. They climbed off the Bahrain launch into a familiarity of crowds, couched camels, known streets, a stiff Gulf breeze. They renewed acquaintance with the dormant plane and the crudely westernized house and the walled compound stacked with supplies and equipment. Before a day passed their minds had taken in fresh images of the fantastic mirages on the *sabkhas*, the tranced motion of the colored Gulf. On their first night they met again, climbing to their rooftop cots, the great dark-blue Arabian sky sequined with stars.

On the dock to meet them were familiar faces. Old Muhammad Tawil, troublesome and officious as they had sometimes thought him, seemed genuinely glad to see them: they pumped his hand, crying upon him the peace of God. Here were the *qadi* and the Amir, smiling and without warrants for anybody's arrest. And here were employees carried over from the previous season – Nasser the mechanic, Saleh the cook, a driver or two, soldiers, guides, all making up the first small core of a westernized workforce.

Discovery!

The original ten Americans were now thirteen. The pilot who had replaced Charley Rocheville was Joe Mountain, distinguished for a Friedrich Barbarossa beard and wide, pointed mustaches. As a third member of the aerial-survey crew, Kerr had Russell Gerow, a mechanic and photographer. Brought over from Bahrain to fill in for Dreyfus during his illness, and now established in al-Hasa, was Al Carpenter, driller, mechanic, boatman, all-around craftsman. They were picked men, and the jobs were of a kind to demand their best. But the new face that meant most to the work at hand, and most to the history of Arabian oil, was that of Max Steineke, an American geologist; and the familiar face that the geologists were most pleased to see among the Arabs was that of Khamis ibn Rimthan, an Ajman guide.

It is conceded by those who worked with him that Steineke was the man who first came to understand the stratigraphy and the structure underlying eastern Arabia's nearly featureless surface. As a field geologist he rated with the best anywhere, and as a man, a companion, a colleague, he could not have been better adapted to the pioneering conditions he now encountered. Burly, big jawed, hearty, enthusiastic, profane, indefatigable, careless of irrelevant details and implacable in tracking down a line of scientific inquiry, he made men like him, and won their confidence. He was a very pure example of a very American type, and heir to every quality that America had learned while settling and conquering a continent. In a man he respected most of all enthusiasm, intelligence, a capacity to do his job; to system and procedures he applied only the pragmatic test: he wanted to know if they worked.

As he would have said himself, Steineke was "no son of a bitch for civilization." Since his graduation from Stanford in 1921 he had worked in Alaska, Colombia, and New Zealand, and was one of Socal's senior geologists, with thirteen varied years of experience, when he wrote to Clark Gester from down under in 1934 and asked to be put on the Arabian venture. A fine shot with either rifle or pistol, a man who loved the outdoors and thrived on work, a "big man with a big arm and a big voice," as the Arabs said, he had worked in the California desert and had packed with mules across the Andes. He never stopped driving, never stopped thinking, and habitually could not be bothered with details.

But if Steineke, now just getting his first curious glimpses of Arabia, represented and epitomized the American, expressed their collective virtues at the highest pitch, gave them a leader and a model and gave the Arabs a standard by which to know the American type, one of the familiar faces on the dock did the same for the Arabs: the guide Khamis ibn Rimthan.

Khamis ibn Rimthan — his first name meant "Thursday" — had come to Casoc no more willingly than Friday came to Crusoe. An Ajman tribesman of al-Hasa, Khamis was about nineteen in 1929 when the Mutair rebellion against Ibn Saud led by Faisal al-Dawish was suppressed, and when the fierce Ibn Jiluwi in revenge for the death of his son all but decimated Khamis' fellow tribesmen. When, therefore, about the middle of October 1933, Ibn Jiluwi sent a peremptory order to Khamis to report to him in Jubail, it was with considerable uneasiness that Khamis complied. It took five days to get there and many hours of waiting, but at last he was told why he had been summoned: he was to be the guide for the foreigners who had come, gossip said, "to search for gold and the relics of the old people."

Khamis, who had no desire to be separated from his family for months, indicated that he was a very poor guide, that there were many better to be had, and anyway he was not a soldier, he did not belong to any form of army. But Ibn Jiluwi had said Khamis, and Khamis it was.

Khamis was a little disingenuous in saying that there were better guides. Though he spoke no English, the geologists soon found him sharply and steadily intelligent, at once a great joker and a man of dignity and loyalty. Considering that he was both illiterate and almost totally ignorant of any world other than his own, he had an extraordinary understanding. Also he had built into him somewhere a foolproof gyroscopic compass.

It was impossible to lose him. He did not use the maps, but ask him in what direction a certain landmark lay, and he would tell you. Ask him how far, and he would know within a very narrow margin of error, although he didn't learn to estimate distance in miles until after he had joined the geologists. Before that, he had used the terms of the desert, reckoning distance in so many hours or days by a specified kind of camel: as "six days by *dhalul*." Even in country which he had not seen before, he had a knack for finding his way, and if the Americans accused him of using black magic he would tell them innocently that he got the information from two good men. How he told reliable informants from others, and how he managed to make such nearly infallible use of the information he got, was his own secret.

During the first season he had worked mainly with Henry and Hoover. During the second, and later, he was assigned more and more often to Steineke's party. In the years to come, Khamis and the Americans he worked for made the sort of cultural exchange that nations wish they knew how to promote. They did not change their known ways to fit one another: they overlapped, supplemented, and informed one another.

If Khamis or the soldiers told stories of raids or battles, the geologists could counter with Custer's Last Stand or the Alamo. If Khamis astonished them with tales of jinns and afreets, they could try to kid him into believing the world was round. If Steineke or Hoover or Koch brought down a gazelle, they might find Khamis sliding in front of them to stoop and turn the gazelle toward Mecca and cut its throat with a swift *Bismallah*: In the name of God, most gracious, most merciful.

What they learned from one another was respect and friendship. Just as the Casoc people who knew him felt that King Ibn Saud would have been a great man no matter where or in what circumstances he had been born, the geologists felt that

Khamis would have stood out in any society as a man of great ability, integrity, and character.

The new season's work was a continuation from where they had left off, an attempt to read the structure of their 320,000 square miles underneath its masking of dunes and *dikaka*, to interpret the enigmatic outcroppings, establish the age and relationships of strata, locate every regional high that might reveal the presence of a dome. There was little enough to go on, and they had as yet none of the gravity meter and seismographic and structure drilling equipment that might have simplified the job. Steineke, looking off the roof of the Jubail compound his first day in Arabia and seeing the Jabal al-Berri, made the same mistake Miller and Henry had made. The Jabal al-Berri looked very like the Jabal Dukhan on Bahrain and the Jabal Dhahran down by Dammam. It was a cinch; the way you did it in this country was to cruise around until you found *jabals*.

But it wasn't quite that easy, as Steineke quickly discovered. The cruising itself was nothing to take lightly, even in cars whose springs and front cross-members had been built up by Dreyfus, Carpenter, and Nasser for off-road work, and whose wheels were now fitted with the new, effective 9.00 x 18 low-pressure tires that Miller had discovered and bought in London. They had not so many soldiers to hamper their movements – Lenahan after his conference with Miller in Cairo had persuaded the government to reduce the guard for each party to ten – but they still had camels enough, and flies enough. The slow, camel-supplied camps settled, and mapped, and moved, and settled again, while other camel caravans went out to establish plane bases and gasoline dumps at Lina, far up on the edge of the Dahna near the Iraq border, and at al-Lisafah, in the flint desert below the Iraq Neutral Zone.

To this latter spot went Henry and Brown for a spell of isolated exploratory work, while Steineke and Koch worked west and south of Jubail, and Burchfiel and Hoover started for al-'Uqair. They found plenty of *jabals*; what else they found was more ambiguous. This was obviously not a hit-and-run job.

September's heat gave way to the warm but pleasant weather of October, and by degrees to chilly fall. One November day in a big *sabkha* south of Jubail, Steineke and Tom Koch snowballed each other with packed hailstones.

They had a crisis when the plane, making an aerial traverse of the as-Sayyariyat region, broke its tail skid and was laid up at al-Lisafah; without too much trouble they cobbled up a jury tail skid of automobile springs for it to come in on. On November 11, 1934, they got their fourteenth man, who arrived off Jubail by dhow and rode on a donkey the final shallow stretch to shore, dressed in Arab clothes and hanging on with both hands. He was a youngster with some business training and some experience as a field clerk with oil companies in Texas and California. Name: Bill Burleigh. He would relieve Allen White of much of the paperwork.

At the end of November, Miller crossed over to Bahrain and brought back the first three members of the drilling crew scheduled for Dammam Dome, and three days after Christmas another contingent of the drilling crew came over in the care of Allen White. On that same launch, looking so terribly civilized that they didn't let him wade ashore like the others but instead had a crewman carry him piggyback through the shallows of al-Khobar, came Lloyd Hamilton, starting a "public relations" tour of the field.

They gave Hamilton a realistic view of the whole operation from Jubail to Hofuf, and though he did not conform to field practice by letting his beard grow, he did start a mustache and he did get into *ghutra* and *agal,* and on formal occasions into a *bisht* as well. He bore up under the osteopathic treatment of desert driving, and he was game for the ceremonial visits — and coffee drinking — all at night because it was the month of Ramadan when no Muslim could eat or drink during the daylight hours.

It was an established Arabian custom for a traveler just arriving in a village to call at once upon the amir, in all the dust and dirt of travel, and pay his respects. After coffee and a brief visit, he was allowed to continue to his destination in the town. In observing this custom, Hamilton and Miller had the experience that was to become traditional with Amir Ibn Jiluwi, one of the most taciturn of men. He was, as Hamilton said in a wild understatement, "a good listener."

After the complimentary tautologies of Arabic greeting, his conversation seemed to consist of the one word *qahwa*, coffee, and at least he used it to fill every awkward pause. At first Hamilton did not hear the Amir say even that. He heard the word, though, sharply spoken, growing louder as it went, repeated down a line of soldiers toward the kitchen. For a moment he thought that something was wrong, that he had somehow violated good manners, until the entrance of the coffee servant with his beaked copper pot and his handful of little cups reassured him.

The ritual was familiar enough to Hamilton by now, though in Ibn Jiluwi's *majlis* it seemed rather more peremptory than hospitable. A dark hand thrust a stack of cups before one's nose, a deft thumb dealt the top cup off, the pot tipped, and a short gush of coffee burst through the reed strainer-plug. One drank it in two or three swallows; there was the taste of cardamom. The coffee servant, clashing his stack of cups, gathering them in from those who wobbled them in token of satiety, constantly stacking the used ones under and dealing the top ones off, was back with another splash of black sludge.

After three it was polite to wobble the cup, but to take fewer than three was an affront. Then one settled back against the cushions and through the interpreter tried to tell Ibn Jiluwi what the geologists had found, what the prospects were, what plans the company had. In the midst of another difficult pause one heard his low murmur, "Qahwa," which was instantly repeated by the shaikh next to him, and in louder tones by the man next, and so on down the line, and the violent chain reaction of Arab hospitality was set off again.

Hamilton counted nine cups of coffee and five glasses of tea that he drank while paying his respects to Ibn Jiluwi and immediately afterward to his son. As soon as he and Miller got to their quarters, his esophagus echoing of cardamom and his bones disconnected by the day's six hours of cross-country driving, he fell on his pallet bed and slept like a dead man until Miller called him at five.

He particularly wanted to be up early: one of the few things Ibn Jiluwi had communicated to him was permission to take movies of Hofuf, something that no one had ever done. He also wanted to get off a telegram to Ibn Saud asking if he might visit the King in Riyadh, and after that go on across Arabia to Jiddah.

He got his movies, and he got his reply from Ibn Saud. The King not only wanted him to come to Riyadh, he wanted him to come on the first day of the Feast of the 'Id al-Fitr that ended Ramadan's month of fasting and prayer.

It was January 5, 1935, the last day of Ramadan, when Hamilton, Miller, Felix Dreyfus, three soldiers, a guide, a cook, and an interpreter left al-Khobar in three Fords to drive to Riyadh.

The first day was the familiar, rough sequence of *sabkhas*, dunes, and then *sabkhas* again to Hofuf, where they telegraphed the customary greetings to the King, Prince Faisal, Abdullah Sulaiman, and Fuad Hamza, drank the customary dozens of glasses of tea and cups of coffee, and lay down to sleep to the dreary howling of jackals sulking around the great oasis.

When they left next morning, the first sun lay rosy against the walls and mud forts of Hofuf, and a jackal stood watching them so curiously that they could have run him down. They might have if he had not looked so much like a bushy-tailed dog. Braced for a rough day, Hamilton found it easier than he expected. Rains had hardened the dunes into giant roller coasters over which they gunned their Fords recklessly: it was by now axiomatic in Arabia

Plate I

Camel caravan east of Medina - 1938 ~ *LS*

Dhows sailing on the Gulf - 1938 ~ *LS*

A well at the Hofuf oasis - 1938 ~ *LS*

Photos courtesy of the following: FD - Felix Dreyfus Collection, LS - Les Snyder Collection, SAW/P - Saudi Aramco World/Padia, SF - Steve Furman Collection, TCB - T. C. Barger Collection, UU - University of Utah, J. Willard Marriott Library, Stegner Collection

Plate II

Suburbs of Riyadh - 1935 ~ *FD*

Hofuf, capital of Al Hasa - 1938 ~ *LS*

Street scene in Qatif - 1938 ~ *LS*

Plate III

Saudi Finance Minister
Abdullah Sulaiman.
Ras Tanura - 1939 ~ *TCB*

Lloyd Hamilton
with Abdullah
Philby at right.
Jiddah - 1936

Plate IV

Burzon House; Henry-Miller expedition leaving Jubail to establish the base camp at Jabal Dhahran. 1934 ~ *UU*

L-r: Soak Hoover, Hugh Burchfiel, Doc Nomland, Bert Miller, Krug Henry and Felix Dreyfus. Jubail - February 1934 ~ *FD*

Dining room at the Jubail compound. L-R: Burleigh, Mountain, Koch, Brown, Dreyfus, and Steineke. Note the fan. 1934 ~ *UU*

Plate V

Fairchild 71, photo reconnaissance aircraft at Jubail - March 1934 ~ *FD*

Joe Mountain and Bert Miller. Jubail - 1934 ~ *FD*

Henry-Miller field party establishes camp at Jabal Dhahran, the original site of the city of Dhahran. 1934 ~ *FD*

Plate VI

Soak Hoover, Krug Henry and Dick Kerr. Jubail - May 4, 1934 ~ *FD*

Fred Davies.
Bahrain - 1934 ~ *FD*

Annette Rabil, Krug's fiancé.
Dhour el-Choueir, Lebanon - 1934 ~ *SAW/P*

Field party to the eastern edge of the concession. Foreground geologists, r-l: Meeker, Barger, Steineke, and Harriss. Rub' al-Khali - 1938 ~ *TCB*

Plate VII

Falconeer.
Jubail - 1934 ~ *FD*

L-r: Translator, Bill Lenahan, Said Hashim,
Guy Williams. Road to Riyadh - 1934 ~ *FD*

First aid and dentistry by Bert Miller. Jubail - 1934 ~ *FD*

1. Hospital 2. Bunk house 3. Club, dining rooms, kitchen 4. Light plant, ice
house, & commissary 5. Fred Davies & Guy Williams' house 6. Office &
warehouse 7. Garage & welding shop. Dhahran - 1935 ~ *FD*

Plate VIII

Three desert guides in Jubail - 1934 ~ *FD*

Children in Jubail - 1934 ~ *FD*

Building the pier at Al Khobar from coral rock - 1934 ~ *FD*

that you drove like a bat out of hell, because to stop was to risk getting stuck. The *sabkhas*, which might have been soft in winter, gave them no trouble.

As they worked inland the land rose, thin ledges and outcrops appeared, the *sabkhas* dropped behind, there was less sand. When they pitched camp at 8:30 that night in the Wadi ar-Rumah their horizon was defined by low cliff-lines, and during the last hours they crept and creaked and crawled in low gear over bare rock ledges, taking it very easy to spare their overloaded springs, and bumping down into patches of sand with the foot insistent, but not too insistent, on the throttle, and blasting through and lurching and crawling again over another stretch of ledge.

Their guide was a worried man; when he got momentarily lost he stopped them and scanned the country with an expression of great anxiety. Their soldiers, too, were anxious. Hamilton and Miller and Dreyfus could not stop for five minutes to stretch their legs, or walk twenty feet from the cars, without a robed figure, crisscrossed with bandoliers and armed with a rifle, at their heels. Evidently visitors to the King were to be looked after with care. Several soldiers had been punished because the government had received relatively unimportant complaints from the Americans, and as a consequence the Americans had quit making complaints. Here, certainly, they had no complaints to make, unless for over-solicitousness.

This was Arabia as a romantic imagination might have created it: nights so mellow that the men lay out under the scatter of dry bright stars and heard the silence beyond their fire as if the whole desert hung listening. Physically, it might have been Arizona, or New Mexico, with its flat crestlines, its dry clarity of air, its silence. But it felt more mysterious than that; and the faces of soldiers and guide and interpreter, dark, bearded, gleaming in teeth and eye as they spoke or laughed, corroborated Hamilton's sense that this was authentic Arabia, hardly touched by the West. The water that he shaved with in the gray predawn light, and the coffee he drank before they started off again, corroborated Arabia further: they were so flavored with mutton tallow from the *ghurba* the water had been carried in that Hamilton felt he could smell sheep all morning.

The Wadi ar-Rumah was four rough hours from Riyadh; they took seven because one car broke a spring, which Dreyfus and the drivers replaced. An hour out, they were met by two soldiers and a driver in a government car, bearing the greetings of the Crown Prince, Amir Saud, and his invitation to stop at the Badia Summer Palace outside the walls of Riyadh. The place astonished them: a Spanish- or Moorish-looking house surrounded by palm gardens and peach and fig trees, with a view down the wide straggling palms of the Wadi Hanifa.

It might have been in some desert part of California, except for the numbers of servants and the amplitude of the space assigned them. They were swamped in soldiers and servants, and adrift in their many rooms. After the somewhat primitive hospitality of Hofuf, this was luxury, with brass-framed mirrors, brass washbowls and water ewers, drapes, cushions, Persian rugs, intricately ornamented walls and rafters, a colonnaded central court surmounted by the jagged crenels and merlons of the wall, and decorated all around with zigzag plaster reliefs. They had barely had time to decide to put all their cots together rather than scatter through a bedroom apiece, when the King sent to ask when he might see them; and they had barely cleaned up when Hafiz Wahba, whom Hamilton knew well as the Saudi Minister to London, came to escort them to the *majlis*.

The meeting was so friendly that its import could not possibly be mistaken, and it brought comfort to Bert Miller, harassed throughout his first season by the suspicions and prohibitions of local officials. At least at this level, suspicion and prohibition did not apply. Even Hamilton, sophisticated in negotiation, felt he was having one of the notable experiences of his life. Miller and Dreyfus, a geologist and a mechanic, could be excused for pinching themselves now and then to test if they really sat here in the council chamber among potentates and guards, in the remote capital of Ibn Saud's kingdom, making jovial conversation with the King and one of his sons and exchanging jokes through an interpreter.

They had taken the first movies ever taken in Hofuf; on the morning after their arrival they took the first ones ever taken in Riyadh, and it is unlikely that any camera bug since has had richer opportunities. That morning, as part of the Lesser Festival, the *'Id al-Fitr*, 5,000 soldiers paraded in a dance of war, long double lines of them brandishing rifles, pistols, and swords while they moved in a slow, hypnotic shuffle and barked out a hoarse antiphonal chant. The air was full of bullets fired at what the Americans thought were terribly flat angles, but they were not nervous for their safety. The King himself had authorized their movie camera, the Amir Saud himself had placed them at their spot of observation, Yusef Yassin himself was their companion, and four of the King's soldiers stood guard at the four fenders of their car.

At every stage of their visit they had impressed upon them the government's friendship and desire to cooperate. In the afternoon, after the war dance, Miller and Hamilton went over with Fuad Hamza, Hafiz Wahba, and Yusef Yassin all the plans for the season's work as well as all the incidents of friction and cultural misunderstanding. It seemed, as they talked, that the difficulties had been fewer than might have been anticipated; considering the strangeness of the Americans to the Arabs, and the equal strangeness of the Arabs to the Americans, everyone had done pretty well.

In Lenahan, the company had a Jiddah representative whom the King liked and whom the ministers could deal with. And in the news that the company planned to drill the Dammam structure the government had the most welcome information it could have received. It was January 1935. The world was still sunk in depression, the hajj would be light again, the Saudi need of money was acute in spite of the second loan, which the company had made in advance of its due date. Needing income so badly, the government from the King down waved aside the warnings of the Americans that there might be no oil down there. They wanted to believe, needed to believe, perhaps, that the result of drilling would be automatic riches.

Two pieces of news came to the Americans at Riyadh. One was that Karl Twitchell had obtained the mining concession in the Hijaz he had been negotiating for and was back in London negotiating for capital to start digging out the gold that King Solomon's miners had left. The other was that the long wrangle between Gulf and Anglo-Persian about the oil concession in Kuwait, the negotiation which had embarrassed and handcuffed the Eastern and General Syndicate and cut it out of the Arabian deal, had finally been settled by a compromise, each company taking half. So more American or part-American enterprise got a foothold in the Arabian Peninsula.

The three days of their visit in Riyadh they found a rich and bizarre experience. The Najd capital was very different from cosmopolitan Jiddah or from the palm gardens and pearling towns of the Gulf. They had penetrated to a place almost unknown, almost as isolated as Mecca was holy, and there had established for the future the pattern of close contact with the King himself. They felt like explorers, and went through all the motions and emotions of tourists, and shot up a lot of film, and over-exposed most of it in spite of the warnings Dick Kerr had given them at al-Khobar before they left, and the instructions he had given them about believing a light meter in the desert.

Jiddah, by the usual standards of driving and with the usual stickings and breakdowns, was four days away. The road led over the Tuwaiq Escarpment by Hassiyan Pass and across 400 miles of broken desert and plateau. At first the country rock was sedimentaries in long flat beds. Later, as they worked westward across the contact line, they came onto what had been the ancient continental mass from which the material of the sedimentaries had been washed, and the country showed them worn granite teeth, and later on, near Birkah, the roughest sort of lava plateau.

Along those 400 miles there were only a few oasis towns, such as Marrat and Duwadami, where gasoline might be available, but except for occasional water they did not need to depend on the country. They moved independently and with speed, and thanks partly to their skill as drivers and partly to their low-pressure tires, they found themselves within two days and a half only a few miles outside of Mecca. From their stopping place below the granite hills they sent a car in to find a guide who could take them around the forbidden city.

The speed of their trip had deprived them of a planned reception. In the spirit of goodwill and optimism that had marked Riyadh, Abdullah Sulaiman, H. St. John Philby, and Lenahan had planned to have tents and a welcoming party at the turnoff from the Mecca road. Now, having been too headlong in their crossing, Hamilton, Miller, and Dreyfus sat uncomfortably near Mecca, wondered if they might already have overstepped themselves, and waited for their guide. While they waited a distinguished-looking Arab drove up and approached their cars. He turned out to be St. John Philby. A little later arrived Abdullah Sulaiman, smiling and apologizing for the fact that the government radio stations had not sent advance word of their arrival.

Lenahan did not come at all; eventually they drove on into Jiddah without him. They were already established in the Bait Americani when their Jiddah representative sneaked sheepishly back into town. He had set out with Bill Griffin, one of the Jiddah Englishmen, and with Najib Salha as guide, intending to camp overnight at ash-Shariah and bring the Hamilton party in from there. But Najib got lost, and they wound up on the very outskirts of Mecca before they recognized where they were. In his hurry to get the unbelievers out of there, Najib Salha blew a tire on a rock, and when they had repaired that, they thought it best to retreat and let the Hamilton party make its own entrance.

The magnificence of the new Bait Americani made up for the lameness of the welcome. The house itself was big and airy and pleasantly decorated, part of the growing European quarter. The furniture, which Lenahan had ordered when in Cairo, was chaste and elegant, the tile floors were spotless, there were bathrooms with both tub and shower, the water closets, to Sir Andrew Ryan's disgust, worked. The drinking water came down from Egypt in large glass bottles – it was safer to import it than to drink the water brought by donkey cart every morning and poured into a tank with a funnel-like opening on the street. The house was, in all, a revelation in modern comfort and convenience, three floors and a roof garden with potted flowers that actually survived the heat and the sandstorms, and with a pair of pet baboons named Micky and Mona for atmosphere.

There were some days of social activity in Jiddah, and rounds of dinners, and conferences with Abdullah Sulaiman, and a general agreement that Lenahan had been very effective in keeping things straightened out with the government, but, now that drilling was beginning, could use an assistant. Bert Miller was prepared to admit that without Lenahan in Jiddah he wouldn't have been able to work in Jubail. In a spirit of holiday he and Hamilton, whom he was to accompany as far as Cairo while Felix Dreyfus drove the cars back across country to al-Khobar, decided to cross to Port Sudan and Khartoum and float down the Nile. They were entitled to their vacation, and anyway, what they did at this moment was not extremely important. The really important events were beginning on the other side of Arabia, on the scabby, barren flanks of the *jabals* near al-Khobar.

Chapter Six
~ The Wildcatters ~

They did not come as settlers, or even as explorers; they were neither the kind that planned to stay nor the kind that evinced much interest in the strange places where they found themselves. One place was much like another; they took change philosophically; they imposed themselves and their own vagrant subculture on whatever spot of earth happened to contain them. They were wildcatters, used to moving on, and when they came wading onto the shores of Saudi Arabia in 1935, they were thanking their stars that they didn't have to stay on Bahrain. Discovery was their business, and they had already done that at Jabal Dukhan. It was all right to get the rig all dirty with the first producer, the one that mattered, but it was another matter just to drill holes where you already knew you would hit oil.

They took the far corners of the earth without excitement because they had already seen a lot of them. Of that first wildcat crew on Dammam Dome, every man had been knocking around the world for years. Guy (Slim) Williams, the slouchy and laconic toolpusher, had had a China tour; so had Jack Schloesslin, a driller, small, fat, ferociously foul-mouthed, and as soft under the crust as Camembert. Both of them had known Bill Eltiste, a general utility man in transportation, machine shop, and garage in

Argentina in 1922. When Eltiste pulled out in 1925 to take a leave in the States, he worked about a month at Taft, in the San Joaquin Valley, and then headed out for Maracaibo, Venezuela. After a year there he went on to Colombia, and there ran into Schloesslin, who had meantime been in Ecuador. Slim Williams had by then left South America for Montana. These were the expected and routine jumps.

When Ed Skinner, who was assistant manager at Maracaibo, was transferred to Bahrain as manager in 1931, he took with him as a crew a bunch of these rough and skillful roamers who had already touched on practically all the places where Socal had had foreign operations. This was by and large the same crew that was sent to the mainland later. The al-Hasa concession was test-drilled by men who had been around.

But they did not – quite – bring all their gods with them into Latium. Missing from the al-Hasa wildcat and from the towns around it were the beer parlors, the dance halls, the juke boxes, the slot machines, the movie theaters. Nevertheless they did manage certain things from the beginning: refrigeration, electric fans, bunkhouse radios, ice cream – and a state of mind that even without beer and movies and the company of ladies was startlingly and unmistakably American, and that involved, among other things, optimism, generosity, carelessness, roughness, high productivity, the habit of exaggeration, the knack of improvising, and a family relationship to Paul Bunyan.

They would have stared in incredulity at anyone who had called them missionaries. Yet if utter faith in a way of life, and an utter conviction that the rest of the world would best be served by adopting it, constitute the essential elements in missionary fervor, these men were missionaries as surely as were Dr. Harrison's Christians over on Bahrain.

The first one over, besides Slim Williams, was Walt Haenggi, a rig builder and construction man who had already done service to the Bahrain crew by demonstrating what happened if you refused to wear a hat or a *ghutra* in Arabia. Haenggi was a big, rugged, oil-field roughneck, not inclined to baby himself. He scorned all head coverings for some time, until one summer day when the temperature was about 120 degrees he suddenly took off at a dead run across the island. The Bapco manager, Ed Skinner, who had been a fullback at California, pursued him and brought him down, and they put him in the refrigerated food locker for a while to cool his overheated skull. When Haenggi arrived at al-Khobar, he was wearing a hat.

Next came Joe Cartwright, known as Joe Khobar, the camp clerk and paymaster. He had worked in Texas, where the paymaster laid a six-shooter on the table to maintain decorum among his clients. The first time Joe Khobar paid off the crew at the Dammam camp – later to be known as the Dhahran camp – there was the six-shooter. He did not last long in Arabia. It was felt that the Arabs would not understand him as the Texans had.

Just after Christmas 1934, on the same launch that brought Lloyd Hamilton on the first leg of his trans-Arabian tour, there came Claude Jared, a driller, Floyd Ohliger, a petroleum engineer, and Frank Dang, a Chinese cook, all wading ashore because there were no dock facilities. Jared was the orthodox foreign-department wildcatter. Ohliger was a freckle-nosed and engaging Pennsylvania Dutchman who had wildcatted in Venezuela and done a hitch on a concession in the Magdalena Valley in Colombia after getting his degree in petroleum engineering from Pitt. Subsequently he had been in California, Oklahoma, and Texas, and then had gone back to Palo Alto to learn some more physics at Stanford.

Frank Dang was something more unlikely. After twelve years spent cooking in a Berkeley sorority house, he went back to China on a visit, could not get back into the United States, and ended up cooking for the staff house of Socal in Maracaibo, Venezuela. Later he returned to China and opened a string of movie houses, but had to give it up. So many of Chiang Kai-shek's soldiers insisted on coming in free that they crowded out the paying guests and put Frank out of business. Now, through the Bahrain cook, Chow

Lee, also an ex-Venezuelan, he was brought out here to Arabia, as erratic a wanderer as any of them.

They located a camp on the terrace near the higher *jabals*, dug a water well, took apart two double-walled tents that had been stored in Jubail since the previous fall, and made them into four tents, which they set up near the spotted site for Well No. 1.

The morning after Ohliger's arrival he had his first taste of how various the duties of a petroleum engineer could be in Arabia. Of two precious and coddled Christmas turkeys the crew had brought in a crate from Bahrain, only one remained next morning – a thoughtful and meditative bird who mused upon the feet, head, and feathers of his companion.

The crew suspected wolves or jackals, but before long, hearing snarls and howls from the well, they investigated and found a saluki dog had fallen down between the wellside and the cribbing that kept it from caving in. For a dog as skinny as he was, he had a suspiciously fat paunch, and he was stuck so thoroughly, and so far down, that at first they couldn't reach him. Hamilton and Miller went off to Hofuf, leaving Floyd Ohliger muttering and scratching his head, and the crew speculating on whether the water would taste better or worse if they left the saluki down there.

Until the establishment of the camp, their assault on Arabia had had no seeming of permanence; they had lived as visitors in Arab houses in Jubail and Hofuf, and in the desert they moved around more than the Bedouins. But at al-Khobar they began at once the thing they were notably good at: construction.

Al-Hasa was a frontier made not with ax and gun and individual initiative over a period of generations, but with the organized industrial and engineering skill of the 20th century over a period of months.

They located their pier by aerial photographs that showed every reef and channel, and they built it according to blueprint, though because they couldn't yet bring in their full industrial armament they had to build it with such equipment and materials as Arabia afforded, and with local labor.

Floyd Ohliger, having engineered his way out of the saluki situation, had as his second job the building of the al-Khobar pier. There was a historic meeting, not thought of as historic at the time, by the fishermen's *barastis* on the shore; its purpose was the first mass employment of Saudis as industrial labor. Ohliger enlisted every available dhow and put the crews to gathering the crusty, shell-like stone the Arabs called *faroush* which low tide exposed along the edge of the Gulf. Within a few weeks there was a long rough finger of stone poking out into the green water, and visiting firemen no longer had to come ashore on the shoulders of crewmen, new employees no longer had to wade ashore, supplies no longer had to be carried on the heads of workmen.

By the time they were well into their first tentative move to change the face of Arabia, there were more of them – almost every one a man of two or more trades. Bill Eltiste was a marvelous and ingenious all-around mechanic who could double as driller and triple as rig builder, and who, though without much formal education, had the endlessly inquisitive and pondering mind of a good scientist. He was big and slow and low-voiced; when he wasn't working he was likely to be lying in his bunk reading engineering handbooks. Jack Schloesslin, in addition to being a driller, was a plumber. George McCoy was a driller and pipeline worker; Alex Zoll a driller and blacksmith. While the geologists and the plane crew scattered across Arabia, filling in the map from Turaif on the north to the Jabrin oasis and the Rub' al-Khali on the south, the drilling crew went about its concentrated business at Dammam Dome.

Then there was the problem of housing: Walt Haenggi and a crew started on a bunkhouse up near the site where the first well had been spotted the June before; it was oriented in an east-west direction so as to admit as few as possible of the sun's hottest rays. There was the problem of water: a hand-dug well in the flat below the *jabals* yielded sweet water of fair quality for drinking; and Eltiste boxed in one of the underwater springs exposed at low tide and got a greater supply of brackish water than could be used for camp and drilling purposes. There was the job of supply, the job of transportation. Across the stretch of dunes between the al-Khobar camp and the site of the well they dragged lumber, cement, equipment, the old cable rig, moving things by camel or car or laboriously and slowly by Caterpillar tractor.

It is a legend in Arabia now that at some point in these early years Bill Eltiste and Dick Kerr, observing how a camel's big squishy feet spread out to the size of a manhole cover in loose sand, commandeered a cargo camel and hoisted him on an A-frame and weighed him and then sat down with a slide rule and figured out the ratio of foot surface to body weight, and so devised the low-pressure sand tires that have since revolutionized off-road work in the desert. They were indeed pioneers in off-road transportation, but neither Eltiste nor Kerr admits to weighing any camel.

If anybody ever did, it was an engineer with the Egyptian Camel Corps who developed the idea of oversized tires with Dunlop, in England, and got them to manufacture 9.00 x 13s with about 12 pounds of pressure for desert work. Miller saw these tires when he was in London in the summer of 1934, and ordered fifty of them for the touring cars, pickups, and station wagons. On the way back to Jubail, when he stopped in Alexandria to meet Lenahan, he saw a demonstration of larger tires for trucks arranged by the Dunlop people with the Ford agency. Because he wasn't quite sure they would work on the Arabian sands, he bought only one set and two spares. As soon as he got back in the field he was wishing he had bought dozens.

The fact is that the earliest beginnings of low-pressure tires in Arabia go beyond Eltiste and even Kerr and Miller. The so-called balloon tires, as used in the United States, were recommended from the first by Twitchell and Hamilton, who had heard about them from others. The cars that Twitchell brought across from Jiddah in September 1933 had the biggest tires he could get there, which were 7.50 x 16s. Even Kerr's Fairchild had big doughnut balloons. In spite of the attractiveness of the picture of Eltiste and Kerr hoisting a camel on an A-frame, truth compels the statement that it was later, and on heavy equipment, that these two made their notable contribution. They took what the Camel Corps engineer had first comprehended, and applied it to bigger and bigger carriers, until by now a rig weighing 400,000 pounds and up goes off across the Arabian Desert on rubber.

By February 19, 1935, the collar for Dammam No. 1 was completed – the hard way. Having no dynamite at the time, they broke up the rock by alternately getting it hot with a wood fire and then drenching it with cold water. Haenggi's crew began erecting the derrick, accepting the help of everybody around, including the engineers and geologists. ("What can I do to help around here?" asked Floyd Ohliger, the petroleum engineer. Eltiste handed him a 10-pound hammer and a handful of 60-penny spikes and pointed to some 3x12 planks on the derrick floor. "Nail down a few boards," he said.) By the middle of April the derrick was up and they were rigging up and digging a sump hole. On April 30, 1935, they spudded in Dammam No. 1 with the old cable rig, starting a 22 ½-inch hole.

This was what they had come for. No problems of expense, policy, public relations, cultural adjustment, logistics, or integration of effort concerned them. Those were office problems. No problems of terrain or location troubled them. Those were the geologists' lookout. The three American drillers with their crews were here to drill a hole and see what was down there, to keep three shifts going night and day, to meet the hourly problems of teaching the Saudi and Bahraini workmen how not to get hurt, how to respect the machinery, how to do the job.

The fact that most of them had only a little Arabic did not bother them. Most of them hadn't had much Spanish either: they gave orders by some combination of gesture, grunt, shouting, and an occasional indispensable word. Slim Williams, confronted by the necessity of communicating the idea "down," and knowing only the word for "up," which was *fok*, managed to convey his meaning by raising his voice to three times its usual volume and adding "no God damn it." Thus, "*FOK*, NO GOD DAMN IT!" came to be a reasonably clear, if slightly crude, version of "down."

The wildcatters were marked, as a class, by great practical skill, a general lack of patience with incompetent or unskilled people, a general lack of comprehension of the fine points of intercultural relations, and a general rough good nature. They were the furthest thing in the world from snobs, and they were jokers and pranksters and were pleasantly surprised to find the Arabs a good deal like them in that respect. Moreover, they were a hand-picked crew, and having been carefully warned against kinds of behavior likely to offend their Arab hosts, they watched themselves. They had the example and the advice of certain ones among the geological crew, notably Art Brown, Allen White, and Felix Dreyfus, as well as one of their own number, Bill Eltiste, who picked up Arabic fast and established friendly relations in Jubail, Hofuf, and al-Khobar.

All in all, relations were healthy. Miller had the expected arguments with Muhammad Ali Tawil about customs and the hiring and treatment of Saudi workmen, but there was nothing even approaching an incident until Walt Haenggi let the heat and the multiple irritations of life work on him in the summer of 1935. Working on him too, perhaps, was the fact that he had been married to a missionary doctor in Bahrain not too long before, and felt frustrated by his inability to have his wife in Arabia with him.

The Dammam camp had more home comforts than the Jubail compound, but it was an even more bleak and unlovely place for a man to live – bald, treeless, blinding with sun and heat. There was not a glass of beer nearer than Bahrain, to which they were seldom able to go, and not a woman in all Arabia at whom they would have dared look. The temperature when one rose of a summer morning around 5:00 would be perhaps 92 degrees, with a humidity so thick that the mere movement of dressing soaked a man in sweat. After breakfast, as the sun climbed and the thermometer rose upward toward its top limit of 125 – once an engineer near the Iraq Neutral Zone read 132 degrees on his thermometer at noon – the humidity fell a little, and at 110 or 115 one often felt cooler than in the early morning. But still it was no Sunday school picnic to work a full shift with your clothes soaking wet, your whole body itching and burning with prickly heat, your skin chafed raw under the belt, and your head aching with the clang of the fierce sun.

A man might be excused for irritability, especially when he had to do a job with a crew of Bahraini or Saudi workmen whose childhood training had fitted them to drive camels and find their way across howling wildernesses, or dive sixty or seventy feet down to the pearl beds, and glean a living from one of the hardest environments in which men have managed to live, but did not at once fit them for jobs involving industrial tools and techniques. They learned, and many of them learned fast, but there were inevitable moments when the boss took his head in his hands, and times when if he had been bossing a crew at home in America he would have blown sky-high.

In the middle of June, Walt Haenggi eventually blew. It is uncertain how high he blew and whether he was really angry, but his outburst came close to getting the whole outfit expelled from Arabia.

He had been having trouble with an Arab workman, a man who had not quite learned that to get a job done well and quickly somebody had to give orders and somebody else had to take them. Apparently the workman had been uncooperative and sullen; apparently he came to work one morning after a series of incidents in which Haenggi had had to reprimand him, and scowled at Haenggi with particular provocation.

Precisely what happened then is lost in rumor and hearsay. Dick Kerr, up in Jubail, heard that Haenggi hung a left hook on the Arab, a half-playful hook that did not know its own strength or allow for the workman's ignorance of the art of self-defense. Miller insisted that no blow was struck. Haenggi himself said he grabbed the man and bent him back across a bench and shook him a little. The workman, in any event, rushed out of the place and reported to government authorities that Haenggi had pulled a knife and threatened him with it.

Haenggi's act, however justified, was the match that they had all feared; the powder train of cultural suspicion flared up hotly. Shaikh Muhammad Tawil was over to the camp as fast as he could get there. He wanted a full explanation, to which he was obviously entitled, and Bert Miller promised him one. He made arrangements for Haenggi to come in from the water-well pump where he was working, and while he and Ohliger waited in the dining hall they tried to placate Shaikh Muhammad. They had with them a young Kuwaiti boy who knew a little English and sometimes served them as interpreter.

Haenggi was slow coming in, having stopped to wash up in the bunkhouse. Before he appeared, George McCoy, who had been on the graveyard shift, banged in and walked across the dining room to get a drink. Shaikh Muhammad took one look at him and blew higher than Haenggi had. He stood up shouting so loud that the scared Kuwaiti boy couldn't even understand what he said, and then he stormed out of the dining hall and shouted to workmen on the rig and on jobs around the camp. By the time Miller and Ohliger recovered from their astonishment, Shaikh Muhammad was on his way to Qatif, and all the Arab workmen in the place, in obedience to his orders, had stopped work.

Tawil telegraphed his story to the King, who told Lenahan to get Haenggi out of Arabia right away. But in Qatif, to which Miller had followed Tawil that same Sunday evening, Shaikh Muhammad had had some explanations that half appeased him. The driller who came through and seemed to show such contemptuous disregard of the Arab delegation was not Haenggi, as Tawil had thought, and Haenggi did not appear to be so clearly guilty as it had seemed at first.

Of three written statements by Arabs which were read to Tawil, two seemed to clear Haenggi of serious guilt. Nevertheless, Haenggi would have to leave Arabia. Miller said he could not agree to that. Guy Williams had vowed that if Haenggi was thrown out of Arabia he was going too; and Miller pointed out that this would leave them without a carpenter and without a drilling superintendent. And Arabia wanted oil. The King wanted oil. All the ministers wanted oil.

As a matter of fact, most of the American crew were agreed that they should be firm; to agree to Haenggi's expulsion would have been a bad precedent. They thought Haenggi had intended no more than a rough joke, or at most a reprimand. They persuaded Tawil, and when Lenahan's telegram came telling them to remove Haenggi, they telegraphed back and persuaded Lenahan and the King. Haenggi stayed, and the work went on, the better, perhaps, for a clearing of the air and a venting of the irritations – and also for the warning of how broad the tolerance had to be on both sides.

Near the end of September, Miller ended his field work in Arabia. He had a long vacation coming, since he had been in the Gulf region for three and a quarter years, but he had stayed through the summer to get information for air conditioning in new construction in Bahrain and Saudi Arabia. Also, he wanted to get the geological parties organized for the next season's field work. Fred Davies relieved him in al-Hasa.

The theory behind drilling oil wells is very simple. You drill a hole in the ground over a place where you have reason to hope, or guess, or believe there is a humped-up dome in the strata, and try to break through into that dome. If there is any accumulation of hydrocarbons there, as gas or oil or a mixture of the two, the internal pressure will force it up the hole you have drilled, and you have an oil or gas well. It is as simple as that. Only the actual doing is complicated. And with the best geological advice in the world it is terribly easy to guess wrong about what is a half mile or a mile or two miles underground.

This is how the testing of a gamble looks when transcribed as a series of cables sent halfway around the world:

May 7, 1935: To Reginald Stoner from Guy Williams: "Well No. 1 . . . drilling in hard gray limestone . . . 260'."

May 14: Stoner from Williams: "Well No. 1 . . . 496' . . . gray limestone, encountered water 312' . . . slight showing tar 383' . . . casing set on shoulder 103' . . . to straighten hole. All well here."

July 15: Stoner from Williams: "Drilled ahead to 1,433' . . . gray limestone . . . All well here."

August 25: Stoner from Miller: "Slight showings of oil and gas at 1,774'. Not important but encouraging."

August 30: Stoner from Williams: "1,886' . . . blue shale. Casing 1,845' . . . dense limestone 1,774'–1,800'; and 1,819'–1,883'; shows oil and gas 1,779'–1,801'; and 1,840'–1,883'; flowing by heads . . . possibly would make 50 bbls. per day. All well here."

September 6: Stoner from Williams: "1,959' . . . casing 1,939' . . . dense limestone oil and gas 1,886'–1,906'. Streaks blue reddish brown greenish shale and dense limestone 1,906'–1,959'. Oil and gas 1,948'–1,959'. A.P.I. gravity 47 . . . hole caved badly . . . lowered casing present depth hole cleaned itself . . . maximum pressure 530' in four hours . . . preparing make flow test. All well here."

September 12: Stoner from Williams: ". . . 21 hours test at the rate of 98 bbls. in 24 hours and 700 MCF gas rate . . . 300 flow pressure ¼-inch bean A.P.I. gravity above 50 . . . preparing to drill deeper."

September 18: Stoner from Williams: ". . . 1,977' deep . . . While shut down for changing control head, flowed by heads approximately 6,537 bbls. per day A.P.I. gravity of 50."

That September 18 cable jarred them back home. It could just possibly be true. San Francisco cabled frantically for confirmation of the figure of 6,537 barrels a day, and to Stoner from the Los Angeles office came a telegram suggesting that the figure must be an error because the well was only flowing "by heads" or by surges. "These figures may need checking before jumping out of window," Los Angeles said a little breathlessly.

Williams steadied them with a cable on September 23. The estimated flow was around 100 barrels a day. It would have been an oil well in Pennsylvania, but not out here. And so back to work and back to the cabled reports:

November 27: Stoner from Davies: "2,271' . . . 6 5/8" casing 2,238' . . . alternating sand and shale 2,236'–2,271'; total of 19 feet sand in three members. Unloaded to test. Strong flow of gas . . . showing of oil. Gauged 1,800 MCF gas with 680 lbs. back pressure. Unable to gauge further because fitting started cut out. Killing well with mud. . ."

January 4, 1936: Stoner from Davies: "Plugged with cement to 2,372' . . . standing."

They hadn't given up on No. 1, but their enthusiasm was dampened. On the same day they plugged it, they started rigging up for No. 2. The parallel with the Bahrain structure was obviously not so precise as they had hoped: the zone that was richly productive on Bahrain was disappointing here. But one of the wells on Bahrain had found oil at a deeper horizon, at 2,832 feet. To go down that deep they needed a rotary drilling rig. Charley Potter brought one over from Bahrain and they went about installing it on No. 1, using the cable rig to start No. 2 on February 8.

In mid-April, a year after they had spudded it in, they had No. 1 down below 3,200 feet, down below the deep productive zone on Bahrain. Through May and June they struggled with sticking drill pipe, cavings, cementings, broken casings, and perforations and acid treatments that had little effect. Their faith in the well was gone, and the excitement stirred up in official Saudi Arab quarters when it blew gas and oil during the tests of the previous August had faded too.

The crew went on tinkering with No. 1 for six months more, then shut it in for nearly a year before they finally completed it as a standby gas well in December 1937. By then no one was paying much attention to it. The attention had long been focused on No. 2, which by May 11, 1936 (after the rotary rig was moved there) was drilled to 2,175 feet and was giving most encouraging indications. On June 20, during a five-day test, No. 2 flowed an average of 335 barrels of 54° A.P.I. crude a day. One week later, after acid treatment, it produced steadily at the rate of 160 barrels an hour – equivalent to 3,840 barrels a day – until it was shut in because the storage was full. Obviously there were some hydrocarbons down there.

Even on the meager showing of No. 1, the San Francisco office had shown strongly bullish tendencies, and No. 2 confirmed the official optimism. On May 22 William H. Berg, then a vice president and director, sent word that if Dammam No. 2 turned out to be a producer, the men in the field should be prepared to drill the Al Alat structure, first recommended by Max Steineke partly because it was the likeliest geological prospect and partly because it was only twenty miles northwest of the Dammam camp and could be serviced from there and supplied from al-Khobar. Inside of six days, on the strength of the developments at No. 2, the Al Alat well was authorized, and early in June the San Francisco office threw the book at Davies and his slim field force by authorizing drilling Dammam Nos. 3, 4, 5, and 6 to test the extent of the structure there.

When Davies protested that even No. 2 had been pushed too fast, and that they really had no idea of the thickness of the producing strata, and that four new wells at Dammam plus one at Al Alat were beyond the capacities of the crews, San Francisco replied by authorizing Bahrain to cooperate with everything it had, and in July it authorized still another well, Dammam No. 7, designed to be a deep test of the so-called Arab Zone which had shown gas, but little oil, on Bahrain.

Authorization of the drilling program also meant authorization to expand the workforce and the camp facilities to meet it. This meant replacing the wildcat camp with a permanent one, and a little group of fewer than two dozen Americans and about two hundred Saudi, Bahraini, and Indian workmen with a very much larger force. It meant reserving for company use another plot of land at Dammam camp to match the reservations already made at al-Khobar, Ras Tanura, and Dhulaifain, on the Gulf north of Ras Tanura. It meant new workers, most of whom would have to be recruited from abroad with inevitable arguments to prove to the

Saudi Arab government that, as yet, there were no technically skilled Saudis available. It meant better transshipping arrangements between Bahrain and the mainland. It meant water wells at Al Alat and new ones at Dammam camp; the drilling they were already doing utilized 15,000 barrels of fresh water daily and worked the pumps on the submarine spring around the clock.

It meant approval of layouts and plans for a permanent camp, approval of housing plans, building of housing for new personnel, and before that the building of housing for the men who would build the housing. It meant enlargement of al-Khobar pier, the surveying of the Gulf to find better channels for deeper-draft ships. It meant laying out and oiling and keeping in repair a road between al-Khobar and the Al Alat wildcat, the last eight miles of it across bad dunes. It meant increasing the size of the camps for Saudi workers and the building of a new one at Al Alat. It meant more bunkhouses, more machine shops, a bigger power plant, bigger storehouses. And almost every new and bigger thing that expansion meant also created new and bigger problems of adjustment between Arab and American, new and bigger difficulties of negotiation, fresh differences of opinion in the interpretation of the all-important Concession Agreement.

San Francisco, convinced after the June showing of No. 2 that they had an oil field, cabled that it was sending four two-bedroom, air-conditioned, prefabricated bunkhouses to supplement the already enlarged one that Walt Haenggi had built. Ten days later, riding a big wave of excitement and optimism, Stoner cabled that he was also sending some air-conditioned cottages suitable for family living. He advised Fred Davies to put his mind seriously on the problem of taking care of married personnel.

Davies was perfectly willing. But he as general manager, and Floyd Ohliger as petroleum engineer, and Guy Williams as drilling superintendent, and Max Steineke as chief geologist, and Bill Lenahan as official government representative, and everyone in a position of responsibility in Arabia, had plenty of other problems to put his mind on. The wildcatters with their bits probing a half mile down in Arabia's crust had immensely complicated all their lives. This was no longer an adventurous exploring expedition or a picturesque outpost. The Jubail compound was still kept as a geological office, but geological headquarters had already, in October 1935, been consolidated into the Dammam camp when Davies replaced Bert Miller in charge of the whole operation.

Some of the fun had gone. The Fairchild, once their pet and darling, was folded up and stuffed in a shed, no longer needed. Its motor, packed in a crate labeled A-1, was shipped off to the United States for rebuilding, the first thing ever exported from the al-Khobar pier. The old concerns – the constant equilibristic job of government relations, the steady exploration of the concession, the drilling of new test wells – would go on, but around them now would grow an increasingly complex net of other needs, other jobs, and other problems; and along the Gulf coast would grow new outposts of industrial civilization, some of them temporary, some permanent.

What had been a frontier was on the boom. But it was on the boom in a way new to their experience. In most parts of the world the discovery of oil or valuable minerals would have drawn in a crowd of fortune hunters, prospectors, floating labor, entertainers, gamblers – plus providers of supplies and services, who would have supplemented the planned expansion by the company. In Saudi Arabia the conditions of remoteness and the exclusive concession left everything to be done by the company, and if that gave them the advantage of greater control, it also left them with the responsibility for greater foresight.

Throughout 1936 they were always behind, always short of something, always getting something half-built and moving into it and using it as a base to build something else. While San Francisco pondered the plan and map of the permanent camp, sent in by Davies at the end of 1935, and while Bay Area laboratories tested various Arabian building materials to see if anything local would do for construction, Davies and Dreyfus visited the King, then visiting Hofuf, and found him genial and pleased with the way they were pushing ahead, confident that very soon now he would have for his kingdom the sort of riches enjoyed by his friend the Shaikh of Bahrain. Such incidents as the Haenggi affair were only locally upsetting. Push ahead faster, therefore. This was even before the spudding-in of Dammam No. 2, which did not come until February 8.

All through the spring, as the bits ground deeper in both No. 1 and No. 2, the supporting operations proliferated. The men broadened and lengthened the al-Khobar pier, and before it was anything but a horizontal rockslide, cars and trucks were scraping their pans across it. Dark roads began to reach out from al-Khobar to Dammam camp, from Dammam camp toward Al Alat, sprayed with the crude from No. 1. In March, Davies negotiated a contract with the Mesopotamia Persia Corporation of Bahrain to bring company freight in by barge or launch or dhow, and immediately the local customs officers, the local government representative, and ultimately Lenahan and the Ministry of Finance in Jiddah were involved in a debate about anchorage fees, liability in case of accident, the proper validation of manifests.

In Jiddah there were quite different signs of growth and strain. Saudi Arabia, which for generations had used the Maria Theresa (thaler) dollar and sometimes the gold sovereign for currency, had, under Ibn Saud, formally outlawed the Maria Theresa dollar and established as its own unit of exchange the silver riyal. There were never enough riyals in circulation, but what had been before Casoc a faint awkwardness now revealed itself as an acute lack. Casoc was interested because it sometimes had trouble making payrolls in the local medium of exchange, always silver because the Saudi Arabs still neither understood nor trusted paper. (Khamis ibn Rimthan, paid once in silver and a rupee note, had kept the silver and thrown the note away.) The Saudi Arab government, to remedy this shortage and to stabilize the fluctuating value of the riyal, had placed an order for the coinage of a million riyals early in 1936 and now wanted to coin another million. For backing it needed gold; it suggested that Casoc might lend it £15,000, and after hesitating from March to July, Casoc did so, since by that time the euphoria brought on by the production at Dammam No. 2 was loosening the purse strings in San Francisco.

This was only one of literally dozens of problems and negotiations that kept Bill Lenahan and his new assistant Bill Burleigh busy in Jiddah. Experience had taught them not to deal with local officials on policy questions, so that now any matters involving interpretation of the Concession Agreement or the supplementary Private Agreement were automatically referred to the Jiddah office by Davies or by Ohliger, who on August 1, 1936, was made assistant general manager.

They handed Lenahan all the old (and persistently renewed) debates about customs liabilities and the size of escorts for field parties and about the company's requests to import foreign labor for specialized jobs that could not yet be handled by Saudis. He acquired likewise such new matters as the police problem brought about by the establishment of a permanent camp. Saudi Arab police assigned to the Dammam and Al Alat camps were local men, and authority did not always sit well on them, even when they thought they knew what this authority was. The precise nature of their jurisdiction within the company reservation, as well as problems of the behavior of policemen, were Lenahan's to solve, though Davies and Ohliger had to deal with specific situations as they arose in the field.

And there was a whole series of government requests, most of them now channeled through Najib Salha, who, always the bargainer, reopened a lot of agreements the company had considered settled. Most of them called for additional company contributions, such as the building of a government house at al-Khobar pier and provision of transportation for the Saudi Arab government representative in al-Hasa. After all, the government argument ran, we would not be having these problems and expenses if you were not here digging for oil. Demands had to be taken up one by one, and parried or allowed as justice and public relations dictated. One thing Lenahan could be sure of: the moment he got one settled, there would be another in its place.

Problems were what made Jiddah stimulating, actually. The gossip and intrigue of its foreign colony were interesting after a fashion, and Lenahan took periodic trips to Egypt or Europe to refresh himself. But it was the problems that he liked. He was a born negotiator, alert and imaginative, and when necessary immovable, and once in a while furious. Paradoxically, his temper rather endeared him to the King, to whom he sometimes went when he found the ministers intransigent. "I like Lenahan because I know him," Ibn Saud said once, "and I know him because I have fought with him so many times."

By the beginning of August 1936, when Ohliger was taking over his new job and they were building the rig for Al Alat No. 1, the company had made its loan to the government, had decided not to compete with Longrigg and IPC for a concession for the Saudi-owned Farasan Islands in the Red Sea, and had obtained land reservations for Al Alat and clearances for Dammam Wells Nos. 3, 4, 5, and 6 as well as a 70,000-acre reservation for the permanent camp and its necessary installations. By that same midsummer dividing line, a company engineer named Charles Herring had reported that a submarine pipeline to the Bahrain refinery was perfectly feasible, and in London Roy Lebkicher, Hamilton's assistant, had had several conferences with the British Admiralty about a hydrographic survey of the Gulf with an eye to the marking of channels and the creation of a major port.

Once committed, there was practically no limit to how far the company might be extended in its effort to develop and market a major oil deposit. It was very willing, even eager, in spite of its uncertain status as a purely commercial stranger in a foreign country. All it needed, actually, was the oil, and that in midsummer 1936 did not look difficult. In the process of finding it, the field was pressing several programs vigorously.

A lean and drawling paleontologist, Dick Bramkamp, came out at the end of August and set up an Arabian foraminiferal laboratory so that they would not have the delay and awkwardness of relying on the lab on Bahrain. From October on, Jerry Harriss and Walt Hoag, a pair of geologists who cordially disliked each other and went for days without speaking, were off in the desert west of Jubail sourly mapping an area of nearly 4,000 square miles as a preliminary to geophysical work there. In November the first structure drilling program, with Krug Henry in charge, began a series of holes at Al Alat, Qatif, and Dammam. Careful study of the cores from those holes, and their coordination with cores from other districts and with the results of surface geological work, would eventually give them a more positive idea of the continuity, depth, and flexure of strata, and make drilling less of a gamble and more of a science.

This was the beginning of the geologists' fourth season in the field, and the findings had been, on the whole, meager. They had discovered at once what they had seen from a distance: the Dammam Dome. They had by surface investigations and Max Steineke's intuitions detected signs of closure at Abqaiq and Qatif, and the an-Nala area west of Hofuf was known to be regionally high and worth further study. The Al Alat structure had been plane-tabled and was now being test-drilled and structure-drilled. But they still did not know the Miocene stratigraphy clearly enough to see the underground organization of the region, and they did not know clearly its relation to the Eocene. They had a great deal of hunting still to do, and by means more productive than surface geology.

Through 1936 that program went on. The camp spread out across the crusty rock and shallow sand southwest of the *jabals*, and the flock of test wells that San Francisco had ordered went down – all by rotary. As reported by cable on April 15, No. 1 had gone down below 3,200 feet without real result. More alarming, No. 2, after its spectacular test at a rate of 3,840 barrels per day, "went wet," and settled down in the later months of 1936 to a production of 225 barrels a day of oil and 1,965 barrels of water; it was obviously going to need some rehabilitation. And what of wildcats Nos. 3, 4, 5, and 6, all hopefully aimed at the Bahrain Zone which had gushed out the June flow of No. 2?

No. 3 was spudded in on July 14 and completed to the Bahrain Zone on November 20. Production was never more than a hundred barrels a day of 28° A.P.I. oil, 15 percent water. It was never flowed except for use as road oil.

No. 4, spudded in August 20, was suspended in the Bahrain Zone at 2,318 feet on November 18. There was not even a showing on this one: a dry hole, a duster.

No. 5, spudded in September 8, was down to 2,067 feet by the end of the year without producing anything.

No. 6, whose derrick was erected in September, suffered from the overload of rush work and from the sagging of spirits when 3, 4, and 5 went to no purpose and No. 2 dwindled. It sat there, a derrick on a cellar, until after the turn of the year before anything was done with it.

In the meantime, preparations had been made for the first deep test hole. It was called Dammam No. 7, and it was spudded in on December 7. What it would find was, by then, anyone's guess, but they all knew it had better show something. Time was running out.

Chapter Seven
~ *Dammam No. 7* ~

There is a time in any wildcat camp when the bunkhouse begins to yield to the family cottage; Reg Stoner had already anticipated that time when he shipped the first air-conditioned, two-bedroom portables out to Saudi Arabia in June of 1936. But it was not until the spring of 1937 that Annette Henry and Nellie Carpenter arrived to make history as the first American wives to live in the Eastern Province of Saudi Arabia. Like rock being cracked by frost, the isolation of Saudi Arabia was broken by a series of small expansions. A cupful of water in a crevice, when it swells into ice, can split a great boulder. The arrival of the first wives was the application of that sort of innocent-appearing but potent force.

Mrs. Henry – the lovely Annette whom Krug Henry had seen, courted, and won in an uproarious few weeks in Lebanon – came down from Syria, Nellie Carpenter from Bahrain. They sneaked up on al-Hasa, as it were, by stages. Gingerly, unveiled and stared-at, they bumped along the al-Khobar pier and were brought to two of the six new cottages that squatted baldly on the stone and sand, without a bush, a spear of grass, a weed even, around them. Their view was of a lone derrick among bare *jabals*, a fence enclosing an acreage of scorched earth, a cluster of gaunt power poles. But there were never two women more appreciated, respected, and revered. The schoolteacher in a Wyoming cow town was a social outcast by comparison.

In September they got reinforcements when Don Brown's wife Edna, Erma Witherspoon, Patsy Jones, and Florence Steineke arrived together on the British-India boat from Bombay. Even the first four American children, as if to compensate for the unlicked masculinity of the bunkhouse, were girls: Maxine and Marian Steineke, Marilyn Witherspoon, and Mitzi Henry.

Pioneers as much as their husbands were, the women owned the camp; they owned it by right of their civilizing force, their function in turning it into a community. Drillers and geologists went out of their way to bring the children presents and pets. Where the Jubail and Dammam camps had specialized in hawks and wolf-pups, the family cottages were shortly flooded with baby gazelles, hedgehogs, and salukis. Chow Lee and Frank Dang brought the wives bread and chow mein from the cookhouse, and for special occasions dusted off recipes unused since Berkeley sorority house days. The cottages, each with its air-conditioning unit, were comfortable despite their dreary yards, and the equipment was new and clean.

And yet it was a hard place for a squeamish, timid, or restless woman. Exaggerated – even groundless – thoughts of unknown snakes, unknown germs, unknown dangers for the children, kept them watchful. Unexaggerated, perfectly understandable concern as to how American wives should conduct themselves in this country (where an unveiled woman was then a shock to the conventions) kept them on edge. They had some anxious preliminary discussions about whether they should or should not go veiled, and what kind of clothes would be appropriate and at the same time bearable in the heat. The decision, made with considerable uneasiness, was against veiling, but the ladies sacrificed the wearing of slacks or shorts.

One of the difficult aspects of their life at first was the combination of convention and company caution that kept them within the camp fence. They were never supposed to go out, and if they occasionally did, they usually huddled inconspicuously in the back of the cars.

But that was at the very beginning. Before long Steineke was taking the women out on field trips and showing them some of Arabia's desolate reaches of dunes and outcrops, and flat brownish *sabkhas* with their horizons afloat in the mirage and a camel loaded with salt grass moving in the distance as tall and black as a waterspout. Later they got glimpses of Bedouin camps and the *barastis* of irregular soldiers by the wells, saw gazelle break down the wadis, and sometimes observed the curious phenomenon of herds of camels that seemed to have been stained and varnished – when their owners sheared them and greased their hides – and down on the shore by Dammam or al-Khobar saw fishermen wading out to the arrowy points of their fish traps, and townsmen washing camels or donkeys in the salt water to remove the ever present lice and ticks.

By an unkindness of fate, only three of them played bridge or were interested in playing it, so they depended on the occasional visitor from Bahrain for a ladies' foursome. The established families traded dinners; occasionally a geologist from one of the field parties, or one of the managerial staff or one of the boys from the bunkhouse, was invited over. Invariably he recorded such an invitation in his letters home.

As if there were not enough lonesome Americans in the camp to mother, the women involved themselves in the lives of the houseboys, the cooks, and the drivers. Over a period of years, they fascinated themselves trying to unravel the marital condition of Chow Lee, who had a wife in China but who had lived in Venezuela with a woman from La Villa de Rosario. It was said that after the Venezuelan venture was closed down and Lee came to Bahrain he had sent two money orders to the woman but that both had been returned. This was mysterious and interesting. So was the fact that almost every year Lee returned to China to visit his wife, and that every year without fail, whether Lee returned to China or not, his wife seemed to have a new child.

Both Lee and Dang were good cooks. They were the sole bakers of bread for the community, and bread was their biggest headache. Dang brought the first riser across from Bahrain and got it just to the bunkhouse when it blew up with the heat; later they had a good deal of trouble keeping loaves from disappearing, because the Saudi helpers looked upon bread as an expendable luxury. Dang, in fact, departed somewhat suddenly from Arabia after chasing one group of helpers out of the kitchen with a cleaver. Chow Lee solved the problem of the disappearing bread by fiercely, and in the sight of all, wiping every loaf of dough with a ham or bacon rind before he put it in the oven. Since his helpers to a man were devout, practicing Muslims to whom pork was forbidden, he lost no more bread.

The wives collected stories too about Shaubi, a Saudi driver and mechanic, a wry, merry, low-comedy character who was always having troubles and always being urged to prepare for them by carrying spare water, spare fuel pump, spare fan belt, spare spark plugs. Stimulated by the prosperity of working for steady wages, he went away for a while, and as he was permitted to do by his religion, came back with a second wife. When the women asked him reproachfully why he went and did a thing like that, he gave them back their own doctrine: she was a spare.

Still, it was not all jolly and amusing. The almost frantic expansion of 1936 put strains upon both company and government, and the company's growing activity forced expansion of the government bureaucracy to handle it. It was not merely that Saudi Arabia as a unified nation was barely ten years old and was still developing its agencies. Problems utterly unknown up to that time in the whole history of the Arabian Peninsula had to be met. In Saudi Arabia, for example, there were not yet any workmen's compensation laws, but when five Arab workers were injured in a dynamite explosion in November 1936, the problem was acutely before them. So was the problem of the Saudi Arab police, most of them Hijazis and under a chief of police who did not consider himself bound to pay attention either to the official government representative for al-Hasa or to Shaikh Abdullah Sulaiman.

In January 1937, the police treated fifteen Bahraini employees so roughly that they quit in a body, and since they were semiskilled men, their loss hurt. Through March there was a series of exasperating incidents. The police assigned to the Dammam camp not only showed little desire to cooperate with the company, which was after all bearing the cost of their wages, but indicated a considerable truculence on occasion, and a willingness to manhandle Americans they caught in some misdemeanor or other. Violence was their heritage, a camel stick their natural form of argument. The camp was on edge, the women were uneasy, the roughnecks of the drilling crews were in no mood to submit to rough treatment, the management was walking on eggs for fear some flare-up like the Haenggi incident of 1935 might bring the whole structure of compromise and mutual forbearance down around their ears.

Floyd Ohliger, upon whom most of the job of protest and countermeasures fell, was a good-natured man, and essentially a patient one, but at a certain point in an argument he could harden like a rock. He hardened on April 28, 1937, when he notified Sayid Ali Sultan, the government representative, that the heretofore innocent, aimless pilferage of company materials had reached such proportions that the company wanted the government police withdrawn. Ohliger knew, of course, that the pilferage was not deliberate stealing but the simple assumptions of simple workers that a company as large as Casoc certainly wouldn't grudge a little item here and there. Until April 28 it didn't. But then the line was drawn, and on August 4, Abdullah Sulaiman relieved the chief of police, and replaced him with a man much more cooperative in handling the company's problem, thus easing the situation considerably.

Other events also helped to counteract the unpleasantnesses. The Saudi government was pleased to learn in April that structure wells Nos. S-A2 and S-A3 at Al Alat, as well as S-A5 at the edge of the Qatif oasis, had encountered large flows of sweet water which was being developed for the benefit of the Bedouins and local farmers.

From the government, actually, whatever the officiousness of the local police, the company continued to receive effective cooperation. In August 1937, it obtained permission to import twenty radios and to distribute them within the camp as it saw fit; that same permission included phonographs. Music was added to the life of bunkhouse and family cottage, and came close to transforming it; it was wonderful how dead hours could be filled by a radio, how a voice from the air could restore contact with the world that sometimes seemed as far away as Mars. Then, the day after Thanksgiving, they attended in the recreation hall the first professional motion picture ever shown in the Eastern Province – and possibly in all Saudi Arabia. Several people had projectors for their 8-mm. and 16-mm. films, but this was the real thing. Everyone in camp was there.

On December 23, as if to bring to a close in good feeling and reassurance a year that had been disappointing and a little tense, Crown Prince Saud came to Dammam with a great caravan of cars, visited the installations and the camp, received everyone in his great outdoor *majlis*, and held a special audience for the women and even the children, who came up to drop scared and hastily-learned curtsies. Since the Crown Prince did not speak English and the ladies, except for Annette Henry, were new to Arabic, there was little conversation beyond the stilted exchange of amenities by interpreter. But the visit demonstrated the continuing friendliness of the royal family, and it thrilled the ladies exceedingly.

One other thing of importance happened in 1937. Max Steineke went across Arabia and back.

The men in the exploration department, charged as they were with surveying and mapping the most remote reaches of the concession, had an early and continuing advantage over the drillers and others tied down to the Dammam camp and the coast area. They saw Arabia at its most free, its wildest and cleanest, and hardly a one of them did not, even with the additional hardships, prefer the desert to the towns. And even for the geologists, a trip all the way across Arabia was likely to be the biggest adventure of the Arabian experience. Such a trip enhanced and justified the routine discomforts by adding novelty, uncertainty, a touch of danger. Lloyd Hamilton, Bert Miller, and Felix Dreyfus had found their 1934 crossing by way of Riyadh the best experience of their lives. Every subsequent trip produced a crop of yarns that remained part of the Arabian canon – stories about cosmic mischances, boneheaded errors, strange encounters, heroic troubles with sand, with *sabkhas*, with wadis in flash flood. Everyone lucky enough to get a trip across Arabia remembered it; everyone lucky enough to make the round-trip was to be envied.

There had not been many round-trips before March and April 1937, when Steineke and Floyd Meeker made theirs, and there was probably never a trip quite so fruitful. For this was the first complete look that Steineke got at the Arabian surface geology all the way from the obliterated features of the Arabian Gulf coast to the basement complex of the Hijaz. On the way from Dammam to Jiddah, the party, which included Fred Davies, Hamilton, Max Thornburg, Steineke, and Meeker, besides drivers and interpreters and a cook, had its mind on problems of government relations; but coming back by themselves, Steineke and Meeker could, whenever they weren't having car or road trouble, look at rocks. In a few days of quick reconnaissance Steineke probably illuminated Arabian stratigraphy as much as all the previous field work had been able to do.

Going out, they had two sedans and three pickups. They traveled without undue haste, and camped in comfort, with a big tarpaulin that stretched across the sedans, parked fifteen or twenty feet apart, and made an expansive tent, almost a *majlis*. As was customary, the party stopped in Hofuf to pay its respects to Ibn Jiluwi. As was usual, the Amir did a good deal of listening. As was his habit, he played his trick of murmuring "Qahwa!" ("Coffee!") under his breath and having his bodyguard repeat the order in a sudden savage shout that startled the uninitiated out of their cushions. And as was common practice, the desert veterans gave – but not until asked – some lessons in cross-country travel to the less seasoned members. Max Thornburg, eating dates at the noon stop on the second day, noticed that Steineke did not pop whole dates into his mouth and spit out the seeds, as Thornburg himself was doing, but broke them and ate them contemplatively by halves. Sometimes he absently threw a whole date away. Thornburg inquired about the idiosyncrasy. He was shown the little worm that sometimes lay next to the seed, and abruptly quit eating whole dates. In fact, he gave up dates altogether.

Outside Riyadh a few miles they paused to change into Arab clothes. Their halt was made memorable by a sound of music around a turn in the wadi. Presently there came in sight an Arab on a donkey, blowing furiously – blowing, not playing – on a mouth organ. When he saw them he stopped in confusion and hid the harmonica under his robe.

Like other distinguished guests, they stayed at the Badia Palace, outside the walls of Riyadh, and like all their predecessors they were awakened by the wild shriek and sliding moan and shriek again of wooden pulleys turning on wooden spindles as two or three hundred donkeys began their day of hauling *ghurbas* of water to the well-brink to dump into the ditches that watered the gardens. They visited with the Crown Prince Saud both in his castle and in Badia Palace, and he showed them the palace, including a room full of old-fashioned clocks, no two of which told the same time. They thought it some whim, that the Crown Prince wanted visibly before him the correct time of each country on the globe, but he smilingly denied any such scientific intention. He just liked to hear them strike and chime.

So as to be sure of a supply, the caravan had sent gasoline on ahead to Riyadh, Duwadami, and Muwaih. Except for the loss of time in ceremonial coffee drinking with the amir of each place, that plan worked well. Water was less easy. The wells they tried to fill up at were generally crowded with camels, and the water hardly fit for animals. Even clean water out of a green *ghurba*, a goatskin with the hair side in, gagged them; it gagged them just as much when they made it into coffee or tea.

About the only good their *ghurba* water did for them was to reassure them that they would not die of thirst; they assumed that at some agonized point the stuff would become drinkable. But they had not reached that point, and their tongues were like leather, when, some hours out of Jiddah, they were met by Bill Burleigh, who had a gallon jug two-thirds full of lovely, clear, unflavored water. They agreed that it was quite good, though it didn't have much *body*.

So much for a routine crossing without notable adventures. They dined with the King and Abdullah Sulaiman, experienced the luxuries of Lenahan's Bait Americani, met Philby again, then headed back.

The mishaps that they had escaped coming over were visited on Steineke and Meeker going back. Coming over the first range of mountains on the road that Twitchell's Saudi Arab Mining Syndicate had built, they noticed a very black cloud with a tail that whipped around like a kite's. A few drops of rain fell on the windshield. A quarter of a mile farther on they topped a little hill and were suddenly surrounded by water. Within a few miles, faced by a wadi running several feet of tumultuous floodwater, they were forced to camp.

Next day they made about twenty-five miles, crossing the wadi seven times in the process. Each time the water was deeper, until it floated the floorboards of the cars. They climbed out and removed the fan belts to keep from throwing water on the motors. When they got out of the wadi and onto the soap-slick clay, they put the fan belts back on. In a little while they had to take them off again. Then they put them back on. Then they took them off, put them on, took them off. Their twenty-five miles of progress had mostly been pushing and wading.

In the morning the ground was a little drier, the going better. They made 125 miles and passed one sign of a changing Arabia: a party of Arabs, including several children, stuck in a broken-down car. Without the spare parts they needed, Meeker and Steineke could not help; they gave the group a five-rupee note as a sign of goodwill and drove on. Another day, and still drying, they made it to Duwadami. The day after that 'Ain Khuff, and this was what Steineke had been pressing to reach, for near 'Ain Khuff was the contact between igneous and sedimentary rock, new rock and old rock. From here eastward, oil could occur; back where they had passed there was hardly a chance. Though their concession did not extend farther west than the Dahna, east of Riyadh, a study of the rocks just here at the contact might illuminate and bring together all the patchy information they had gathered.

They spent a day around 'Ain Khuff examining synclines and anticlines and hunting fossils, and on March 30 moved camp to the foot of Hassiyan Pass below the Tuwaiq Escarpment. More fossil hunting, with some finds that indicated a narrow band of Paleozoic rocks separating the Mesozoic Tuwaiq Mountains from the crystalline and volcanic plateaus they had recently crossed. Clues. They went into Steineke's field notebook and, more important, into his head.

That night the unpredictable desert dumped another cloudburst on them, and flash floods from the mountains nearly washed them away. Struggling to the summit of the pass the next day, they found a suitable Arabian April Fools' joke: drifts of hail four inches deep, some of the stones still as big as marbles after lying on the ground all night.

There was nothing much that Floyd Meeker – accompanying Steineke on this foxhound sniffing among the rocks and the outcrops – could have said for sure was done; there is nothing much for a historian to summarize as the accomplishments of that geological reconnaissance. They simply went over to Jubail and Steineke looked around, they went on down through Riyadh and on April 3 arrived in al-Kharj.

Steineke's examination of that region, with its slump beds, its great lake-like *'ains* in the hollow rock, its *dahls*, or caves, in the formations that Steineke determined were Jurassic, its fossils, including petrified logs, and its exposure of the clear nonconformity marking the contact of the Aruma beds with the Nubian sandstone, took six days.

They had no further adventures, though there was a scare one night when their helpers thought a camel driver at 'Ain Wasia was a party of Bedouin raiders. They had a little grouse shooting, and Floyd Meeker had the opportunity, not especially relished, of drinking bowls of camel's milk proffered by that same "raider." He also had a chance to taste the flesh, reputed to be like chicken, of a two-foot lizard called a *dabb*. Meeker stalled by saying they were just about to take off for Dammam. But he did not escape; his new friend brought the *dabb* along, across the Dahna and into Hofuf, and up through a *shamal*, or sandstorm, to the home camp, and there presented him with the whole thing.

They arrived in Dammam, with a pleasant sense of coming home, to hear the latest news – that the first wives were coming – and to hear the word, none of it too encouraging, on the deeptest well, Dammam No. 7. Nobody thought of them as having done anything special, though they were envied their glimpse of greater Arabia. But in Steineke's notes – and in his head – were geological jottings that gave them for the first time some inkling of Arabia's structure, and that some years later would lead to the discovery of both the Abqaiq and the Ghawar oil fields.

The company file on Dammam No. 7 begins with a carbon copy of a cable on torn yellow flimsy. It is dated July 7, 1936, and it says that the wildcatters want to start the deep-test well as soon as the heavy steam rig now en route arrives. For the next five months there are reports on building the derrick foundation, digging the cellar, erecting the derrick, rigging up. On December 7, they began drilling. On March 8, 1937, after a series of exchanges on reamings, cementings, and delays while waiting for drill pipe, San Francisco revealed its eagerness and optimism: "Well No. 7 . . . When will reaming job be completed? When will married quarters be ready?" Davies cabled back that the reaming would be done about April 1. By that time, three cottages would be ready, and by April 15 another two. (These were the houses that paved the way for Annette Henry, Nellie Carpenter, and the other pioneer wives.)

No. 7 had at least the usual number of accidents and delays. On April 10 they were rigging up to fish for a lost bit. On April 16 Davies cabled E. M. Butterworth, who was assistant manager for Socal's new foreign division producing department in San Francisco: "Well No. 7 . . . cleaned out with 24 ½" bit 726' solid bridge caving, large boulder falls in – plugged with cement 200 sacks – located top of cement at 704'."

By May 1937, everybody around Dammam admitted that the well was in bad shape and was going to be slow. There was a spurt in July that took them down to 2,400 feet, then delays again. On October 6 they had reached 3,300 feet. Tests then, as well as on the 11th and 13th at slightly greater depths, produced the same report: "No oil, no water."

At 3,600 feet, on October 16, they got their first showing of oil – about two gallons, in a flow of thin gas-cut mud. On the last day of 1937, with the hole drilled to 4,535 feet, the well blew out when the control equipment failed. After contact was reestablished, measurements showed the well making 30 million cubic feet of gas a day against 1,600 pounds back pressure. Because of the high pressure they let it blow for seven hours while mixing mud to kill it with, and then killed it without difficulty. There was no oil in the gas it blew.

San Francisco, beginning to worry, watched the progress of the well anxiously. More revealing than any of the communications dealing with stuck drill pipe, broken rotary chains, or fishing expeditions was the cable that Skinner, now in San Francisco as manager of foreign producing, sent Ohliger on November 10, 1937. It reflected the reaction from the uninhibited optimism of 1936, for by now, with No. 2 dwindled to a bare 100 barrels a day and none of the new wells in the Bahrain Zone productive, the board was getting restive. The company had pulled out of foreign wildcats before; it could pull out of this one too, and perhaps should, before more millions went down the hole to join those already poured in. Skinner's cable of November 10 instructed Ohliger to do no more work on any of the shallow wells without submitting a detailed proposal first. San Francisco wanted to make a full study of anything more it spent on those holes. And it wanted to see what No. 7 did before it spent anything at all.

Skinner and Davies had agreed long before that it was a waste of money to drill only to the Bahrain Zone, and that the best bet was the Arab Zone. Already the "small board" made up of department heads was beginning to demur at the expense of additional equipment, and Reg Stoner, as general manager, was quietly "borrowing" equipment from Taft and other California operating points for Arabia. That way, it wouldn't have to be accounted for until the end of the year, and by that time Stoner, Gester, Lombardi, and the other hopeful ones believed something might have happened.

Distance frustrated them; inadequate communications balked their desire to get close to what was happening. Early in 1938, Gester recalled Max Steineke for consultations, and they had a series of long, intent, speculative conferences over the geological maps. It was a terrible country to prophesy about, for the surface indications were obscure, and structure drilling and geophysical work had barely begun. Worse than that, some of the areas where they most wanted seismographic information had hollow limestone formations that reverberated too much for intelligible results.

Should they or should they not? Stoner had heard enough reverberations of discontent from the limestone members of the board of directors to be uneasy. The expenses of Arabia had already run to a good many million dollars, and in late 1937 and early 1938 dollars did not grow on trees. The stock market was nearly as low as it had been at the bottom of the Depression; five years of "recovery" seemed to have left them right where they were. They pinned Steineke down. What did he honestly think of the prospects?

Steineke did not like to recommend drilling until he had run the geological and geophysical evidence through a wringer and convinced himself that the gamble was justified. As one of the early geologists put it: "He wanted to know exactly *how* you knew what you thought you knew." But, once he was convinced, he never hesitated about committing himself; he never took refuge in scientific caution; he never alibied by saying, "If we had another season's work, then we would *know*." He was never embarrassed or hesitant about changing his opinion if new data proved him to be wrong. But his opinion had been crystallizing. On top of the geological data that Bert Miller had bequeathed him, remarkably perceptive considering the speed with which Miller's three geological teams had gathered it, he could now put what he had found on his trip from Jiddah with Meeker.

Now here he was, pinned in a corner by the San Francisco department heads, fighting an internal war between his scientific skepticism and his personal enthusiasm, and the enthusiasm won. He had some guesses that he wanted to prove out; he believed in the Arabian venture; he sold them on it.

While he was selling them, Ohliger's crew was drilling past the "fish" that it had been unable to pick up, and on March 4, 1938, San Francisco got the word that blew it back again into the euphoria of the summer of 1936. Tested on that day, No. 7 flowed at the rate of 1,585 barrels a day. Tested three days later, it flowed at the rate of 3,690 barrels. The drilling party stuck the tester in the hole and couldn't get it out, and the well, flowing as nearly open as possible through the stuck pipe, went on producing at a rate that made them cheer.

Rather than burn the oil, for which there was no storage, they flowed it back into No. 1 in an improvised junction operation, and they let it run long enough so they could tell something about the continuing productivity of the C member of the Arab Zone. They were lucky, although they didn't realize it at the time. Unlike Bahrain oil, which is "sweet," the crude that they were getting was "sour," having a high content of toxic hydrogen sulfide. In Iraq, several of the crew that brought in the discovery well had been fatally poisoned by walking through a small ravine where hydrogen sulfide had accumulated. All that the Dammam crew knew was that the oil and gas from the well smelled bad, and none of them smelled it enough to be hurt.

This was the way it went: March 16, 2,130 barrels; March 17, 2,209; March 18, 2,128; March 19, 2,117; March 20, 2,149; March 21, 3,732; March 22, 3,810; March 28, 3,420; March 24, 3,275; March 25, 3,308. And so on through April 22, when Ed Skinner cabled Ohliger that from San Francisco's point of view there was no reason to continue the test. By then, the total production was over 100,000 barrels. Ohliger estimated that No. 7 could produce 2,000 barrels a day without impairing the reservoir conditions. Soon thereafter, No. 2 and No. 4 were deepened to the Arab Zone and also turned out to be good producers. Dammam was a commercial field.

This was the music that San Francisco liked to dance to; at once it began to dance. Bill Eltiste had come back to Chicago early in 1938 to persuade some tire company to make molds for special desert tires, and also to get some automobile manufacturer to design experimental cars and trucks for off-road use. He got from Marmon-Herrington a promise to build a big heavy-duty 10-ton 6 x 6 truck, mounted on 13.50 x 20 six-ply dual tires, and extracted from the company reluctant permission to have Autocar Corporation build a few smaller trucks using balloon tires of the same size. By the time he got to San Francisco from his automotive conferences in Chicago, the strike in No. 7 had been made, and Eltiste was dazed with offers of mechanical aid. Stoner no longer had to steal what Arabia needed. Experimental trucks? Sure. How many? You ordered one? Better order four or five more. Autocars? Sure. Get enough so you can operate. Wire now and increase that order to 36.

Nothing was too good for al-Hasa after March 4, 1938. Within five days of the cable announcing the strike, San Francisco had notified the field that it was sending out a central air-conditioning plant for the bunkhouses and mess hall. What had died down to a feeble guttering flame spurted into a great flare as oil from the Arab Zone flowed into it.

They had never, no matter how wearily they might have desired it, been able simply to explore their concession area and drill holes in its crust in search of oil. Inevitably they had become a loan agency, a training program, an unofficial department of water supply, a geological and geodetic survey, a mapping bureau, a port-construction authority, a highway commission. Now the Crown Prince Saud involved them in international diplomacy by inviting the Earl of Athlone and his wife, the Princess Alice, to visit Saudi Arabia early in 1938.

The reaction in certain quarters was prompt and furious. Mussolini denounced the visit as a bald effort on the part of Great Britain to curry favor with Saudi Arabia and to "interfere" in the politics of Asia and Africa. The Princess Alice was, after all, a granddaughter of Queen Victoria and second cousin to King

George VI of England; her husband was the brother of Queen Mary and uncle of the king. The throne could hardly have been more directly represented except by the king and queen themselves. But Mussolini's fulminations did not deter what the papers liked to call "the royal pair." Far from canceling their trip to Jiddah, they let it be known that they might go on to Riyadh and perhaps all the way across Arabia to the Arabian Gulf and the island of Bahrain. On the strength of that chance, Lloyd Hamilton wrote Lenahan suggesting that the Saudi Arab government might appreciate it if the Earl and Princess Alice were invited to visit the Dammam camp. He also suggested that the company's cars might be better equipped for desert travel and in better mechanical condition than the government's, and that if Ohliger could spare a little transportation it would be a pleasant gesture to offer it.

Lenahan hesitated to make any such invitations or offers. For one thing, as the commercial representative of an American company, he did not want to intrude on a strictly British-Saudi show, or interfere between host and guest. For another, Britain and Saudi Arabia had a disagreement going about the undefined boundaries where Ibn Saud's kingdom shaded off into British protected Aden, Dhufar, Oman, Muscat, and the shaikhdoms of the Trucial Coast, and since Casoc's concession ran to those same disputed boundaries, it was maintaining a scrupulous neutrality on the issue for fear of getting embroiled. But for the moment, at least, Lenahan need not have worried. When he met Princess Alice at a reception in Jiddah she told him she would love to visit the oil camp, and Prince Faisal, who was arranging her itinerary, said that his brother, Crown Prince Saud, had enjoyed such pleasant hospitality at Dammam the previous December that he was sure the Princess and the Earl would find it delightful.

That put Casoc in the visiting dignitary business — where it has been ever since. Lenahan cabled Ohliger to prepare overnight accommodations for the Princess and the Earl, a secretary, a maid,

Hafiz Wahba, the Saudi Minister to London, and Charles Gault, the British Vice-Consul, and to have two station wagons at al-'Uqair to meet the party as it came over from Hofuf. Next day he raised the number of important personages who must be accommodated from six to seven.

That was the exact day, March 4, when they tested No. 7 and got their jubilant cable off to San Francisco. Royal visits in the circumstances were likely to be a nuisance, but Ohliger took his eye off the well long enough to cable that he could find accommodations for six, not seven, and he could have one station wagon and a truck at al-'Uqair, but not two station wagons, and not to make any offers of additional transportation because he didn't have it.

On March 12 Lenahan forwarded to Ohliger an urgent telegram from Hafiz Wahba, requesting eight cars and guides to meet them, not at al-'Uqair, but at Hofuf. In the midst of the hullabaloo of the flow tests, Ohliger managed to throw somebody temporarily out of work and steal his transportation. While he was sending two sedans, a station wagon and a truck to Hofuf on March 14, King George of England was congratulating Ibn Saud, through Princess Alice, on the discovery of Dammam No. 7 that so happily coincided with her goodwill visit.

In Jiddah Lenahan was explaining to one excited minister after another that the discovery of oil did not necessarily mean discovery "in commercial quantities," and that extensive flow tests would have to be conducted, and another well or two put down to the Arab Zone, before commercial production was assured and the gold payments that it entailed were due. On the Jiddah pier an Italian ship was unloading a shipment of field guns and ammunition, sold by Italy to Saudi Arabia, perhaps, as a futile answer to the British goodwill tour.

These were considerations that did not greatly trouble the Dammam housewives. What troubled them was the suddenly appalling thought of entertaining royalty, and doing it in these unpretentious cottages crouching on the flats under their naked power poles. Since there was no other place to put them, the royal party would have to be content with the married cottages; the married couples temporarily doubled up to make room. But what did royalty eat? And what did you say to royalty when you were introduced? And which foot did you put back of you when you dropped a curtsy? Or did you curtsy at all – did you maybe just shake hands and say how-do-you-do?

It is to be feared that the visit of Princess Alice and the Earl of Athlone preoccupied the ladies of the camp rather more than the continuing good news from the tests of No. 7. They plotted and rearranged, furnished the guest cottages with their combined best. They chose Fay Rector to cook for the party because she was the best of them in front of a stove. As for the problem of how to address royalty, they never did solve it. The Princess solved it herself. Appearing among them full of energy and charm, utterly unfazed by her trip across Arabia, curious about everything, overlooking their clumsy attempts at court manners, she had them talking before they knew how it happened, and when Mrs. Rector stopped short in the middle of a sentence and said half in laughter and half in confusion, "You know, I don't know what to call you," the Princess said at once, "Why, call me Alice." "All right," Mrs. Rector said, "if you'll call me Fay."

Alice was tremendous. She was a greater success than Dammam No. 7. When she left she was on terms of intimacy with them all, and the first thing she did when she got back to London was to write for the recipe of Fay Rector's angel food. Fluttered by its second royal visit in three months, Dammam settled back to being an oil camp again, but for some time there was a brisk exchange of letters and recipes between the Arabian Gulf and the United Kingdom.

Chapter Eight
~ Into Production ~

Bill Lenahan announced commercial production to King Ibn Saud on October 16, 1938, making a special trip to Riyadh to do so. The King hardly needed to be told what the news, long anticipated, meant. There had never been a time when the money needs of his kingdom could be kept down to the level of the income. Besides that, he told Lenahan that he was personally gratified: some of his ministers had never been quite confident of Casoc's ability to push the exploration and test drilling through to the final end of producing commercial oil. He let it be known, through Abdullah Sulaiman, that Saudi Arabia had recently rejected approaches for concessions from other companies, and that it had done so because of its goodwill toward Casoc. And the King said again, as he had said to Fred Davies when the two talked in Hofuf in 1936, that he would like sometime to visit the oil installations in the Eastern Province.

They were, by late 1938, beginning to be extensive. There were the wells among the *jabals* at the place which in February of the next year would be officially named Dhahran. There was the permanent camp a few hundred yards southwest, a fenced, transplanted, prefabricated community with a recreation hall and a movie theater. There was the enlarged al-Khobar pier with its customs house and a small storage and shipping terminal from which oil had begun to go by barge to the Bahrain refinery in September. And forty miles north on the sandspit of Ras Tanura, construction crews from Socal's engineering department, working under Walt Miller, were creating a major port facility.

On completion – to its first specifications – it would have crude oil tankage for 670,000 barrels, plus submarine loading lines and moorings for the anchorage of deep-draft vessels 3,000 feet offshore. It would be tied to the wells and camp at Dhahran by a service road and by a 10-inch pipeline. Still in blueprints, but shortly to be authorized, was a stabilization plant to remove from the "sour" oil of the Dammam Dome the toxic H_2S gas.

The whole Ras Tanura complex was scheduled to be completed by spring of 1939. And the King, Abdullah Sulaiman, Lenahan, and the company management decided that on or about May 1, 1939, they would hold a great celebration marking the moment which five years of effort had been aimed at: the loading of the first tanker.

May 1, thereafter, was the deadline toward which everything worked. But before it could be reached, a major job of negotiation lay ahead for Lenahan, for the word he had got in Riyadh about the government's turning down a bid for competing concessions turned out to be, to put it gently, premature. Stimulated by Casoc's strike at Dammam, competitors had begun to cast speculative eyes on the uncommitted parts of Saudi Arabia and on any possible territories that Casoc might relinquish according to the terms of the 1933 agreement.

In 1935, Petroleum Concessions Limited had been formed with the same ownership as IPC. Its function was to create affiliates in each country to develop concessions. In 1936, Hamilton's old competitor, Stephen Longrigg, signed a concession for areas of the Hijaz and 'Asir, and Petroleum Development (Western Arabia) Limited was formed to develop the concession.

Then, in February 1938, the Jiddah manager of Petroleum Development (Western Arabia) asked Lenahan if Casoc's preferential rights could be canceled if the Saudi Arab government repaid the loans Casoc had advanced it. Since the terms governing the preferential rights had never been published by the Saudi Arab government, this was clearly a fishing expedition on IPC's part. In September, a little while before Lenahan went to Riyadh to announce commercial production, J. Skliros of IPC wrote to Hafiz Wahba making a blunt offer for a renegotiation of Petroleum Concessions Limited's agreement in order to include the parts of Saudi Arabia not previously granted, plus the two Neutral Zones. The offer was for £100,000 gold as a bonus, and a rental of £15,000 per year thereafter. This was the offer, presumably, that Lenahan was told the government had rejected. But a few days later, in Jiddah, Najib Salha gave Lenahan to understand that it might be a good time for Casoc to make a matching offer for the same territory.

Lenahan thought so too. So did Hamilton in London. So, after consideration, did the boards of Socal and The Texas Company, which by then was sharing in the Casoc venture. But when in early December Lenahan received authority to match the IPC offer, Shaikh Abdullah professed to be supremely scornful of such a pitiful proposal. The least he would transmit to the ministers was an offer for twice those figures.

This was the beginning of a negotiation as careful and drawn out as the one which Hamilton and the ministers had conducted in 1933. It brought Hamilton down to Jiddah in January 1939 to try to deal directly with the King. He did, but the result was disappointing. The King did not want to negotiate for anything but the Kuwait–Saudi Arabia Neutral Zone; moreover, he tried to talk the two Casoc men into agreeing to some relinquishment of their preferential rights.

This the company refused to consider. It did, however, skirmish around looking for possibilities of some joint approach with a

British group, perhaps IPC, to the Kuwait Neutral Zone. But when Lenahan came across from Port Sudan on the same boat with IPC's negotiator, who was again Longrigg, he took the opportunity of telling Longrigg the unpublished facts about the Casoc preferential rights to the Kuwait Neutral Zone. Longrigg agreed that Casoc was impregnable there, said that the asking price for the Kuwait Neutral Zone was too high in any case, and indicated that if he couldn't negotiate for the Najd he would go on home.

Lenahan chose to do nothing while Longrigg dickered for two portions of the Najd that his company wanted. Before Longrigg left Jiddah, however, he had demonstrated that the government was, after all, willing to listen to that kind of proposal. Lenahan therefore put the central Arabian areas back in, and renewed his own offer of December to match the IPC proposal. When it was rejected, he withdrew from further negotiations.

The King told Shaikh Abdullah to notify Lenahan that in that case the company would have to relinquish its preferential rights to the Kuwait Neutral Zone. Lenahan, quoting the 1933 agreement, stood pat. Abdullah Sulaiman after a few days suggested some counterproposals. So it went. Through March they jockeyed each other closer to some mutually acceptable terms, and as they did so it became clear to Lenahan that others besides Casoc and IPC were interested in Arabian concessions.

One was a likable and very able German named Dr. Fritz Grobba, thought to be the head of the Nazi espionage system in the Middle East. He was accredited as German Minister to Iraq, where his principal monument would be the Rashid 'Ali rebellion, which he apparently fomented. He flew into Jiddah with his entourage, sniffed around, dropped hints, made everyone like him, but made no overt offers. He was allied, in ways which were obvious in their general direction but dark in their details, with the people in the Italian Legation, who indicated a desire to bid on the understanding that if they got the concession they would develop it in cooperation with the Germans.

Then on March 26, a delegation of Japanese arrived in Jiddah from Egypt with the announced intention of signing a trade treaty with Saudi Arabia. In the delegation were the Japanese Minister to Egypt, a geologist from the Imperial Geological Survey of Japan, and a secretary. The Minister went off to Riyadh almost at once, leaving the geologist behind to pump Lenahan with detailed and extensive questions on the oil operations of Casoc and the stratigraphy of Arabia. Lenahan gave him freely whatever information was public knowledge, and none of what was not. But he took no chances that the Japanese, hungry like the rest of the Axis for oil, might buy something with a fabulous offer in Riyadh. He telegraphed Floyd Ohliger, who was also in Riyadh, to keep his eyes open.

The company could not have had a better representative there. By 1939 Ohliger was becoming something nearly like a son to Ibn Saud. They had spent many hours talking, talked all night sometimes. Ohliger was completely convinced that Ibn Saud was one of the great kings of history, and the King looked upon Ohliger with trust and affection.

They had had several strong disagreements, but the effect was as it had been in Lenahan's case: a man who stood up to the King earned his respect. So now Ohliger talked to him with privileged frankness, learned that the King thought the company's terms were too "strict," learned that the Japanese were indeed trying for an oil concession in the areas disputed between IPC and Casoc, and learned between the lines of the King's talk that he was much too acute to get caught in any such alliance, even though, as Najib Salha reported later, the Japanese offers reached "astronomical proportions."

The Japanese Minister returned to Jiddah on April 13, but his talks with the ministers there did not trouble Lenahan. Though by the terms of the 1933 agreement Casoc was obligated to meet any bona fide offer in order to insure its preferential rights, the King had shown no signs of wanting to use the desperate Japanese offer as a lever under the company. It was the IPC offer which needed to be met. March and April saw long epicycloidal arguments on what constituted "meeting," and suggestions that Casoc hurry up and relinquish some of its unwanted territory so that the government could sell rights in it to someone else. Lenahan settled the relinquishment suggestion by reminding Shaikh Abdullah of the words of Ibn Saud in their January conference, when he said he wanted all of al-Hasa to be operated by no one but Casoc, and that he was therefore in no hurry to force relinquishments until the company was ready.

That was where they were, writing letters full of mutual respect, but still a long way apart, when it came time to go to Ras Tanura and turn the valves that would change the future of the Kingdom of Saudi Arabia.

In the months preceding that historic occasion there had been a subtle change in the men who had pioneered the great search. Of the first group of geologists – the ten-man beachhead team – not one remained since Krug Henry had departed for Egypt. Fred Davies, now manager of Bapco's producing division, was only temporarily back on Bahrain from the States for discussions concerning an additional concession area there, leaving Steineke and Bramkamp the oldest living geological inhabitants of Saudi Arabia. Of the earliest drilling crews, a few, Ohliger and Bill Eltiste among them, remained; others such as Jack Schloesslin and Alex Zoll were scattered around Saudi Arabia drilling water wells. Bill Burleigh was in Jiddah. But in the main, Dhahran camp was staffed by replacements.

One of the newcomers was a man named Phil McConnell, a seasoned production man who had met Floyd Ohliger in California and been talked into going to Bahrain. When he made that rather impetuous decision, Floyd's bride Dorothy invited him for Thanksgiving dinner east of Suez. Four months later he arrived, and on November 23 made his first trip across to al-Hasa. He was in good and experienced company. His traveling companion was Charley Potter, who had brought the first rotary rig to Arabia and had developed the new drilling technique of the floating mudcap; the man running the launch was Felix Dreyfus.

Just before dark they nosed in close to the low shore; all around them, long slim fish, two, three, four feet long, were feeding on the schools of sardines. They came up out of the shoals with an incredible arrowy rush, shot into the air as much as ten feet, fell twisting like divers to go back in nose first.

Phil McConnell was an exceedingly companionable man, full of jokes, songs, anecdotes, insatiably curious about the life that he had come into in middle age, and still rather surprised at himself for what he had done. So lively a man was popular; most of the married group was at the al-Khobar pier to meet him – the Ohligers, Gavin and Erma Witherspoon, Don and Edna Brown, Oliver and Edwina Boone.

Immediately McConnell got an initiation into the difficulties that Ohliger and Witherspoon dealt with daily. At the customs house, a small masonry shack on the barren shore, the door was locked, the place dark. Ohliger swore: he had arranged to pay the government extra in order to have a customs man on duty there 24 hours of the day. Soldiers appeared and explained that the customs man had gone to the old town of Dammam a few miles away up the coast. The passengers went on to Dhahran camp leaving their baggage behind, and the Ohligers and McConnell started for Dammam to root out the customs officer.

There were no roads that McConnell could see, only sand, rocks, the stare of a *barasti* in the headlights, the straining blackness beyond the lights that suggested an appalling emptiness. Then they stopped and Ohliger backed a little and started on another tack and McConnell saw what the blackness was: their wheels were practically in the Gulf.

By methods which McConnell observed with awe, Ohliger found his way along the black coast, into the black town, up black openings to a building. They pounded on a door. Somewhat grimly, they advised the customs man of his duty; somewhat grimly, he prepared himself and came along. Back at the customs house an hour later he gave their bags the most excruciating and careful examination and let them through.

Nothing in the slightest unusual happened on that three-day visit. McConnell had the best steak he had had since leaving the States, he ate waffles for breakfast until he had a heavy list to starboard, he took a ride through the countryside and up as far as Qatif with Floyd Ohliger, he saw all the stigmata of great hurry, great expansion, the pipeline heading out for Ras Tanura, the new bunkhouses and cottages and shops, the derricks of wells that were being drilled or deepened. In Dammam he saw a sword dance put on by the villagers to mark the end of Ramadan, and at the Ohligers' belligerently American house he watched Floyd Ohliger make his first attempt to carve a turkey. It did not seem odd to him or to any of them, probably, that the resident manager of an operation involving millions of dollars of investment should be a youthful-looking man of thirty-two who had never dissected a Thanksgiving bird.

Next morning he had the opportunity of observing the qualities of decision and firmness that were there under the freckled boyish look. As they were starting on a drive, the new government representative for al-Hasa, Ahmad Lary, appeared to protest Ohliger's action in returning after Ramadan to a daily schedule of eight hours and fifteen minutes of work. Ohliger told him that working hours were supposed to be a matter between the company and the central government. Ahmad Lary leaned on the door and talked, while Dorothy Ohliger sat patient but immovable. Ahmad Lary was unhappy that Mr. Ohliger was angry. Obviously he had not understood Ahmad Lary's meager English. Ohliger assured him that his English was excellent, and that he had understood all of it. But working hours were not the concern of the local representative.

Ahmad Lary suggested that Mr. Ohliger get out of the car and come and talk it over under more appropriate conditions.

Ohliger indicated that there was nothing to talk over. They sat for two hours while the manager politely turned away the representative's arguments, and then they drove on.

Across the Peninsula in Jiddah, meanwhile, other newcomers were settling in. One was Anita Burleigh. Anita Burleigh was the first American woman to live in Jiddah, and at first she didn't mind a bit. Living with the Philbys in the Green Palace outside the wall, she and Bill found the social life bright and lively, with many dinners and receptions and teas, moonlight fishing excursions on the Red Sea, visits to ships anchored in the harbor, and sometimes a dance over which the stained glass at the end of the Philbys' court cast a diffused glow of colored moonlight that for an hour or two made every romantic preconception of the mysterious East look true.

Later, in her own house, she encountered a few of the East's problems. Water, for instance, was of three kinds, each with its own system of supply and distribution. Drinking water came by ship from Egypt in oversized bottles. Cooking water came from the city's condensers. The rest was delivered to street-level tanks by a water boy with a cart (unless he missed, in which case the house ran dry for a day) and pumped to the roof tanks by hand.

In its devious course to the kitchen and bathroom taps it followed a labyrinth of pipes installed by Jiddah's best plumber. He was a hard and persistent worker, although at first he spent hours trying to make the bathtub drain fit into the washbasin, and once tried to hook up the pipe supports for the shower curtain so that the water would flow through them. The Burleighs had a lovely apple-green bathtub from Germany, but hot water had to be carried in gasoline tins because their hot-water heater, coming across to them from Dhahran, had been dropped somewhere in the desert by one truck and picked up by another. It still hadn't shown up.

Like other Jiddah houses, theirs was open, or nearly open, on two sides of each room. The wooden shutters started at waist height and went to the ceiling, the windows slid up or down to cover either the upper or lower half of the shutter. No matter how they juggled it, something was half-open always, a condition which gave them lively times moving the kerosene heaters around when the wind was cold, and filled them with despair when the sand blew. For greenery they had some sick nasturtiums, zinnias, bachelor buttons, petunias, constantly dying and being replaced, and one durable white-flowered vine given them by the Italian Minister. And they slept under cumulus masses of mosquito netting in an atmosphere smelling aseptically of Flit.

On the other hand, they looked out over the Medina Gate and the sea beyond, and in the evenings the air was soft and mild, and at parties the women wore filmy dresses and the men "Red Sea kits" – whites with cummerbunds. At all times the city clamored and howled and brayed and snarled with a bedlam of animal noises, with once in a while a midnight shot as some irritated Englishman potted a prowling pariah dog. The street merchants pushing carts or carrying baskets through the street had their little songs, plaintive, tentative, ending always on a minor.

It was a pretty romantic place, actually. It was even more romantic when Anita Burleigh found that she had permission to cross Arabia (which no western woman but Princess Alice and Lady Rendel, wife of Sir George Rendel of the British Foreign Office, had ever done) to attend the festivities at Ras Tanura on May 1. Most romantic of all, she would wear the clothes of an Arab man, to keep from being conspicuous.

The Burleighs and Bill Lenahan left Jiddah together on April 15, 1939, traveling in the caravan of Abdullah Sulaiman, and this was very different from the rough pilgrimages of the geologists. True, their two hundred cars crawled in an antlike line across the highlands, hanging up on high centers, sticking in sand, sending downwind a long high dust like a bank of fog. But despite the terrible road, there was not even a pretense of roughing it. At Hadda they had coffee and tea while they waited for the trucks to catch up. At al-Jumum they met a group of merchants on a five-day picnic, and took lunch and more coffee with them in their rose-lined tent while a musician played a homemade stringed instrument called a *rababah* and sang tribal songs. In the warm spring weather the Wadi Fatima was lovely, every water station pleasant.

They had dinner at ash-Shariah, coffee at Sail al-Kabir, another dinner at Ashirah Wells, where they were greeted by Abdullah Sulaiman's nephew Sulaiman ibn Hamad at his hunting encampment. Their tent, put up for them in a great hurry by servants and soldiers, was lined with bright striped cloth, floored with Persian carpets, furnished with cots, mattresses, chairs, a table, a Coleman lamp.

Their boy woke them at five o'clock bringing hot water and coffee. Their breakfast was chicken, goat, hot Arab bread baked over an open fire. While they ate, the tents came down so swiftly that it seemed jinns must have struck them, and they were off before six o'clock, to come to rest again at Muwaih, where the Finance Minister had pitched his tent while he went hunting.

To the tent of Abdullah Sulaiman, here and at the night camp at 'Afif, came visiting desert Bedouins, dignified and holding themselves below no man. They came as guests or hosts or equals, drawn by the word that went ahead of the caravan by Bedouin telegraph, and drank coffee as befitted guests, or proffered wooden, brass-studded bowls of camel's milk as befitted hosts, or gave gifts as befitted equals: sometimes a camel, their only one.

At 'Afif there were encamped 450 people, with many tents and a multitude of fires after dark. Here the desert "lived," the sheep and camels had been grazing. Sitting before the tent on Persian rugs with the smell of sweet desert wood smoke fragrant across the camp, and sipping spiced coffee and sweet tea, Shaikh Abdullah gave Anita a gazelle head with twenty-one rings adorning its horns.

Their road was sparsely dotted with forts, settlements, way stations with echoing names: al-Qai'iya, Duwadami, al-Kifaifiya. The fort at Duwadami provided the first bath of the trip, the welcome variety of a room, a dinner of chicken, mutton, bustard, Turkish sweets, an evening of relaxation with Shaikh Abdullah, Najib Salha, and Muhammad Ali Reza, a member of one of the great Jiddah merchant families and later Minister of Commerce, who often left his car to ride with the Burleighs.

On the fourth day they rose at two thirty to cross the Nafud "while the sands were sleeping," and after hours of beautiful changing light on the mesas and buttes came into Marrah, the walled city of the poets, for a ten o'clock breakfast. A siesta, another meal, another magical folding of the tents, and they were on their way through colored rock formations and old dry ruins to Riyadh. There they found Jack Schloesslin, the driller, living as a cherished guest in the palace.

That in itself was a sufficient marvel, one of the quaintest meetings of irreconcilables in all the contacts between Arab and American. Sent to Riyadh to drill a water well at the King's request, Schloesslin changed his accustomed manners not by the slightest hair. His mouth was as full of innocent obscenity as when on Bahrain he had distributed Christmas presents to every ragged kid he could find. Watched by the lowly and great alike as he spudded in the well with the old cable rig, he went about his business with a wad of tobacco the size of a tennis ball in his jaw, and in defiance of all he offered a chew to any Arab who expressed the slightest interest.

At one point Shaikh Abdullah asked him to pull the bit to show the King how the thing worked. Jack replied that that was too damn much unnecessary work. Shaikh Abdullah, not used to being argued with, insisted pretty sharply. The King stood by, an interested spectator. Jack refused again. Abdullah angrily ordered him to do as he was told. Schloesslin spit in the sand. "Who's diggin' this well, you or me?" he said. His truculence so tickled

Ibn Saud that he named him Mr. Jack the Engineer and had him in frequently for conversations, like Harun al-Rashid making merry company with Abu Hassan the wag.

Now, here he was in a real palace of a real ruling king, a fat and grubby roughneck with a heart of 24-karat gold. He was already legend, and it would not be long before he won the British upper crust of Jiddah as thoroughly as he had won the royal family of Saudi Arabia. He was as remarkable an exhibit as there was in Arabia, what Sir Reader Bullard called "one of Nature's gentlemen."

Anita Burleigh was herself something of an exhibit. She slept in the Queen's palace after a sybaritic hot bath, and waking between pink satin quilts to what she was sure was the screaming of damned souls, looked out on palm gardens and saw the donkeys trotting back and forth in sloped runways, drawing up *ghurbas* of water that tipped and flowed in the ditches. In the *suq*, people stared at her and speculated whether she was woman or boy. To those who inquired, Najib said she was the wife of the American Minister – a thing that did not yet exist. Here in Riyadh the contact between the ancient world and the modern was lightest; neither in Jiddah nor in most of al-Hasa would the sight of a woman's face have caused this amount of staring, but then Anita Burleigh was only the third of her kind to pass this way.

The addition of the King's caravan, which they joined at Ibn Saud's hunting encampment at ar-Rumahiyah, brought their total numbers to nearly 500 cars and 2,000 people. The dust was choking, the heat intense, the metal of the cars too hot to touch and charged with static from running in the sand as they labored and rocked and scraped up over the ar-Rumah Escarpment.

The King's soldiers paraded late in the afternoon, and the guests had the experience of ducking as machine-gun bullets whistled over their heads in a demonstration of war. That evening Anita was led into the King's tent in her *agaasl* and *ghutra* and *aba* and presented first to Ibn Saud and then to the Crown Prince.

Like the ladies at Dammam camp, she found the contact with royalty exhilarating. Najib told her that not over a dozen foreign women had ever been presented, and that not even wives of ministers rated an audience.

Others of the company who had crossed this way – Hamilton, Miller, Dreyfus, Steineke, Thornburg, Floyd Meeker, Jim Staton, Ted Lenzen, Ike Smith – had had business on their minds and discomfort for a traveling companion. Anita Burleigh need not worry about the attitudes of the King or of Abdullah Sulaiman: she was their guest. And she needn't worry about discomforts, for insofar as that thousand-mile automotive steeplechase could be made comfortable, this was how it must be done, with swarms of servants, feasts every night, rugs, cushions, silk-lined tents.

They were no lonely little clot of cars struggling across the desert, but a mighty caravan of the proportions and the color of a crusade, or a counter-crusade. Saladin, if he had traveled by automobile, might have headed such a procession as this, and been guarded by just such a bodyguard hung with just such festoons of warlike hardware. As the caravan boiled out of Riyadh and headed out along the ar-Rumah Plateau toward ar-Rumah Wells, they seemed to Anita a most exotic host indeed.

For their crossing of the red sands of the Dahna, which Anita noted in her diary, perhaps not quite accurately, as "the second most feared desert in the world," they were lucky: the wadis were running muddy water from the night's rain, and the choking dust cloud that had hung over them most of the way was quenched. They drank from a wadi, straining the sand out through a handkerchief and blessing water that for a change did not taste of tallow, and they filled their radiators and all their extra *ghurbas* before taking out across the fifty-mile river of sand. Even so, radiators were boiling dry, and the royal party and its guests were sustaining themselves on canned fruit juices and oranges, before the King's guide brought them out of the sands at Ma'aqala.

At Ma'aqala, after seven days of disguise, Anita met the 20th century again in the form of eleven young Americans, applying seismograph and gravity-meter to the reluctant Arabian crust. It was reassuring to find them there; as the Burleighs breakfasted with them the next morning they seemed the finest of young men. One of them, Tom Barger, spoke remarkably good Arabic; two others, named Olson and Phillips, good-naturedly devoted themselves to following them and pulling them out whenever their hard tires spun and settled them to the axles in the sand.

Twelve miles west of the wildcat camp of Abu Hadriya, another American car came tearing out to meet them. It held Dick Kerr, in charge of the seismographic party in that area. Poor Kerr, unprepared by any precedent either American or Arabian to have the all-male world of exploration invaded, did not recognize Anita Burleigh in her Arab robes. He blistered the air, Anita, and after an appalled moment his own soul, with the profanity of his greeting to Bill Burleigh. But then, recovering, he charged ahead of them into Abu Hadriya and introduced them proudly to an innovation as unprecedented as Anita herself: an air-conditioned house. To Anita, after the open desert, the cottage seemed stifling. She liked better the great camps that rose as if at the rubbing of a lamp and came down the same way, the rituals of Arab hospitality and politeness, the fragrance of many fires, the overarching stars.

The geologists at Ma'aqala and Abu Hadriya, however, were inclined to show off the wonders of modern industry. They had received new, improved transmitters, and suggested that the King might like to talk by voice radio with Shaikh Abdullah at Abu Hadriya. Tom Barger may have been especially interested in showing the radio off because he had been the object of Dick Kerr's considerable scorn during the days when they had all had to learn Morse code and use a bug. Barger was one of those to whom Kerr, who knew Morse as well as he knew English, used to give sarcastic advice about taking his foot off the key.

Now they had this modern improvement that removed such embarrassments and gave the King a chance to see what they were doing in his kingdom. They cranked up the generator and got it going, and called Abu Hadriya and got it among the customary squawks. Barger motioned for the King to speak. The King, apparently not quite sure how loud one should speak into a transmitter, shouted one word: "Abdullah!"

That was all. The static howled him out. But on the other end Shaikh Abdullah, hearing that sudden royal shout, sprang to the instrument and shouted back. It howled at him. The sweat came out on his brow: the King's word might have been the beginning of a command, a reprimand, a cry for help, anything. The crew fiddled and cranked and adjusted in vain. At the Ma'aqala end, Barger and Ibn Saud yelled tentatively into the dead machine. But it was in vain. Modern industry had fallen flat on its face.

From Abu Hadriya the great caravan went on to Dhahran, the cars sticking by the dozens in the *sabkhas* and being pulled out by company trucks posted along the road. After the ten-day trip, Anita Burleigh shed her romantic disguise and reluctantly began to learn again to sleep under a roof and in conditioned air. But not the King's party. They decided against the cottages which had been evacuated for their use, and eastward from the *jabals* a white tent city arose like a bed of mushrooms from the sand. And that evening from the hill above the camp, Florence Steineke and her two little girls watched more than 2,000 Arabs at their prayers, facing in long lines back westward toward Mecca, with the King before them all, leading them.

Not only the Steinekes came out to watch. Man, woman, and child, the population of Dhahran hung around the great encampment like village children around a newly arrived circus. They poked noses and cameras into the great kettles where whole sheep were boiled, they peeked at the fringes of the crowd before the outdoor *majlis*, they gawked at soldiers, drivers, servants, cooks, shaikhs, and amirs. At night, under a blue-black sky, with hundreds of campfires flickering back the flicker of the stars, it might have been a camp of the host of Sennacherib – if Sennacherib had had certain modern conveniences. In preparation for the city of 350 tents, which was to house the King and seventeen other members of the royal family, besides 400 Hijazi police, numerous ministers and dignitaries and amirs, the Shaikh of Bahrain and his brother and a party of 100 guests, and servants and police, to bring the total population of the camp to 2,700, Modern Industry had laid down more than 15,000 feet of three-inch water mains.

Ibn Saud had reached Dhahran on April 28. After two days of banquets and inspections, during which the American population of Dhahran shot up all the film it owned, and during which the whole number of women and children was presented one by one to the King in his great pavilion tent, they moved on to Ras Tanura.

The royal party, as well as the Socal dignitaries – A. S. Russell, a director, plus Davies, Ohliger, Lenahan, Burleigh, Gester, and James Stirton, the engineer who had designed the Ras Tanura complex and would live to design practically every company installation of the next twenty years – were entertained on the broad deck of the tanker *D. G. Scofield*, after which they went ashore and read telegrams of congratulation from William Berg, president of Socal, and Torkild Rieber, chairman of the board of The Texas Company, now in partnership with Socal. The King and Abdullah Sulaiman were presented with automobiles, Najib Salha with a watch and chain, others with gifts in proportion.

Then Ibn Saud reached out the enormous hand with which he had created and held together his kingdom in the first place, and turned the valve on the line through which the wealth, power, and responsibilities of the industrial 20th century would flow into Saudi Arabia. It was May 1, 1939. No representative of the United States was present, even as an observer. The United States had not yet accredited any representative to Saudi Arabia.

Following the celebration, Ibn Saud paid a visit to the Shaikh of Bahrain, where Phil McConnell, destined later to be a wheelhorse of the al-Hasa operations, caught his first glimpse of the Saudi Arabian King whose legend lay from the Red Sea to the Gulf like the shadow of a colossus. He talked with exhausted Americans from the mainland, unanimous in admiring the King and equally unanimous in believing that if his camp at Dhahran had stayed another week they would all be in the hospital.

On May 10, returning to the mainland, Ibn Saud entertained the whole American force of 200 at a banquet in his tent city. It was everybody's conclusion when his caravan boiled away through its own dust toward Riyadh that his visit had been worth every riyal and every foot-pound of energy it had cost.

One effect of the big visit was that it gave Lenahan a chance to talk over the Najd and Neutral Zone negotiations with other Casoc officials. Steineke and the geologists were optimistic about the Kuwait Neutral Zone, having found a structure just below the border that might well lap over on the north. About the two portions of the Najd they were by no means optimistic; exploration had shown no promising signs in either. On April 30, Lenahan cabled San Francisco from al-Hasa proposing that the company let IPC have a free hand in negotiating for the Najd in exchange for the same in the Kuwait and Iraq Neutral Zones. But at that time, all the government relations department correspondence went to London and was passed on to San Francisco with comments and recommendations.

London recommended avoiding all collaboration with IPC for fear the Saudi Arab government might suspect collusion of some sort. In the end, they let Lenahan's last offer stand for both Neutral Zones and the two Najd areas.

On May 9, 1939, the day before he gave his banquet for all the 200 Americans, Ibn Saud asked for the resumption of negotiations. Yusef Yassin came into the discussions with demands for many additional changes, all of which Lenahan rejected. The King also rejected them, assuring Lenahan that he wished to deal with no one but Casoc, but he insisted upon certain changes of his own, which Lenahan thought it wise to grant.

They were ready to sign when Ibn Saud saw the map of the supplemental concession with its corridor through the central Najd joining the north and south concession areas. That would not do; that was the heart of the old Wahhabi country; he did not want any exploration by foreigners in that section around Riyadh, because it was too likely to cause tribal unrest and uprisings.

Redrawing the map reduced the area under consideration, and Lenahan conferred by cable with San Francisco. San Francisco thought he had better close, even without a corresponding reduction of the bonus and annual rental. He wired for, and got, an invitation to follow the King to Riyadh, and on May 23 he was there. For a week, living in the palace, he hammered out the conditions point by point with Yusef Yassin and the King, won a few and lost a few, and finally brought the negotiation to an end.

The supplementary agreement which he and Shaikh Abdullah signed in Riyadh on May 31, 1939, gave the company a sixty-year right to an area of 49,900 square miles in the north, against the Trans-Jordan and Iraq borders, and of 66,900 square miles in the south, backing up against 'Asir, Yemen, and the Hadhramaut, besides the Kuwait Neutral Zone of 2,000 square miles and the Iraq Neutral Zone of 2,500. The bonus was £140,000, the annual rental £20,000 after the first year.

The company obligated itself to build a small refinery and to provide the government free of charge with stipulated quantities of gasoline and kerosene. The government for its part reaffirmed the company's preferential rights in the central Najd for sixty years from the date of the supplementary agreement, and agreed by a separate letter not to negotiate with anyone for that area for a period of five years.

These additions, together with the preferential rights extending westward from the Dahna to the contact between the igneous and sedimentary rocks, gave Casoc rights to an impressive share of the potential oil lands in the Arabian Peninsula, except the Qatar Peninsula and the coastal regions south of it.

In mid-1939 the fashion was to be optimistic, to count the long tons of crude flowing into the tanks at al-Khobar and Ras Tanura, to emphasize good relations, to minimize problems, to take satisfaction in having beaten out the company's competitors again. On June 26 the old tanker *El Segundo* started regular trips every sixty hours to Bahrain from Ras Tanura. In August, the United States government finally gave belated and limited recognition to Arabia by accrediting the Hon. Bert Fish, Minister to Egypt, as Minister to Saudi Arabia as well. He paid his first visit to Jiddah and expressed himself as most struck by the scrupulous and balanced code of relations by which the Casoc management had been guided in dealing with the Saudi Arabs.

The company thought his praise both pleasant and deserved, and history concurs in that opinion: the five years of Casoc's operations in Arabia, from the original concession to the supplementary one, from exploration to commercial production, had been an entirely new sort of foreign economic development in a so-called "underdeveloped" country. The company had operated by agreement and not by coercion; its status, in fact, was markedly tentative and insecure, subject to interference and the political and economic whimsies of the Saudi government. It had tried, and only the men in the field knew how hard, to be scrupulous in living up to its agreements and to be careful in avoiding clashes of religion and culture between its people and the Saudis. At the time of its discovery by the American State Department, it was something of a showpiece, a markedly successful demonstration of cooperation between the industrial West and the conservative East.

Everything was coming along, they had a right to congratulate themselves. Then on September 1 Germany invaded Poland, and the shadow of the swastika fell across the world.

Chapter Nine
~ The Second Wave ~

Saudi Arabia, a kingdom established over a period of a quarter century through the union of many amirates, sultanates, and shaikhdoms, was never a clear image: its edges, or many of them, were blurred. The geographical unit of the Arabian Peninsula was not a political unit, and the precise line where the territory claimed by Ibn Saud met the territory of Yemen, Aden, the Hadhramaut, Dhufar, Oman, Muscat, the Trucial Coast, or Qatar was a matter of vague tradition and of agreements between Great Britain and Turkey that dated back to 1913 and 1914 and by which Saudi Arabia, for one, hardly considered itself bound.

Where Ibn Saud's territory joined the new state of Trans-Jordan was a matter of dispute. Where it met the Shaikhdom of Kuwait, the buffer areas called the Kuwait and Iraq Neutral Zones, and the new state of Iraq, had been generally established between Ibn Saud and Sir Percy Cox at the 1922 al-'Uqair Conference where Frank Holmes got the first oil concession for al-Hasa. The Protocols of al-'Uqair described the boundaries between these northern neighbors and Saudi Arabia, but there had never been a survey, and the only available map was the Asia 1:1,000,000 Geographical Section, General Staff War Office 1917–1918, which

Casoc surveyors had demonstrated to be inaccurate by as much as twenty-five miles at some points. Neither was there an adequate hydrographic chart of the Arabian side of the Gulf.

It was inevitable that the company should take an interest in these blurred edges, for the concession ran to the boundaries of the country on south and east and north. But the Concession Agreement specifically prohibited any interference by the company in the political affairs of Saudi Arabia, and the company therefore could make no move to try to define its concession borders more clearly. It did, however, take the initiative in the hydrographic survey of the Gulf. And it did at the government's request provide its surveyors on two occasions, once to survey in connection with an Iraqi party the border region along the north, from Kuwait to the Trans-Jordan border, and once to establish astronomical stations in the region around Selwa, at the foot of the Qatar Peninsula.

The hydrographic survey dated from the flurry of expansion in 1936, when Roy Lebkicher in London had several conferences with the British Admiralty to see if the Admiralty, either by itself or in collaboration with the company, would complete its soundings of the Gulf waters on the Arabian side and survey the possible channels for the proposed company port at either Dhulaifain or Ras Tanura. Though the Admiralty was friendly and the Saudi Arab government raised no objections to the notion of a joint British-Casoc survey, it shortly developed that the Admiralty did not have a ship or men available at the time. In the end the company provided them, Captain Ike Smith of the *El Segundo* making the soundings and charts, and Charles Herring of the engineering department doing the coastal hydrography with a crew that at various times included Theodore F. Clausing, Jerry Harriss, J. Dougery, Hank Trotter, and James Anderson.

There was a good deal of debate about the relative merits as a port site of Dhulaifain, which had high ground, and Ras Tanura, which was a long low sandspit sticking out into the Gulf. Ras

Tanura won, and Lenahan applied for the reservation of land there for company use. Subsequently, survey crews carried the coast hydrography along to the vicinity of the Neutral Zone border. They were at it off and on from July 1936 to September 1939, when Ras Tanura began regular delivery of oil to tankers.

By that time Casoc had begun to turn over its data to the Admiralty, and the Admiralty was incorporating the information in its charts. The channel for twenty miles was ultimately marked, not with the poles stuck in the bottom which had guided in the first ships with construction materials for Ras Tanura, but by permanent beacons. The lights were put in by Walt Miller and were serviced by tender.

Charlie Herring, who started out in charge of the hydrographic survey, was not there to see the end of it. The day after the Fourth of July 1938, he and his wife, Pauline, started for Bahrain in the *Calarabia*. The weather was clear, calm, and hot; the sand bar, as they went half-speed through the shoals out from al-Khobar, was black with cormorants, and in one place they saw sea cobras lying inert in the water. Al Carpenter, in charge of the launch, loafed and smoked at the wheel; the four crewmen, barefooted and stripped to the waist, were making things shipshape. Cranky but very fast, the *Calarabia* straightened out in deep water and tore a long rip in the placid Gulf astern.

To Pauline Herring it was still romantic and exciting, almost as exciting as it had been when she was in charge of the drawing files in Socal's San Francisco office and catalogued draftsmen's sketches of the Arabian operations, before she met and married Charlie Herring. Now, sitting aft with her husband, enjoying the whip of the breeze and shouting to make herself heard, she was planning things she would buy in Bahrain's *suqs*.

About halfway to Bahrain, the *Calarabia's* whole stern blew apart, killing her instantly.

Herring, terribly injured himself, managed to swim to her and hoist her partly onto a floating hatch cover. The water was littered with smoking fragments and bits of gear; the launch was already gone. A little way off Al Carpenter, badly burned, was half-floating, half-treading water with a piece of wreckage for support, while two uninjured Saudi crewmen put together a raft from a half-burned life preserver, an empty fire extinguisher, and bits of planking lashed together with a piece of manila line. Onto it the three crawled or hooked their arms; onto it they pulled a third Saudi deckhand, hurt and half conscious, and supported him there until he died.

The hatch cover that held up the Herrings had drifted a good distance away. Al Carpenter called, but got no reply. It appeared to him that Pauline was surely dead. He called again to Herring that they should tie themselves together, but Charlie either would not leave his wife's body or could not hear him. A little wind bobbed them, moved the floating wreckage around the edges of the oil slick. The great sky glared down, cloudless, nearly white with heat. Borne by winds or currents, the two little clusters of bodies drifted slowly farther apart.

About one o'clock that afternoon Dick Kerr came in from Bahrain on another launch and noticed that the *Calarabia* was not at her berth. He inquired of the pier gangpusher, who said that she had started for the island. The gangpusher had also seen smoke out in the channel, but thought it was a steamer at Manama. Kerr had imagination, and he was by that time a four-year veteran of Arabia, with a good notion of what trouble in that country could mean. He rounded up Oliver Boone, and the two of them sent out boats to search. That evening they got in touch with Bahrain: the *Calarabia* had not come in. Bahrain too began sending out boats. In al-Khobar they cursed the restrictions on their use of radio for ship-to-shore communications.

About noon the next day Boone's boat found Carpenter and the two Saudi deckhands, still clinging to their patchwork raft. Carpenter, burned, broken, dreadfully sunburned, and in deep shock, was there only because the two Saudis had hung onto him for hours and refused to let him slip into the sea. Boone raced him to shore, while the other boats went on searching for Herring and his wife. That afternoon they found them floating close together, both dead. Still later they picked up the body of one of the crewmen, torn by barracuda.

That was the first bad accident involving Americans in Arabia. It saddened them all, for they were a tight little group, and Charlie and Pauline Herring had been very well liked. But the courage and endurance of the Saudi deckhands was the sort of demonstration that bound Arab and American together: there is no surer bond than shared disaster.

In the early days in the Arabian Peninsula, no one paid much attention to territorial boundaries. Even in 1922, when Sir Percy Cox attempted to pin down Ibn Saud's borders with Kuwait and Iraq, they came up with two Neutral Zones, one snuggled into the corner between Kuwait, Saudi Arabia, and the Gulf, the other a diamond-shaped affair with its eastern point in Wadi al-Batin and its western point at Ansab (Nisab). From there the northern boundary of Saudi Arabia ran to Judaidat 'Ar'ar, from there to Mukur, and from there to the Jabal Anaza, situated in the neighborhood of latitude 32° north and longitude 39° east, where it terminated against the border of Trans-Jordan.

Since the land then was used for nothing but the grazing of sheep and camels, and the only valuable things along it were the water wells, which were used indiscriminately by Bedouins from both sides, no one cared exactly where that northern frontier lay, and for seventeen years no one really knew.

Now, however, with an Arabian oil concession reaching up to the line, and a Kuwait oil concession reaching down to it, it became vastly important. Realizing that ownership of an oil-producing structure that lapped only a mile or two over on one side or the other might be worth many millions of dollars, Saudi Arabia and Iraq decided they had better do something. They appointed a joint commission for a survey.

As was by now customary when a problem involving industrial or engineering know-how arose, the Saudi Arab government turned to Casoc, and Casoc rented out two surveyors who, with Amir Abdul Aziz ibn Zaid (later Minister to Lebanon and Syria) as political representative, met the Iraqis at Wadi al-Batin on April 5, 1938, to launch a survey.

According to their instructions, they were to make, in conjunction with the Iraqi surveyors, sketch maps of the "corner" or "angle" points established by the Treaty of al-'Uqair, and connect and reference these by a system of triangulation along the boundary. They were also to collate topographical information regarding wells, towns, and prominent landmarks for about three miles on each side, and this the surveyors, Charlie Herring and Al Parker, set out to do. Herring, however, was transferred three weeks later and assigned to the hydrographic survey that would, three months later, lead to his tragic death.

Herring's replacement, Dick Hattrup, a young engineer fresh out of Stanford, worked with Parker and the Iraqis until near the end of May, at which time they had finished about 40 percent of the triangulation by methods which, according to mutual agreement, were to be of approximately third-order accuracy. The country along the border was broken and craggy, higher and rockier than the desert southward, and in winter grazed many camels that were gathered in summer around the wells.

They knocked off the survey during the heat of summer, returning to it in September and proceeding methodically through the completion of the Iraq Neutral Zone and on northwesterly until they were within thirteen miles of Mukur in-Na'am, the Well of the Ostrich. And here they struck a snag. The al-'Uqair protocols carried the line from Judaidat 'Ar'ar to Mukur, but it developed that no one knew exactly where to start in Judaidat 'Ar'ar, which was a cluster of several wells. Did one start in the measured middle of these, or did one take some easily distinguished landmark within the area as a triangulation point, or did one establish by astronomical means the precise map location of this lost dot of human settlement on the 1:1,000,000 War Office map and use that?

The Iraq survey party, now under an Englishman named Godfrey, chose to establish its starting point by fixing the map location; the Saudi Arab and Casoc party disagreed. So they went northwestward through the wilderness, triangulating two distinct nets along lines a mile or so apart. And then, when they began to look around for Mukur, they found that the word *mukur* meant simply a well, and that there were two dozen localities containing the word *mukur* within a distance of 100 miles, and no clear indication which of them the treaty-makers had had in mind. Worse, the treaty-makers themselves had worked mainly on information provided by local guides, so it was doubtful that anybody knew.

Since this was a problem not for surveyors but for politicians, the survey parties closed up shop for the summer in early June 1939, and referred their difficulty to their respective governments. In July there was a conference at Riyadh. Nothing came of it, but the survey parties were ordered back to the field anyway, and from October 31 to sometime in December, Hattrup and his two helpers, John C. Wells and "Dutch" Schultz, sat in their camp near Mukur in-Na'am while the Iraq party sat in its camp sixty miles away, neither side able to continue and neither willing to give up the premises which had landed them that far apart. The government conferences went on, and the parties sat, sometimes driving back and forth to pay visits and exchange dinners. It was on one of those trips that they shot the ostrich.

Dick Hattrup accuses Roy Lebkicher of starting the story that he shot the ostrich. He insists that he did not shoot, but only shot *at*, the ostrich, a featherless and most ungainly-looking bird that popped up out of a wadi, escaped Hattrup's surprised and buck-fevered snap shot with the .22, but succumbed to a slug from the army rifle of the amir's soldier-servant a little farther down.

Hattrup's glory is only partially dimmed by his miss: he is the only Casoc or Aramco employee so far uncovered who even got a shot at an ostrich, a bird which was then rarely found anywhere in Arabia except in the Great Nafud to the southwest of where they were then camped, and has never been seen since.

By that time, as it happened, the government representatives had come to an agreement, and soon the survey parties were able to get together again. Triangulation proceeded amicably to the Jabal Anaza, where a Trans-Jordanian delegation met them, listened carefully to the explanation of what had been done up there, and held its counsel.

Later, after years of negotiating, Saudi Arabia and Jordan agreed on their boundaries and conducted a joint survey which appears to have satisfied all concerned. But from the time when the parties shook hands and parted on leap year day 1940, no more substantive accomplishments can be reported on the Iraqi-Saudi boundary. The survey data and the maps rest in the files somewhere, waiting political approval. Casoc and Dick Hattrup, having done their engineering part, and having no political part to play, went back to other jobs.

The best history of any action is the experience of the men who lived it. The history of Aramco in its early years is only very partially the agreements and contracts and transactions of the company, its negotiations with the Saudi Arab government and its balance sheets and its effect on the world oil market and the policy of nations. It is also Fred Davies and Floyd Ohliger, Bert Miller and Krug Henry and Max Steineke and the other geologists, Bill Eltiste and Guy Williams and Jack Schloesslin, Felix Dreyfus and Dick Kerr, and after them the second and third and fourth waves of replacements and reinforcements – Jim Sutton, Les Snyder, Floyd Meeker, Dick Hattrup, Don Mair, Tom Barger, Walt Miller, Charlie Davis, James McPherson, and dozens of others.

Perhaps what makes the early years memorable to them all is the freedom they had then, the absence of regulation and the bookkeeping of civilized business. On this frontier they were thrown on their own resources, they were given a job and trusted to do it, they worked twice as hard and faithfully as if they had been driven to do so, they had what in spite of the discomforts they knew was a grand job. They were attendants at the birth of a world. The "bug" might chase them out of Arabia, but frustration never would, and their morale was expressed in the words written home by a recruit who had just picked his way into their midst along al-Khobar's rough pier in 1936: "It's a great bunch of guys here, and the boss is a prince."

That feeling was shared by many recruits, some of whom didn't turn out to be such bad guys themselves: as a sample, one could do worse than record the experiences of Tom Barger, who would later become president and then chairman of the board of the Arabian American Oil Company (Aramco), the corporate successor to Casoc.

Tom Barger, brought up in Minnesota and North Dakota, got his first experience as a mining engineer in Canada and Montana. While he was riding out the Depression working as a miner in Butte, he was hired to go to Arabia by Doc Nomland, chief geologist of the Standard Oil Company of California, who told him: "Fifty percent of the business is getting along with your partner, 40 percent is surviving in the environment, and 10 percent is professional." Nomland also told Barger that the Arabian venture did not look too promising, and that he might not be there long. If they pulled out of Arabia, however, he could expect to be sent to the Dutch East Indies. Meantime they wanted him badly in al-Hasa. Barger took Nomland at his word and broke all records on trips out to Arabia – he got there in twelve days – only to discover as he came down the pier that the demand for his presence had been somewhat overstated. "A man with a big jaw and a big grin introduced himself as Steineke," Barger would relate later, "and said he didn't know exactly what he was going to do with me, but was happy to have me there." So much for breaking records.

For the next couple of days Barger read reports and tried to absorb in forty-eight hours the total known geology of the region. Then he drove up to Jubail with Walt Hoag in a Marmon-Herrington station wagon, and got bewildered and scared trying to get through the narrow, ditch-cut, and crowded streets of Qatif.

Two or three days after that, Steineke found a job for him: he could help make some astronomical observations and determine the precise location of several points down by Selwa, where an unsettled border dispute between Saudi Arabia and the British was creating friction. The company was making these observations at the government's request, as basic scientific data to be used in talks with the British. On the way down, Steineke broke the rookie in with some more desert driving, first scaring him to death with roller-coaster churning across the dunes south of al-Khobar, and then turning the wheel over to him across the *dikaka* beyond al-'Uqair. Because he was scared of getting stuck in the sand, Barger drove like a madman. Steineke sat cradling the chronometer in his lap and let him go, at the mortal risk of his neck. He had a relaxed habit of letting a young man find his own way; it was a habit that endeared him to them for life.

Down at Selwa, Walt Hoag and Jerry Harriss, still hating each other cordially, were housed in a corrugated iron storehouse. Steineke dropped Barger and the chronometer off and drove back to Dammam, and for a couple of weeks the three surveyors made observations in the disputed zone. Barger understood that these were somewhat important to the Saudi government; he did not understand until later how much political tension quivered along that border ready to be touched off, or that his first job in Arabia — so casually did important jobs fall to them in this environment — would involve him in an international problem that would smolder for years and eventually erupt in near-violence near Buraimi in 1955 and again in 1957.

They finished that detail and came into Dammam camp for Christmas. Hoag's distaste for Harriss was so unlimited that he demanded a transfer and was sent to Jiddah to supervise the drilling of some water wells the government wanted. That made a team out of Barger and Harriss – Tom and Jerry – and threw the raw recruit into the field in the most difficult, unknown, and exciting section of all Arabia, the Rub'al-Khali, the Empty Quarter. On its northern edge, in the company of Harriss, a half-dozen *khuwiya* or Bedouin soldiers, a cook and houseboy, and two or three Arab drivers, he spent the first four months of 1938.

No one else in camp except Harriss spoke English. Barger lived with his copy of Van Ess' *Spoken Arabic of Mesopotamia* open in his hand. Others had learned Arabic well and fast: Art Brown, Felix Dreyfus, Allen White, and Bill Eltiste for four, and Harriss' erstwhile partner, Walt Hoag, best of all.

Many others never got past the pidgin-Arabic stage. Steineke spoke Arabic always in the second person, feminine gender, and present tense. But Barger learned it with a speed that astonished them all. By April he was talking not only with the soldiers and guides of their party, but with Bedouins whose dialects and pronunciation were markedly different from those of the townsmen.

Fortune could not possibly have been kinder to this tall, husky, and very competent young man. He had not been raised on the edge of the West for nothing; he had the proper frontier skills. He was a better shot even than Steineke, and there was no quicker way to win the respect of the Bedouins. He had a talent for laughter. And a good deal of his quickness at picking up the language came from the fact that the Arabs respected him and talked freely, and the further fact that Barger was a shirtsleeve democrat fascinated by the Arabs and their rugged life.

Also he was lucky in the guides assigned to the party. One was Abdul Hadi ibn Jithina, a member of the wild Murrah tribe that had sheltered Ibn Saud's father when he was in flight from the Rashidis. The second was an old 'Amiri, Salim Aba Rus, wrinkled and bearded like a wise man out of the Bible. The third, who rapidly became Tom Barger's close friend, as he was Steineke's, was Khamis ibn Rimthan.

In few places on the world's surface could an American meet so much that was strange, unwritten, unknown. Only two Europeans had ever crossed the Rub' al-Khali: Bertram Thomas in 1930 and Harry St. John B. Philby in 1932. Barger and Harriss, working its northern edge from a base camp at Selwa, were only a few years behind the first western explorers, and in the course of their work they inevitably touched dozens of places where an American or European foot had never stepped. Many of the Bedouins who came warily out of the great wilderness into their camps had never seen a car. Old Salim the guide had never ridden in one until they came. About the only thing he knew about the foreigners was that they could cure ailments, and the first night Khamis brought him in he requested treatment for three: his back bothered him, he couldn't hear out of one ear, and he was constipated.

In those days, field parties carried a variety of drugs, and geologists prescribed with great confidence for many diseases. Old Salim's back was easy; analgesic balm would do the trick. His ear was harder. When Jerry Harriss questioned him, he found that Salim had once been a professional pearl diver, and that he hadn't heard out of that ear for seven years. Jerry asked him how the other one worked. It worked well, said Salim. "God is merciful," said Jerry. "Praise be to God that you can hear out of one ear at least." That didn't exactly cure Salim's ear, but it left him without any recourse except to admit that God *was* merciful.

Now the constipation. They gave him a compound cathartic pill. Salim appeared in the morning and complained that he had not been cured. Vowing to cure him or break records for effort, they filled a tomato can half full of a mixture of mineral oil and castor oil. Salim sniffed it and balked. When they warned him of all the things that would happen to him if he didn't drink, he said he was afraid his stomach would throw it out again. Barger found an orange, the last one of a sack left by Steineke when he visited the camp. Salim had never seen an orange before, but eventually was persuaded to drink the oil and eat the orange for a chaser.

In the morning he was wreathed in smiles. His stomach had "walked." And all through the next two or three days he talked earnestly to Khamis in the back seat as they drove. He had never in his life felt that he needed more than a camel, a woman, and a smooth piece of sand to keep him happy. He had now added oranges to the list.

Down in the Khor Qada region, near the great salt flat of Muttia, where the wells gave only salt water, and tribesmen of al-Murrah lived for months on camel milk, the party stopped at a salt well to fill their empty drums and cans with water for the car radiators. A band of Bedouins was there drawing water for their camels, and among them was an albino, a man who looked like a Scandinavian, with a snow-white beard and pale skin reddened by exposure. They christened him the Lost Engineer, because Khamis jokingly suggested that he was an American *muhendis* (engineer) whose car had broken down.

But they were the American engineers whose car had broken down: a few miles farther on they broke the drive shaft on their station wagon. Deciding to go on with the traverse in their other cars and return to this one later, Harriss took Abdul Hadi ibn Jithina and Ibrahim the driver back to the well to find a Bedouin to help guard the station wagon. They found only the Lost Engineer and his family still there. A colloquy ensued.

"Peace be unto you."

"And to you, God's peace."

"How are you?"

"I am very well. How are you?"

"I am very well."

"Praise God. God give you health."

"God give you health."

"God give you eyes."

"God give you eyes."

"God give you strength."

"God give you strength."

These amenities went on for another five minutes. Then: "We have a broken car, and we have come to see if you will assist in watching it."

"For how much?"

"A rupee a day."

"I will come for two rupees."

"One rupee."

"But it is necessary for me to have two rupees."

"One rupee is the price."

They kicked this around for ten minutes. The Lost Engineer was sad at such a low offer until they took pictures of him and his family, and then he agreed to come for one rupee while his family looked after the camels.

Riding back to the station wagon, he sat on the car seat with his feet folded under him. Abdul Hadi, who had now been with the party some weeks and had superior knowledge, showed him how to sit with his feet reaching down to the floor. He and Ibrahim also explained to the Engineer certain things about the car. Harriss threw it into second, raced the engine, blew the horn, and beat on the side of the door. "Hear it roar," said Khamis and Salim and Abdul Hadi as the motor raced. "Yes," said the Lost Engineer, awed. "Hear it scream," they said as the horn blew. "Yes," said the Lost Engineer. "See how it needs to be encouraged," they said as Harriss hammered on the door. "Ah yes," said the Engineer, who understood this from having worked with camels.

Leaving Ibrahim and the Engineer, the party went on south-southeast for about fifty miles, Khamis being the guide, though this was country he had never been in before. The second day they traveled about sixty miles in an angled course southeast, then south, then southwest, and finally northeast. The third day they drove northwest until noon, turned north a while, and then swung northeast to complete the traverse. For three days they had had no clear landmarks, no *jabals* or wadis, nothing but an expanse of rolling sand hills. Toward evening, Barger asked Khamis to give them a compass reading on the station wagon they had left. Khamis squinted a moment and raised his arm. "How far?" Barger asked. Another moment of thought. "About eight miles," Khamis said.

To test his "Bedouin triangulation" they pointed the cars on the course he set and took off across the roadless and characterless country. At a little more than seven and a half miles they came upon the station wagon. With some guides, they would have been able to rely on neither the direction nor the mileage, nor even the recognition of landmarks. The three guides they had in the Rub' al-Khali were all good, and Khamis incomparably the best of them. They learned to trust him as fully as they trusted their compasses and speedometers. In camp it turned out that Ibrahim was disgruntled. He had been visited during their absence by many of the Lost Engineer's friends and relatives, all of whom, it seemed, had to be fed – they were *mukhtal*. Being told this, Ibrahim had fed them without protest. In his dialect, *mukhtal* meant "crazy." He didn't learn until too late that in the Lost Engineer's Murrah it meant only "hungry."

During the evening the Engineer demonstrated that he was a true Arab, and no Scandinavian masquerading. He reached over and punched Harriss on the leg.

"Ya, Harriss! And will you pay me?"

"Yes."

"Ya, Harriss. How much will you pay me?"

"Three rupees for three days."

"But aren't you going to pay me six rupees?"

"No. The price was one rupee a day."

"But I am a poor man."

"The agreement was for one rupee a day."

A shrug. It was evidently useless. But it was worth a try.

Somewhat later, when they were fed and sitting around the

fire and the time of talk was upon them, Khamis questioned the Engineer.

"How did the broken car behave?"

"Oh, well, well."

"Did it complain of its pain?"

"No."

"Did you feed it?"

"No. "

"You expect to receive a rupee a day and you didn't even feed the car?"

"I did not know it wanted food. It made no complaint."

"Did you water it?"

"No. "

"Three days, and you gave it neither food nor water? Sahib, I do not think you should pay this man anything."

"O.K. We will not pay him."

"But Sahib . . ."

"Well, maybe a rupee or two. He has after all put in his time. But from now on, Muhammad, when you watch a car, give it water and food. It suffers even though it cannot talk or complain. . . ."

Thus the wild tribesmen on the edge of the great sand waste. They said of Khamis that he could bury a rupee in the sand and come back in five years and find it again. They might have said too that in any crowd of Americans kidding a greenhorn, Khamis would have found his way just as surely. It is not on record that he ever sent a Bedouin out for a set of sky hooks or a bucket of cold steam, but that is a matter of mere terminology.

Tom Barger was still with Harriss down in the Rub' al-Khali when the word came in March 1938 that No. 7 was a big producer. That was fine, but it did not immediately or drastically affect Barger's life, except possibly to keep him from being sent on to the Dutch East Indies. He went on doing the jobs that needed doing. For a while, after a brief return to the Dammam camp in April, he was doing surface mapping at Dick Kerr's seismograph camp at Abu Hadriya. When he had finished that he accompanied Max Steineke and Max Thornburg, then vice president of Caltex, on a trip up the coast as far as the border of the Kuwait Neutral Zone. None of their parties had been up to that boundary on the ground; Barger mapped it, and thus had a part in the establishment of another of Saudi Arabia's uncertain borders.

Back in the Dammam camp, he cleaned up the maps of all the field work he had participated in that season while Jerry Harriss prepared the geological report. Barger also prepared an appendix in which he included, with the brashness of youth and a mere six months' acquaintance with the country and the Arabic language, a description of the flora and fauna of the Rub' al-Khali, a list of the Arabic names of the plants and animals, and a list of geographical names in Arabic, using an Indian interpreter in an attempt to get the spellings right. Khamis, who later in his career would become the chief adviser to the Arabian research section of Aramco on matters of place names, was considerably amused.

The geological report was still unfinished when Steineke sent Barger and Harriss off to Kashmir to follow the example of the first geological parties and do their paperwork in the mountains. Harriss did not make notable progress on his report during their month at Srinagar; the last three days of their leave they spent down on their hunkers in a Karachi hotel room, frantically drawing contour lines onto maps. But they still didn't have it done when they arrived on Bahrain, and when Harriss had to go into the hospital there for an operation there was still further delay. Then Harriss fell in love with his nurse, a fact which made his recovery remarkably slow. In mid-September he was still not back, and the report was still not done. Rather than let him sit around doing nothing, Steineke sent Barger up north of Abu Hadriya to help Bill Seale measure a base line from which to begin an accurate triangulation net.

It sounded simple, Barger said later, but almost from the day he arrived it began to go sour. One day, for instance, after staying up all night futilely trying to stave off the arrest of their mechanic Shaubi (the man with the "spare wife") and their cook for a local offense, they returned to learn that they had a dead tractor out by the seismograph camp. "Just stopped," the driver said. They also learned the heat waves were so bad they were unable to work in the daylight and would have to work that night.

Greasy with sweat, Barger rolled in and tried to get a few hours of sleep. Almost immediately Booger Arnold came over from the seismo camp and woke him to suggest going gazelle hunting. Bill Seale went instead and Barger went to sleep again. In a few minutes he was being thunderously thumped by Dick Kerr, overflowing with good nature and noise. He watched Kerr and Jim Cary eat lunch, and at one thirty took to his bed again, his head thick with a cold and his prickly heat in full blossom. That evening when he cranked on the generator for the radio transmitter he couldn't make it go. Two days before he had had the whole thing apart. In his whole time on this station he had got about two messages through to Dammam; most of the time what he sent was as intelligible as a fire siren.

That night he took the radio over and had John Lewis at the seismo camp work on it. The next morning he spent cleaning sand out of the tractor's carburetor and getting it started. When he returned to camp to communicate with Dammam, the generator had conked out again.

He sat and looked at the generator a long while. He had had it apart enough times to know that it was useless to take it apart any more. It was cranked by a rope wound around a flywheel, like an outboard motor. After long thought, Barger jacked up the rear wheel of one of the pickups, started the engine, and put the pickup in gear. Then he pressed the generator's flywheel against the rear wheel of the pickup, which spun it much faster than he could do with the rope. After a little tinkering, he got it running and could turn his attention to greasing a couple of the Fords, a job Shaubi would have done, if still at liberty. And on the following evening Ramadan would begin. That meant workers tired from fasting by day and staying up to eat at night.

It was a peculiar way to be a geologist, but it was the standard routine for making veterans in Arabia.

Chapter Ten
~ The Ten Days at Dammam 12 ~

Dammam No. 12 was the fourth large producing well in the Arab Zone. Spudded in on October 23, 1938, it was down to 4,725 feet on May 31,1939, and by June 7 the drilling crews had finished cementing the casing. Oil well drilling in 1939 was a great deal different from what it was in the early years of the century, when a gusher was expected to drown half a county in valuable and irrecoverable crude before they got it bottled up. No. 12 was bottled from the beginning. They had her curbed like a dangerous horse.

On June 21 they began test-perforating at 4,565 feet, let the well flow for a while, and got a test of 1,700 barrels a day. Below the perforated section lay 150 feet more of productive strata. By July 8 they were ready to perforate the next stage of it under the direction of Harry Rector, who was acting as resident manager in the absence of Floyd Ohliger. Now that the camp had got past its hectic time and its gala time and settled into a routine, Floyd and his family were en route to the States for a vacation, by way of Rome and London.

On a mid-afternoon in July in the Eastern Province the heat does not beat down as it does in drier climates. It pours in a great engulfing tide, down from the brassy sky and up from the blinding rock and sand, and breathes like a steam boiler through every wind that moves. Even with dark glasses, the eyes have trouble taking in all the light, and photographers, in the beginning, all think their light meters have gone crazy. The attention is inclined to wander, the body and brain to focus on minimum survival, on the mere exhalation and inhalation of hot wet air, on the heavy pound of the blood. Since they learned about them, there had been a stiff consumption of salt tablets among the drilling crews.

Against the fierce sky around No. 12, the derricks of neighboring wells shimmered, crawled, almost disappeared. The jabals over toward No. 1 did their special July dance. If an American fell into a daydream about the beach a few miles to the east of them, he adjusted his daydream to the realities, to a cool drink and a shower: the Gulf lapping the fringes of this white-hot shore would have been steaming like a fumarole.

Up on the stabbing board, twenty feet above the derrick floor, Bill Eisler and a helper had got the perforating gun into the lubricator (on top of the casinghead connections) and were preparing to lower it into the casing. In another minute, they would have come down from the stabbing board. A worker in khaki pants – the doctor objected if workers were allowed to work around machinery in their loose robes – was under the floor at the one-inch equalizer valve. Three crewmen stood outside the rig at the remote controls of the $6\,3/8$-inch master valve, awaiting Eisler's orders to open the gate. Monte Hawkins, the second American on the crew, had started for the hoist 150 feet away. Over in the shack three or four petroleum engineers, greasy with sweat, tried to keep their forearms and spongy hands from sticking to the papers they worked on.

That was when Dammam No. 12 exploded.

All Monte Hawkins heard was a sharp hiss as if the air hose of a compressor had been cut. Then he was flat on the ground, dazed and scrambling. Inside the shack the engineers felt the walls ram inward as if something soft and very heavy had hit them. Almost simultaneously they heard a dull, mushy BOOM! and a massive deafening roar like a waterfall or a hurricane swept over them and around them. They rushed to look out, their hair blown back, it seemed, by waves of overwhelming sound. They saw each other's open mouths but heard nothing except their own shouting, faint and far away, as they took in the incredible scene uncoiling before them.

At No. 12 black smoke, shot with red and yellow flames, boiled out of the cellar. Up, through, and around the laced steel of the 135-foot derrick it rose and bent stiffly southward in a wind they had not known was blowing. Then, one shocking instant later, a column of flames 200 feet high shot into the air like something played from a hose.

The men in the shack did the frantic, random things that great excitement makes men do. They rushed toward the fire, they grabbed up papers as if their own shack were burning and they must save the records, they seized the telephone and gabbled in it, as if the explosion would not have shocked the whole camp alert in a split second. Ernie Wichern, like the man who points and clicks his camera instinctively as the *Hindenburg* blows up in the air before his eyes, rushed outside and stood spraddle-legged, trying to focus on the boil of flame and smoke with the derrick's tower almost hidden in it.

Up nearer the rig, the action was more critical. Some said afterward that at the first hiss, as the perforating gun fired prematurely in the lubricator, Bill Eisler shoved the worker beside him off the stabbing board, clear of the fire. Blown or pushed, the worker never moved after he struck the derrick floor. A second or two later, as Monte Hawkins was scrambling to his feet, Eisler himself jumped, hit the derrick floor, and lay where he had fallen.

Hawkins, looking back, saw Eisler begin to crawl, and without a moment's thought went back into that terrible heat to get him. His face shriveled, his eyes slitted, and his lips drawn back from his teeth, staggering, half-blind, being cooked alive, he struggled toward Eisler and was chased back, gathered his arms before his face and drove in again. Eisler was hitching himself along, a broken and agonized animal. Hawkins caught at his hands; the skin peeled off in his grip. He got hold of armpits, wrists, the remnants of clothes, and dragged and rolled him and got his arm and lifted him and pulled him along with his burned arm hooked around his neck. The crewmen who had been at the remote controls of the master valve were by now with him, helping, and Roy Hollingsworth, the first man from outside to reach the fire, skidded up in a sedan. Together they lifted Bill Eisler into the car.

Now others were there to help. From over at the camp the cars and trucks were roaring in. It turned out that the worker who had been under the floor had crawled out miraculously unhurt. It was just as well he had; about this time the fire began setting off the caps and powder on the derrick floor to add their bit to the conflagration.

They sent Eisler off to the hospital to die. Before the car had turned around, within ten minutes of the explosion, the crowd standing back away from the heat, not yet organized for anything, saw the derrick begin to lean. Before their eyes the steel girders at its base melted like wax. Wichern, his film running out, got a shot as the derrick lurched downward toward the blown funnel of smoke, and then ran a few yards closer, behind some rolls of roofing paper, and squinted through his finder again.

The derrick was gone, flattened out in the smoke, not even the crash of its falling audible over the howl and rush and roar. Things less combustible than steel might have melted, and things taller than derricks fallen inaudibly, in that holocaust. Oil at tremendous pressure, coming from nearly a mile down, was feeding the fire at the rate of probably 10,000 barrels a day.

Nobody could ever quite reconstruct how it had all happened, except that, somehow, the perforating gun went off in the lubricator. The worker below the floor had opened the one-inch equalizer valve, and this might have caused a surge of gas to kick the gun up to the top of the lubricator, where it hit its firing pin against the "go-devil" that normally is dropped down the hole later. Or the wire line might have tightened up enough to pull the gun up against the top of the lubricator and the go-devil. Whatever it was, it was enough. Some tiny tick or scratch or jar, some bubble of gas as inconsequential as a hiccup, and all that enormous curbed energy erupted in destructive flame.

For the 200 American men of Dhahran, isolated, remote from the equipment and expertise of experienced professionals, the fire at Dammam No. 12 was a staggering challenge. It was one of the world's most spectacular oil-well fires, one that brought people to emergency stations halfway around the globe, and to fight it, Harry Rector, facing the worst emergency in the company's history, had not a single professional to call on.

He had cabled San Francisco. He had advised Bahrain. He had intercepted Ohliger at Rome. But he couldn't wait for their answers: the emergency was now. Inexperienced he may have been, but then and there he and Herb Fritzie, in charge of one crew, and Bill Eltiste in charge of another, were the best there was available.

The first step was obvious: assign priorities. Because No. 12 was a good distance from the other wells, there was no serious danger of the fire's spreading. The real danger was that the master valve and the connections on the main casing would be destroyed, which would probably destroy the well, and might also spray the entire camp with burning oil. Besides, if the well ran wild, it might seriously deplete the whole oil field by releasing gas pressure and possibly channeling water into the oil zone.

Later there would be the problem of the toxic gas being released. If they put out the fire without controlling the well, a shift in the wind could wipe out the whole camp. The women, therefore, might have to be evacuated. But that would come later. Now, they would focus on the casing valves and fittings.

The fire fighters started water flowing continuously into the cellar to carry off the unburned oil from there and from the immediate surroundings of the well. They also flowed water onto the casing fittings to help keep them cool. They strung together about 400 feet of eight-inch pipe and with a side-boom tractor shoved one end of it into the head of the fire to carry away the oil and gas, and burned these fuels as they came out the other end.

Herb Fritzie and a drilling crew went to work on one of the six-inch lines normally used to pump oil to al-Khobar for the Bahrain refinery and, after installing water pumps at al-Khobar, converted the line to carry water back to Dhahran. But the pumps could deliver only about 300 gallons a minute, and a minimum of 400 gallons was needed for the Casoc fire engine.

So Fritzie's crew ran a pipeline to Dammam No. 8, which had been completed in salt water, and got enough water from that well. John Ames and the other drilling crew, working all night, laid steam lines from several of the boiler plants adjacent to No. 12, and rigged steam nozzles to blast the fire away from vital connections. Then they installed steam jets in the eight-inch line to boost the oil and gas through, so as to get these fuels away from the fire more rapidly. Steam nozzles were also used to keep the flames from blowing in the faces of the workmen, but they were only partially effective. The fire engine was used to pump water through the nozzles.

Efficiency was their trademark. Long before dawn they had a first-aid station, a motor pool, a stockpile of all available pipe and fittings, awnings under which exhausted men could rest in the shade during the day, and a field kitchen where Chow Lee dispensed coffee and hamburgers.

A little after two thirty in the morning the word came down from the hospital that Bill Eisler was dead. Red-eyed, exhausted, they went on setting up their battle gear, and after daylight they went off to their shifts on other wells, and the crews which had been working at these wells all night replaced them at the fire.

Production was what they were all there for; it could not be stopped just because of a fire.

By daylight, asbestos screens had arrived from Bahrain. Bill Eltiste and Herb Fritzie pushed a screen up as close as they could stand, while men with hoses, coming behind, kept them wet and steaming. They thought they could see that the fire was coming from a broken side line in the cellar below the master gate, and their baptism of fire convinced them beyond any doubt that they needed asbestos suits, more screens, extra fire hose, fog nozzles, gas masks, and Bullard fresh-air masks.

Rector wired San Francisco to get them started, and Skinner telephoned Roy Lebkicher in London, asking him to enlist help from Abadan and Basra, and to send down by chartered plane what London could provide. Lebkicher ran into difficulties, for in midsummer of 1939 London was in the midst of war jitters and was desperately preparing for anything. He couldn't get any equipment released in London, but by hunting all over the United Kingdom, he and the others in the London office managed to pick up gas masks, asbestos suits, and other gear and to put it aboard an Imperial Airways plane at Croydon airport within forty-eight hours after Skinner's call.

It turned out that the shipment could go only as far as Rome, but Floyd Ohliger there arranged a transfer to an Italian plane; the Italians were remarkably eager to cooperate. The British, harassed and in trouble, but not likely to permit Italians to fly over and among their oil strongholds of the Middle East, intercepted the Italian plane at Basra and took the equipment on from there. That was July 13. Meantime, some asbestos suits, together with additional fresh-air masks, had been sent by Bapco from Bahrain and by Anglo-Iranian (formerly Anglo-Persian) from Abadan. Bapco had also sent over Mollie Brogan, a registered nurse, with special medicines and supplies.

Since it was summer, the geologists had returned to camp to work on their reports, but Max Steineke had a futile time trying to keep them away from the fire. Dick Kerr and others were helping at the well every night. All over the camp, crews finished their regular shifts and were drawn irresistibly down to No. 12. Shop men who had worked all day spent all night helping to lay water lines, making special wrenches and devices that suggested themselves to the fire fighters. They were getting constant advice, much of it good, from San Francisco and elsewhere, but advice wasn't what they needed most. What they most needed was to get a clear idea of where the main trouble was; then they could devise ways of fixing it.

Fritzie, Walt Sims of Bapco, and especially Eltiste did it for them. First Fritzie and Sims, in asbestos suits, with wire cable around them, went in behind a screen, right to the base of the roaring, boiling column of flame and smoke, and fought to close the upper and lower Shafer gates. Before they were driven back, writhing and almost insane with the heat, they closed one wheel two turns; there it stuck. The control rod of the other was bent, and would have to be straightened before the gate could be closed off. But the stuck one might yet be broken loose; they tried it again next day, four of them on a four-foot wrench, working behind a bigger movable shield that the shop had built overnight.

With the hoses and fog nozzles spraying over their laboring bodies and soaking the ground and the hissing, steaming shield, it was like working in the throat of a volcano during a cloudburst. But heaving together on the wrench, they broke the wheel loose and started it around, staying in the furnace blaze until it could not be borne another second, and still hanging on for one more turn, and another. Then the control rod broke clean off, and they were dragged back to safety. But when they could look again they were cheered; the flame was definitely lower. They could not tell whether the roar was less or not; they had a feeling they would never hear properly again.

Now it was Bill Eltiste's turn to go in behind his screen, clear to the cellar wall. He could see the source of the fire — it came mainly from the split swage nipple on top of the control valve. And it seemed to him that there were better ways of working on it than by trying to straighten the bent rod of the second wheel and get the lower Shafer shut that way. He was a big, easygoing, low-voiced man with the kind of imagination that inventors draw on, and a brain as orderly and reliable as a good watch. He found a pencil and a scrap of paper and he drew a picture of what seemed to be a huge iron spoon. The "spoon," he said, would partly cap the nipple. John Box took the drawing and went to work in the machine shop.

Next day, Box brought up the iron spoon he had made to Eltiste's specifications. Eltiste had already had his crew join together two hundred feet of eight-inch pipe. Box fitted the spoon to the end of this pipe, and a pair of side-boom Caterpillar tractors picked up the pipe and shoved the spoon into the center of the fire. It took some steering; they jockeyed and probed through the heat and smoke, with Eltiste trying to direct them from behind the shield. Then suddenly the spoon slid over the broken swage nipple and the column of fire dropped as if a burner valve had been turned down. At the end of the two-hundred feet of pipe, the oil gushed out in a thick stream that blackened the sand and flowed down into a low spot and began to puddle. The noise fell with the column of fire; they found themselves shouting more loudly than they needed to.

With the flames reduced by half, Eltiste, Cal Ross, and Ed Braun got closer to the valve than they had been able to before, and as soon as they got a look they gave up both the plan to straighten the bent rod and the notion of trying to close the Shafer. There was an alternate plan, suggested from San Francisco, that they tunnel in from sixty or seventy feet away and put a "hot tap" on the main casing fifteen or twenty feet below the cellar.

A hot tap is a routine procedure by which an intercepting line is attached to a main line while oil is still flowing through. Engineers simply weld a fitting to the line to be tapped, attach a flange to the fitting, and bolt a valve to the flange. Then it's a simple matter of inserting a specially fitted tapping machine through the valve and cutting a hole into the main line. Through the intercepting pipeline that is attached to the valve, oil can be drawn out or, as San Francisco was suggesting, mud could be pumped into the well, to block the oil shooting upward from below.

Everybody knew it was going to take a good deal of time and might be dangerous, because gas might seep into the tunnel through the porous and cracked limestone near the bore hole, so Tom Barger, once a mining engineer, was assigned to work it out. He drew up his plans during the night, and work started at daybreak. But this plan was abandoned too. Eltiste, Ross, and Braun saw that it would be easier to put a hot tap on the four-inch bypass line that emerged from the casing below the main valve, and force mud in that way.

By now, though they had worked with only snatches of rest, going from routine shifts to fire-fighting shifts and back again for a solid week, they were doggedly determined to get the rest of that fire out – and by themselves. The word had got around that not only was Anglo-Iranian coming in with men and equipment, but that Charley Potter, the drilling superintendent on leave in the States, had started by plane from Los Angeles to New York to meet Myron Kinley. Kinley, the most famous oil-well fire fighter in the world, was on his way with a crew from Texas, and had announced that he was prepared to fly the Atlantic in a chartered airplane to kill the fire. This was not something many people had done in 1939, but the tired boys in Dhahran were not impressed. "Nuts!" Ed Braun is supposed to have said. "This is our fire." So while they owned it, they made the most of it.

The one-inch equalizer valve was burned and could not be closed. On July 15, a week after the fire broke out, they decided to try to pinch off the one-inch equalizer, although they recognized that it would be a dangerous job: a split in the already burned pipe at the pinch point could spray the crew with blazing oil.

Nevertheless, seeing no alternative, they put a clamp on a twenty-foot torque tube, and very slowly, expecting the pipe to crush or split at any moment, they screwed down on it and pinched the pipe shut. Again they were cheered, for the fire and noise fell abruptly.

By now they had reduced the flare to a quarter of what it had been in the beginning. Ohliger, who had sent his wife on to London and flown back to Dhahran, cabled Skinner that there were only 1,000 to 2,000 barrels a day coming through the swage nipple now. Skinner began to slow up on his assembling of worldwide help; Potter held Kinley in New York pending developments. While the professionals were hesitating, the amateurs closed in.

There were two valves on the four-inch line from the cellar connections: one near the casing head, and one at the top end, near the rim of the cellar. They knew that the top one was closed, but they could not get near enough to open it because of the intense heat. They hoped and believed that the lower one was open, so that an effective hot tap might be put on the line between the two valves. After the shop built the hot tap, they screwed the nuts on one by one under the protection of shields, with their heads and shoulders hanging over into the cellar, which even at one-fourth of its original fury was a fair substitute for hell. Ross and Braun put the nuts on, alternating, being dragged out half dead and going in again after a rest. It was a job that called for muscle and bravery, and it took two days.

On July 18, ten days after the explosion seared the flesh from Bill Eisler's bones, they tested the connections for the last time. Haggard, blistered, scorched, exhausted, they got the word that things were about ready; they dropped back and waited, watching the diminished but still fearful flare that roared into the summer sky and the smoke that blew thick and rolling across the *jabals*. Their unheard shouting fell away. Somebody, somewhere, gave a signal – a nod, a lifted hand. They felt how the bit began boring into the side of the bypass line. Unable to see what they knew was happening, they could only watch the column of smoke and fire for the hoped-for results. If it worked, if the lower valve *was* open, mud would rush down the bypass line into the well as soon as the bit broke through. If it didn't work – well, then they would have to try something else. They waited, watching the apparently quenchless column of smoke and flame.

Then they sprang from the ground, they turned to pound one another on the back; the shouting that for ten days had gone unheard in the roar of the fire burst hoarsely into an abrupt stillness. The fire had gone out like a turned-out light.

There was some self-conscious understatement, a certain controlled pride, in the cable that Ohliger sent Skinner. It spoke for the whole two hundred amateurs. "Fire extinguished," it said. "Hole full of mud. Professional fire fighters not needed."

They proved themselves on No. 12. If they had not been initiated before, they were now. The fire cost the company vast amounts of money and deprived the government of substantial royalties; it cost the crew two lives and ten days of heart-bursting work. Shaikh Abdullah expressed everybody's most fervent wish when he cabled that he hoped this would be the last accident of its kind. But as a test of what was in them, it could hardly have been better devised. Every capacity that they possessed had a chance to shine during those ten days, and in celebration of the way they had handled themselves, the government – for this one occasion – relaxed its prohibition law, and the first beer that was ever in al-Hasa came across from Bahrain, and the firemen really tied one on.

Chapter Eleven
~ *The Unicorns of the Dahna* ~

The German invasion of Poland on September 1, 1939, made its repercussions felt even to the shores of the Gulf. The news came as no special surprise – the company had been fearing war, and stockpiling against the possibility, for some time – but the outbreak of actual fighting meant an immediate threat. It seemed plausible that the Axis, fully aware of the importance of Gulf oil to the British fleet, might have planted troublemakers, saboteurs, and possibly even armed groups in the area. Technically neutral but feeling threatened nevertheless, Dhahran pulled in all the geophysical and geological parties from the desert and put the exploration crews, with their cars and trucks, on 24-hour-a-day patrol around Dhahran and between Dhahran and the other wells, camps, and installations. Twenty-four hours a day operators monitored everything that they could get on the radio, English, German, French, Italian, Russian, and American. The boys in the bunkhouse – they had set up one of the field radios to keep track of events – concurred in liking the French news best: it came on in a soft, feminine voice.

While Tom Barger, who had been recalled from the field along with the other geologists, led a reconnaissance group on a swing around the concession area, there were long conferences in

Dhahran on the possibility of air attacks, on problems of logistics and supply, on security measures. But Barger and his party, talking with every band of Bedouins and every local amir they could find, came across nothing suspicious. Everyone received them with hospitality; no potential saboteurs looked at them out of the corners of their eyes in the *majlis* or around the campfires.

Eventually Dhahran decided it was safe to send the field parties back to their work. People wrote reassuring letters back home, but the optimism had a certain nervousness about it. It struck them all that the home office in San Francisco didn't seem to be sufficiently alarmed. San Francisco was not sitting on an important and logical target, and San Francisco was not in frequent contact with the British on Bahrain, who as active belligerents and custodians of Britain's oil supply were sobering companions.

Actually, after the first scare, the war did not much affect them except by the gradual choking off of their supply lines, and in the beginning that result was not too apparent. Other difficulties crept back to absorb them more – the routine, day-by-day problems of reconciling their heavily-mechanized industry with local habits and with the local Arab representatives and police. Compromise and agreement were easier at the policy level, between Lenahan and Najib Salha, say, than between the men in the field and the local Saudi officials. Here in the Eastern Province the contact was man to man, and since each man was the product of a culture profoundly different from that which had formed the other, there were inevitable incidents of misunderstanding, prejudice, conflicting notions of law and justice. One of them, on December 19, 1939, involved John Ames.

Ames was one of the Bunyans. As a by-product of drilling oil wells, he created legends, often in the company of Hank Trotter, once an all-American at California, or of Bill Eltiste, Steve Furman, or Homer Florey, a boilermaker whose hands were so stiffened from using hammers and sledges that they used to lay a silver rupee on the bar and bet him that he couldn't pick it up. They told, and still tell, a good many stories about John Ames.

They said, for example, that once Trotter, Ames, Furman, Florey, and Dr. T. C. Alexander were gazelle hunting up near Kuwait. The country was *dikaka* and gravel plains, rough but without serious hazards. Nevertheless, in the midst of the flint plains where only a genius could have found a rock bigger than a teacup, Florey and Alexander found and hit a rock three by six feet. They moved it about a yard, mostly inward upon the bumper and radiator of the pickup. The crowd, all of them capable, if necessary, of rebuilding the pickup on the spot, swarmed out of their cars to fix the thing up.

A block on the sand, a few twists of the jack handle, and they had the front end up in the air. John Ames crawled under, and lying on his back began to hammer and pound. In a minute he had pounded the pickup off the jack and brought the truck's front cross-member down across his chest. Pinned down, he swore, briefly. Then he said, "Get the damn thing off me." Trotter stooped, got a grip, tightened, grunted, and lifted the front end off the ground. "How's that?" he said, meaning was the car high enough for Ames to crawl out. But Ames, who thought Trotter had knocked the car off the jack in the first place, crawled out swearing at Hank, resisting Alexander's attempt to examine his chest and implying humorlessly that it was kind of a bum joke to drop a truck on a man. In a minute he crawled back under to resume work, saying to Trotter, "Now stay away from this car, God damn it!"

The Bunyans were of a breed loud, tough, strong, rowdy, good-natured, superbly adapted to the hardness of the life they lived and the job they did, and by and large trying seriously to live up to company policy and get along with Arabs and respect Arabian customs. They were considerably better behaved, probably, than they would have been at home: Heine Snyder, a driller, once complained that "there wasn't a decent fight in the whole damned four years." It was a queer oil field. It appeared even queerer when John Ames, driving through the Dhahran camp at about sixteen miles an hour on December 19, struck a boy who darted from behind a parked tractor. Ames stopped within eighteen feet. He picked up the boy and took him to the company hospital and waited around anxiously while it was determined that the victim had a broken leg and lacerations on the head, but was in no danger of dying. While Ames was waiting, the Saudi police descended and yanked him off to jail; because he was contrite and sorry about what had happened, he went peaceably. But it at once appeared that he was in serious trouble.

Just how serious was the question. Striking and injuring a pedestrian with an automobile is a grave offense anywhere, and Saudi Arabia is no exception. Further, all residents in the kingdom, including Americans, were subject to the Shari'ah law, a code with some troubling differences if compared to American practices.

On the official side, there was confusion. Ahmad Lary, al-Hasa representative of the Bureau of Mines and Public Works, was inclined to one line of action; Ghalib Taufic, the chief of police, to another. Ames sweated in jail while the argument went on. Ohliger, unable to obtain Ames' release, protested against the local attempt to treat him as if he were a common criminal and insisted that the police regulations in matters of this kind should be discussed with higher authorities.

Dhahran got on the radio to Lenahan, and Lenahan took the case up with Najib Salha, and Najib instructed Ahmad Lary to release Ames into Ohliger's custody. After that, the police and the company would be allowed to present their arguments and evidence separately to their Jiddah offices, whereupon the *qadi* would consider both sides and decide the amount that Ames was to pay as indemnity to the parents of the injured boy. From the beginning, Najib held that Ames should pay hospital and doctor bills as well as the wages the boy would have received during his hospitalization. And if the boy died, he added, Ames' guilt would not be decided according to American practices, but by the *qadi* in accordance with Shari'ah law.

As it turned out, the boy not only lived and collected his reparations money, but emerged from the hospital fifteen pounds heavier and cured of malaria, scurvy, and an enlarged spleen. But the possibility that an American might be subject to Shari'ah law was enough to make a man thoughtful. The Americans may have been largely ignorant of Shari'ah law, but they did know there were some disturbing possibilities. For if it was a small case, by the standards of Americans grown callous to death by automobile and geared to handle accidental death or injury in specific legal ways, it was not small in Saudi Arabia, where everything from food and housing to the most basic law of the land was under pressure along the frontier contact of cultures.

Most of Arabia, even the Dahna and the Jafura sands, is laced and crisscrossed with camel tracks. But beyond 'Ain Muqainima, the last well on the edge of the Rub' al-Khali – an old well to judge by the ten-foot bank of camel dung around its mouth, and indispensable in spite of the hydrogen sulfide stink of its water – there were no tracks. Southward between the Dahna and ar-Rimal reached the long, perfectly flat gravel plain called Abu Bahr, the Father of the Sea, and for miles there was nothing to break the incredible flatness or the equally incredible barrenness.

As the Texans say of the Staked Plains, you could look farther and see less than almost anywhere in the world. Not a *jabal*, not a sandhill, not a dune, not a shrub or a blade of grass, not a rock bigger than a pebble. Tom Barger's party made their traverses across it by sticking a piece of adhesive tape on the windshield and another below it where the shadow of the first would fall, and marking the shadow with a pencil. Then they set the car on the compass course they wanted, and every twenty minutes stopped to correct their course as the shadow moved leftward. It was the nearest thing to marine or aerial navigation that solid ground could provide, and it went on without a break until nearly noon. Then the country ahead began to roll, and the Dahna dunes closed in from the right. Here, as the Arabs said, the desert "lived." A recent rain had moistened it, and now there was grass in a narrow, yard-wide band along the foot of the dunes on the south side. When the desert "lived" here, the Murrah said, there might be hunting, since the *wudayhi* sometimes strayed up from the depths of the Rub' al-Khali. This was unlikely since the *wudayhi*, or oryx, were among the rarest of Arabia's animals. No one in the party, even the Arabs, had ever seen a wild one. Still, as Barger squatted behind the sedan, sheltering himself and the mercury from the sand that had begun to blow, and shot the sun, Khamis the guide continued to talk about the possibility.

Then they climbed back into the car and started to turn around and saw three – as fabulous as beasts out of a fairy tale, as improbable as three unicorns.

Today, it is forbidden to shoot most game in Saudi Arabia. Like other parts of the world, Saudi Arabia has learned the need for conservation. But then things were different, and within seconds, as the oryx broke and ran, the sedan and the pickup were roaring after them.

Johnny Thomas, a recruit from the University of Washington, had cut loose with the shotgun, and one of the two bigger *wudayhi* was down. Barger, driving the sedan, waved at the soldiers to look after it, while he tore out in pursuit of the other big one. The third, a calf, they ignored.

The oryx was not as fast as a gazelle; they gained on him. A little too anxious, Thomas fired with the shotgun before they were quite within range. Khamis emptied the .22, but because of the angle he hit him in the side and hind quarters. Then the bull stopped, and Khamis dropped him with a shot in the head, but before they could come up to him he was on his feet and running again. Tom Barger slid over, reloaded the .22, and shot three times. The oryx went down to stay. Meantime the soldiers in the pickup had had their own thrills. When they drove up to the cow that Thomas had shot, she rose up and charged them. Soldiers scattered in every direction. Some of them got to the truck just ahead of her two-foot horns, which rammed into the spare tire like bayonets. Then she also went down to stay.

To complete their sweep, they tracked the calf to where he had stopped among the dunes nearly a mile away. Barger pursued him slowly while Thomas and Khamis crouched on the running board, and at a propitious moment Khamis dove off like a bulldogger in a rodeo and had him.

For the next day or two they ate the best meat that Arabia provided, and they kept the calf, Butch, force-fed with a medicine dropper. The soldiers scoured the country for miles to bring in bunches of grass, but then they ran out of condensed milk, and the inhospitable reaches of Abu Bahr provided no more stubble. For a while Butch existed on Klim, which left him a little pale and sickly, but not too sickly to butt anything that came close. He gave it to a soldier who came in to get his eyes treated, and he knocked the wind out of a sheep who wandered into his orbit. At night he refused to sleep outside, preferring to root and scoop an illusory hole in the matting they spread for him in the tent. He submitted to being wrapped in a flannel shirt on cold nights, and when he wandered outside and got tangled up in the tent ropes, he blatted for help like an airbulb auto horn.

He was everybody's baby. But he was symbolic of the losses that accompanied the gains of the industrial invasion. Butch's parents had been unable to escape hunters chasing them in a car, the kind of hunting that was to virtually wipe out both oryx and gazelle before conservation laws were put into effect. And Butch himself, treated more kindly by the newcomers, died of their kindness; born to subsist on an occasional wisp of grass, he fell so greedily upon the alfalfa they brought him in the supply truck from Hofuf that he bloated up and perished in convulsions.

Within two weeks they came across five more oryx. They had broken down a truck in the Abu Bahr and removed the whole rear assembly, axles, differential, and all. They had to pull it apart with the lorry while one side was anchored to the pickup, and then they had to dig the broken bearing fragments out of the differential, install new bearings, and put the truck back together. They were feeling in a mood for a change of chores when Khamis spotted the tracks of five *wudayhi* moving northeast. By a coincidence which they nudged just a little, they too were working in that direction. At lunch, for a laugh, Barger rigged up a lasso out of a piece of rope and demonstrated for the soldiers how cowboys caught cows in America. They were not impressed.

A half hour after lunch, however, they ran into the herd, and as two calves veered off, Barger decided he would show them that the cowboy method was not as silly as they thought it. He climbed out on the running board, and hanging on by his eyebrows while Thomas brought him up beside a fleeing calf at thirty miles an hour, he lassoed her on the fourth cast. Then they ran down the other one and he hindfooted it and spilled it neatly on the very first throw. This time the Arabs were impressed, and complimented him many times on his "idea." If there had been any more *wudayhi* in Abu Bahr that season, he might have started a cultural revolution and turned the Bedouins into vaqueros.

The boy from North Dakota was developing into a man of real stature in the field. He had every frontier competence in addition to sound scientific training and personal qualities that set him apart. From the beginning he had been the one who carried the conversation when the field parties found themselves invited to drink coffee with Ibn Jiluwi or local amirs, once or twice with the Crown Prince Saud when he was camped near them, and most notably when King Ibn Saud came through on his visit to Ras Tanura. Though he might go visiting in a pair of pants whose seat had long been gone, and which he had to cover by a woolen *bisht* that drowned him in sweat, Barger could hold his own in most conversations, stumble through a more formal visit with the Crown Prince without the necessity of an interpreter, and even get a "Praise be to God" out of the taciturn Ibn Jiluwi. He had a native grace, and a sensitiveness to Arab notions of decorum. Not only did he know much of interior Arabia better than almost any company man except perhaps Steineke, but he knew Arabs.

One day Steineke came down to the Jabrin oasis that was their base for the Rubʿ al-Khali exploration and said that he had been approached by the government relations department to see if Barger could be wooed away from geology. Steineke left it up to him: Barger had a long leave coming, his contract was about up, his second could be negotiated on the old basis or on the new. What was certain was that he could come back either way, to a promotion and a raise. He was the kind who grew with the job.

Tom Barger did not think, then, that he wanted to go into government relations, where he had no training to build on except a knowledge of Arabic. Time and the accidents of the war period would change his mind. His knowledge of the Arabic tongue and the Arab people was more valuable to the company than all the training he had slaved through in geology and mining engineering. But before he made the decision that would move him over into the area where Bill Lenahan, Bill Burleigh, Roy Lebkicher, Floyd Ohliger, and Gavin Witherspoon worked, there was a last job in the field: an exploratory trip to the towns of Layla and Sulaiyl, at the foot of the Tuwaiq Mountains, and a look at the new concession area south of Sulaiyl which Lenahan had obtained in his negotiation of May 1939. No one from the company had ever seen any part of that country. Layla was all but virgin territory. The only westerner who had ever visited it was H. St. John B. Philby, and he had been there only once, in 1917.

Max Steineke, prevented at the last minute from going, sent Dick Bramkamp, the paleontologist, in his place. While they waited for Bramkamp to arrive with Shaubi, the mechanic, Barger and Thomas amused themselves by planting sixty frogs in the wells of the Jabrin oasis, so deadly with malaria that the Bedouins came there only at date-picking time. It was the geologists' pious hope that the frogs would eat the larva of anopheles and that the names Barger and Thomas would be immortalized in the medical journals. They also had a bath and shampoo, the first of either in two weeks, and Thomas oiled up his hair and beard, which in ordinary times were full of dust and practically felted. They had a contest to see who could find the longest hair in his beard, a competition which Barger won by a sixteenth of an inch with a hair just about three inches long. But Thomas' beard proved more useful, if not so ornamental, because his whiskers were perfectly round, and Barger found that he could use them as crosshairs when adjusting the sextant.

When they had all that taken care of, and were sitting in the tent enjoying the itch of unaccustomed cleanliness, a sudden windstorm struck them, blew all their papers off the table, filled the tent with fine sand, swung the lights. They staggered out with their eyes full of grit and tightened the ropes and got the tent secured and came back in. It had lasted only minutes – just long enough to dirty everything up again and fill Johnny Thomas' oiled beard with a new collection of real estate.

Their destination was so deep inland, and the isolation of the inhabitants from western contacts so complete, that Ibn Jiluwi sent an extra ten soldiers from Hofuf to accompany them. The eyes of Saleh the cook popped when he saw them. Their amir, Muhammad ibn Mansur, was Ibn Jiluwi's tax collector and right-hand man, and came by the special command of Ibn Saud. The nine "soldiers" were all prominent men, four of them amirs themselves. Physically and in every other way they were a very superior lot.

They loved a joke and they took the trip as a picnic, and because Ibn Jiluwi was in Riyadh visiting the King, his own tea-maker came as one of the Hofuf detachment – a stout and cheerful man named Faraj, loaded down with a rifle, a Mauser pistol, and two bandoliers of cartridges. He had a trick of adding rose water to the tea, which gave it a touch of sumptuous, oriental splendor. Faraj carried the rose water in an old Scotch bottle, and he treated it with great care.

Two Autocar lorries, two pickups, and a sedan, loaded with fifteen soldiers, two geologists, two cooks, a houseboy, and three drivers, left the Jabrin camp and made the Dahna sands by noon. That night they camped in a desolate waste of rocks on the Huraisan Plateau, and the following afternoon, as they came from the east across a great plain, they saw black islands of palm groves floating on the mirage, and mountains beyond. That was Layla, the capital town of al-Aflaj. Hordes of ragged boys and a good many men poured out of the towns of Layla and as-Sayh, to the south, and stared at them where they camped, but none came close. Amir Muhammad ibn Mansur sent word of their arrival by three of his soldiers; somewhat later, he dressed in his best and took his whole army in to pay a call on the local amir. Later still, on invitation, the entire party went in to dine with the son of the amir, acting as host in his father's absence.

This they were used to – the great platters heaped with layers of wheat gruel, rice, whole sheep, chickens. Tidbits were piled on the plates of the guests, so that they didn't have to enter the tugging contest, all with the right hand, by which the Arabs wrenched boiled mutton off the carcass. When they had had enough they rose, wished the blessings of God on the host, and held out their hands for the servant to pour water over them. Being guests, they were lucky: first whack at the towel.

Layla was surrounded by old mud forts, most of them from the time just before Ibn Saud brought peace, but some of them reputed to be of the time of 'Ad, king of the mythical lost city of Wabar (which some think is Ophir) in the Rub' al-Khali. West and southwest of the town were the clear blue *'ains*, or wells, of the Aflaj, called wells presumably because there was no word for lake among the Arabs of Arabia. One the Americans measured was eighty-five feet deep, and one they swam in was a quarter-mile wide and three-quarters long. From all of them covered canals led out, some of them into barren sand long gone back to desert. Along the canals were the stone manholes, designed to be built up above advancing dunes, that they knew from Qatif. Where a dune had moved on, the manholes were left like a row of chimneys across the desert.

After the first excited outpouring from Layla at their arrival, the inhabitants stayed out of sight. The visitors moved uneasily, conscious of being watched. Muhammad ibn Mansur and his soldiers disliked the place intensely; no one would *salaam* them, and people refused to sell them meat, calling them servants of unbelievers.

Other people of the region were less standoffish. At Wasit, up the Wadi Hamar in the Tuwaiq Mountains, they could hear a mile away the mighty drone of voices as the inhabitants came running to look at the first foreigners and the first cars they had ever seen. These were friendly. So were the people of Sulaiyl, southward along the Tuwaiq Escarpment, which they reached two days later after examining the surface geology of the wadis that emptied every few miles into the desert, and after a thunderstorm had soaked them in the night. Sulaiyl, at the mouth of the great Wadi Dawasir, was a round of dinners and visits and coffee; the Hofuf soldiers, who had sworn that if they went back through Layla they would hand a beating to anyone who would not salaam them, mellowed under constant hospitality.

At Sulaiyl, too, Barger had the often-repeated opportunity to play doctor, which could be heartbreaking when it was not, as in old Salim's case, funny. The first patient brought to him was a ten-year-old boy who had hurt his leg weeks before by falling off a camel. "God lengthen your life, O my uncle," he said in greeting, and lay without whimpering as Barger examined the leg, evidently broken, much swollen, and scabbed with continued infection. Barger told him to soak the whole leg in hot salt water twice a day and keep a clean rag over it. Beyond that, it was with God. *Allah kareem* – God is kind. The boy came back next evening and, magically, the swelling was very much less. The doctor prescribed more of the same treatment, gave the boy a couple of Maria Theresa thalers (dollars) and some clean rags, and had done everything he could. Another boy, paralyzed from the hips down, who was brought in by his tearful father on a stretcher, he could not help. "This sickness is from God, and if He wills, He will cure it. *Allah kareem*. I can do nothing for him."

Down in the new concession area, at the well called Hisy, where a donkey drew water under the protection of a mud fort, they met a very old man, wrinkled like a monkey, whom the soldiers nicknamed the Old Man of Hisy, the Brother of 'Ad. "O, Old Man, how old are you?" they said to him, and grinning with wrinkled gums he croaked in his low old voice, "*Mubty*" – ancient. He would not accept a ride in the sedan back to his fort. "I will go by foot," he said. "I have gone a long way on my feet." He had never seen an automobile before, but he was not surprised by it. If such a thing appeared by his '*ain*, it was God's will.

'Ain Hisy was their deepest penetration into unknown Arabia. Three days later they were back at Layla, where they stopped only for water. Their meat needs did not need to be satisfied by the Layla *suq*; they had been having great gazelle hunting. The soldiers, who preferred the certainty of buckshot, were a little astonished to see Barger pick off a running gazelle (and gazelles had been clocked at nearly forty miles an hour) with a .22 from the backseat of the sedan.

From Layla they went back toward Jabrin, stopped while Thomas, Barger, and Dick Bramkamp made some important geological examinations just west of the Dahna, and got into Jabrin camp in the midst of boiling heat on the 18th of April 1940. Within a month Barger was on his way to Dhahran, and in a couple of months more on his way home on long leave.

When he came back in 1941, the war would have sharply restricted company activity, field work would be suspended, and after driving Roy Lebkicher across Arabia as a temporary replacement for Bill Lenahan, who was leaving after eight years, Barger would find himself a government relations man. Garry Owen would arrive in the spring of 1942 to take over Lenahan's work, and Lebkicher would return to Dhahran as manager of relations. The camp at Dhahran would have been pinched in upon itself, into what Phil McConnell would label the Time of the Hundred Men. For quite a long time the new country Barger and Bramkamp had opened up would stay unvisited, as remote as if it still belonged to 'Ad, the King of Wabar, or his ancient relative the Old Man of Hisy.

Chapter Twelve
~ Air Raid! ~

The night of October 19, 1940. The sky is full of light from a late three-quarter moon, the purity of its cup is broken only by one trailing film of cloud, the stars are pale but very many. Over the Gulf, where sometimes a heavy fish splashes in water still as oil, the lower air is faintly pearly. Bahrain lies afloat, its houses dark, the crooked alleys of Manama blackly rutted among the moon-white walls. Only the refinery blazes with light, a hub at the center of lighted spokes of roads, throwing its harder, brighter, five-and-dime glitter back at the softer glitter of the stars and the cooling metal of the moon. Five hundred yards to one side, the gas flares gush flame.

A little after three o'clock the Bapco guard in the field gave a warning that there were planes going over. Somewhat later, he warned again, worried about who they might be. At the Sitra terminal a worker outside having his past-midnight lunch saw them and called William Gentry, who in turn called Ward Anderson. Anderson got up and put on his pants and went out on the porch. That was just about the moment when a jolting roll of explosions shocked the McConnells out of bed. Gertrude McConnell, shocked awake before she had had time to stop sleeping, groped around on the floor under the impression that there was an earthquake and that she should be down where falling objects wouldn't hit her. Phil McConnell cursed the elusiveness of a man's pants whenever an emergency arose, found a pair neatly laid out and started to drag them on, threw them aside because he realized they were good ones that might get dirty, rushed to the closet for another pair, and finally made it outside.

Directly over the Bapco refinery's bright stare of light, between that and the moon, hung two tremendous stars, too big and bright to be real. Phil could have read a magazine in his yard. Next door, Ward Anderson's door slammed, then his car door, then his car shot gravel as it zoomed out into the road. McConnell yelled to him vainly to turn off his lights, and Gertrude McConnell yelled vainly at Phil not to go out, and Phil yelled again at Mrs. Anderson to ask if Gertie could come over, and in a minute or two he was headed down the road after Anderson, but with his lights turned off.

It was perfectly clear that Bahrain had been, or was being, bombed. By the time they had gathered to check the damage – Fred Davies, Lloyd Hamilton, McConnell, Milton Lipp, Don Hanna, a collection of bosses both resident and visiting – the intense magnesium flares had winked out and rumors had begun to come in. One of them said that some men interrupted at a late poker party had been hurrying home just now when they thought they saw flares in the sky over Arabia, and thought they heard muffled explosions.

In Dhahran many people had heard those same explosions. "Spike" Spurlock, the lawyer who had drawn up the papers for the incorporation of Casoc in 1933 and who had until recently been in the London office, lay there awhile listening for something more, and then rolled over and went back to sleep. But Spurlock was a philosopher by nature, so unexcitable that his friends swore a self-winding wristwatch would invariably go dead on his wrist. Others, not so calm, ran out in shirttails, pajamas, or less, to discover what went on. Bill Eltiste dashed out of his quarters, and his neighbor, Mrs. Dreyfus, out of hers, and together they talked for a while before Bill realized he had neglected to dress. He denies indignantly, however, that he was naked. "I had my shoes on," he says, and besides, as if in mitigation of the informality of his attire, "it was dark."

By then the Italian planes, which had dropped two or three dozen small fifty-pound fragmentation bombs on Arabia and more than eighty on Bahrain, were a long way off to the west in the shining metallic sky, headed for Eritrea. They had come, it appeared later, from the Dodecanese Islands. Since no wreckage was ever found, it was presumed that they made their African sanctuary on the fuel they had. Why they had bombed the refinery on Bahrain was obvious enough, but why they had dropped bombs on Saudi Arabia, a neutral country whose government they were trying to woo, was a harder one. And when people got out in the morning and began to inspect the damage they had done, everything disintegrated into guess and speculation and incredulity mixed with ribald humor. If the bombers had been manned by Mark Twain's version of James Fenimore Cooper's Indians, they could not have performed more ineptly.

On a night shining with moonlight, the planes had come over Dhahran, flying at 6,000 feet and in no hurry. Below them the blaze of lights from the wells and the gas-separator plant glittered up at the sky's illuminated dome. They flew with stern directness over the gas-oil separator plant. They may be presumed to have squinted through their bombsights. Presumably young men aboard the aircraft grew tense. There came an order. Deadly missiles tumbled out of the planes' bellies and lit with devastating effect at the edge of the *jabals*, several hundred yards from anything, puncturing an oil flowline and cutting a water main.

Then the bombers, having done their deadly work, circled once to observe it, and bored on through the night to Bahrain. Below them there the refinery was jeweled with lights like a Texas oil town. They circled at least once, looking it over. No one bothered them, no alarms went out, no planes rose, no ack-ack came up at them. Bahrain, as a matter of fact, was thought to be so far away from enemy bases that it needed no defenses at all. There it lay, lighted up like a California supermarket opening.

Carefully the raiders dropped flares – more or less the equivalent of lighting a match to look into a movie projector's beam. Again came the order. Again deadly missiles tumbled out of the planes' bellies. This time they played havoc with a coke pile. Then the bombers turned westward again and droned away toward Africa.

It was simply inconceivable that they should have missed, not once but twice, from that height and under those conditions. Some thought they must have missed on purpose – that the raid was made as a stunt, to scare the British into diverting part of their already inadequate guns and planes from the Mediterranean or elsewhere to defend Bahrain. Some thought it had been done for propaganda reasons and therefore wasn't concerned with doing damage. Yet if you had your enemy right in your sights, why would you deliberately miss him? Some believed that the Bahrain refinery was missed because it was an American neutral installation, though effectively part of the British war effort. These same people thought the bombs dropped on Dhahran were a mistake, the result of some Italian pilot's confusion about exactly where he was.

The explanation that satisfied more people than any other was that the raid suffered from too much care, not too little. In both Dhahran and Bahrain the bombs fell well clustered, and in each case near the flares. But the flares at Dhahran had been moved farther away from the installations within the past week. A man carefully briefed to sight on the flares might possibly have stayed with his instructions even though the brightly lighted GOSP and wells suggested that other targets might be simpler and more effective. Over on Bahrain, also, the flares had been moved farther from the refinery shortly before the bombing. Having arrived at the Arabian flares thinking he was over Bahrain, a well-briefed but unimaginative squadron leader might have realized his geographical error and flown on to Bahrain to repeat his tactical blunder. And if that explanation didn't satisfy you, what theory had you to offer?

When the flowline was punctured at Dhahran, a stream of oil flowed down among the houses where many of the Saudi workmen lived; Dick Kerr and Charlie Davis had the job of routing everybody out before somebody's *barasti* fire or a carelessly tossed match should touch off a blaze. Everybody stayed up all night, and at about six o'clock, Cal Ross heard the official Italian announcement over his radio: "Bahrain has been destroyed. Fires were left burning that the pilots could see for a hundred miles as they left the scene."

The next morning at Dhahran there were about fifty or sixty Americans, along with a number of Saudis, scratching around in the line of small bomb craters that ran along a level stretch of ground, then up and over a rise and down the other side. They were searching for bomb fragments to keep as souvenirs. All at once Oliver (Danny) Boone burst from one of the craters, running as if for his life. The others, following his panic-stricken, backward-straining gaze, saw two Saudis who had just come over the rim, each carrying a dud bomb. Within seconds there wasn't an American in sight – only a pair of Hofuf sandals that Joe Carroll had run out of in his dash for cover.

From behind a rock, Boone screamed at the Saudis to put the bombs down. He did not have to resort to Slim Williams' form of Arabic; he knew the right word for down, which was *taht*! But he nearly swallowed his tongue when the innocent Saudis took him at his word and tossed the bombs wonderingly aside. Before the Americans went back to their scavenging they assigned Cal Ross and Bill Eltiste the job of disposing of the duds. Nobody was curious enough to disassemble them and see how they worked or why they hadn't gone off. Eltiste and Ross laid a stick of dynamite beside each one and detonated them from a good safe distance.

Whatever the explanation of this most futile of all air raids – and no one knows the real answer yet – there was one instant effect. If the motive was to scare the British, the raid was a success. It also scared the Americans, who as neutrals had less cause to stay there and be shot at. Before another night of moonlight rolled around, the Bahrain refinery was blacked out and shut down while the crews worked on air raid shelters.

In Dhahran, a few people took to the dunes and slept outside, but most of them, including the wives, refused to budge. The contemporary members of the tinkerers and gadgeteers society of Saudi Arabia began what would turn out to be a four-year series of experiments in meeting the threats of war. They sprayed the whole town with oil to keep streets and sidewalks from shining, and made it a housekeeper's nightmare; they began rigging air injection systems – venturis – on the flares, and turned them into giant Bunsen burners that threw a blue and much less visible flame into the sides of the *jabals*. And a lot of them, including some who had stayed after the Italian declaration of war in June only because they hoped Arabia would be outside the war zone, began to get out.

The women of Bahrain started moving with the first British-India boat. Gertrude McConnell went on that, not so much because she wanted to go for herself as because her friend Gretchen Foley, pregnant and frightened, didn't want to leave without her. Some women from Casoc were aboard, and a few men whose contracts were up anyway, or who for one reason or other were about to leave. In a day or so planes took out some more.

Then Floyd Ohliger got approval to use a tanker. He put an emergency launch aboard it to augment the lifeboats, the shop built life rafts to be slung on the deck, and a whole crowd of evacuees started the five-day trip down the Gulf to Bombay. On November 12, a couple of weeks after the Bahrain refinery had cautiously opened up again, ninety-nine Casoc and Bapco evacuees sailed for home from Bombay on the *President Garfield*, leaving Bahrain practically bare of American women and Dhahran with only a watchful handful, waiting to see if anything more would happen.

In February 1940, Dhahran had been a community of 371 American employees, 38 American wives, and 16 American children, plus a force of 3,300 Saudi Arab, Bahraini, Indian, and other employees. In fact, the whole Casoc operation was getting so large that in September 1940, it was separated from Socal's foreign producing department and made an independent entity, with its own board of directors and Fred Davies as president. But within a few weeks after the *opera bouffe* bombing, the American group in Dhahran was down to 226 employees, 19 wives, and 5 children. By May of the next year the camp was totally womanless and childless, and many men with families and obligations in the States were leaving. The company, on the principle that staying in Dhahran was a kind of war service that no one should be required to do against his will, did not try to hold them.

Operations shrank as the labor force dwindled and the flow of supplies was pinched off. Everything they obtained – and for two or three years they had trouble getting anything – had to come to them around the Cape of Good Hope. Industrial parts, cars, trucks, tires, food, equipment of all kinds grew harder and harder to obtain, and at length impossible, and though they tried to stockpile everything they could, they were crippled by shortages that threatened, but were never quite able, to shut them down altogether.

When the war interfered, they were on the verge of being one of the major oil producers in the world, with the most extravagant prospects for expansion. Although the Ma'aqala wildcat had been closed down in March 1940 as a dry hole, Abu Hadriya No. 1 had struck oil that same month at a depth of 10,115 feet, and a second well had been started there to test the extent of the field. Just after the bombing, in November 1940, the drillers dirtied up the rig with a big new producer at Abqaiq No. 1, about thirty-five miles southwest of Dhahran.

The second Abu Hadriya well was suspended and the first shut in immediately after the bombing; Abqaiq No. 1 was shut in the following February. But even by that time they knew enough of the potentialities of the Abqaiq field to know that it was incomparably larger and more important than that at Dammam. Perhaps Max Steineke's greatest single achievement had been the series of intuitions that led to this suspicion of closure at Abqaiq, later demonstrated to be one of the world's great oil reservoirs. He had weighed and collated such random and uncertain clues as the occurrence of salt flats, the occasional patches of Tertiary outcrops, even the alignment of the sand hills. He had suggested the use of structure drilling and by that means had corroborated his guess that there was around Abqaiq a well-defined domal feature whose surface features had been all but obliterated. The test well was spudded in on August 4, 1940. In November, San Francisco cabled its congratulations. According to a memorandum by Terry Duce, one of the directors, just before the well was shut in, in February 1941, "the drill-stem test . . . indicates that the well was flowing at the rate of 405 barrels an hour or 9,720 barrels per day. . . . These are of course only drill-stem tests and merely indicative that we have a big well . . . with the possibility of a big new field."

Considering that in the United States, where competitive leasing and drilling put a maximum of holes down into a field, a well that produced 100 barrels a day was a good one, and that some wells, with constant pumping, produced 12 barrels or less, Mr. Duce's restraint seems almost chilly. Abqaiq No. 1 was a better well than any at Dammam, and if Steineke's guess about the structure was correct (as it proved to be), the field itself was many times greater.

Instead of developing it, they closed it down. They had to. Without adequate manpower or adequate supplies, they were able, by great effort and ingenuity, to keep the Dammam field producing, though the 12,000 to 15,000 barrels a day that they got through the stabilization plant, down to al-Khobar by the six-inch pipeline, and by barge across the channel to the Bahrain refinery never satisfied the home office, and would not have satisfied themselves if they had not known their daily production was more than they were entitled to in the circumstances.

At Ras Tanura the crude oil tank farm stood idle, the pumps were still, the port facilities went unused. The 3,000-barrel-a-day "teakettle" refinery, which had been completed on the Ras Tanura sandspit in the autumn of 1940, was shut down the following June. The twenty miles of channel beacons leading into the port no longer flashed their lights down the shallow Gulf. No crude coursed through the pipeline from Dammam, no tanker followed the course of the *D. G. Scofield* to the moorings, the *El Segundo* was off on more pressing business. Any tankers plying the Gulf, and any naval vessels in need of refueling, were headed for Bahrain or Abadan, where they could obtain refined products.

But what isolated them from the world and from the clamor of great events made their own problems more absorbing, their little society more cohesive. One effect of isolation and shortages was to return them to the frontier makeshift and ingenuity that had prevailed before the big growth year of 1936. Another was to return them to the bunkhouse way of life by withdrawing all their wives and children and suspending everything that had made Dhahran a sort of home. Still another was to put the Saudi Arab government in a bad hole financially, since both oil royalties and the hajj fell off sharply.

By now, when the Saudi Arab government got in a hole, it automatically consulted the company. Fortunately its need coincided with the enforced release of many company geologists, engineers, and relations men from business duties. Instead of expanding its oil operations, Casoc found itself expanding its goodwill activities. The revolutionary, disturbing, but increasingly

195

fruitful meeting of cultures that had begun in 1933 was accelerated, not halted, by the war. Al-Hasa was still a frontier, with everything that implied.

Chapter Thirteen
~ The Time of the Hundred Men ~

Pearl Harbor caught the greatly reduced contingent of men in Dhahran, as it caught nearly everyone else, by surprise, and their surprise was like that of Americans everywhere, complicated by the sharp increase in anxiety that went with being made without warning into combatants. In spite of general sympathy, they had been a little aloof from the problems of the English on Bahrain. Now, no longer protected by the neutrality of their country, their shipping no longer even nominally safe, both their supply lines and themselves exposed and many of their lines of communication interrupted or cut, they felt themselves at loose ends; they were driven by a grim and unsatisfied desire to contribute.

There were only two women in Dhahran now, both nurses, and about the middle of December one of them, Mary Margaret Bours, announced that she had been married some time previously, and thus took herself out of circulation. Immediately after that, as if to make the most of what little remained to them, Bob Williams of the accounting department announced that he was going to marry the other nurse, Anna Mary Snyder.

No Christian marriage had ever been performed in al-Hasa. It took special permission from Ibn Saud himself before the

Williams-Snyder marriage could be held in Dhahran. Because of the general atmosphere of isolation, scarcity, and anxiety, the couple had planned a private wedding, but Floyd Ohliger and Bill Eltiste, looking around at the morale of the camp, suggested that they make it public and invite everyone. Among the guests were two Saudi government officials, happily turned tourist to observe the quaint customs of the foreigners.

There were only three women to take care of the details: the bride, Mary Margaret Bours, and Mrs. G. D. Van Peursem, wife of the Dutch Reformed minister from Bahrain who was to perform the ceremony. It was to be held in the auditorium, which they decorated as they could – Arabia, except in the time of rains, was then an almost flowerless country. For music they had only a phonograph. What they would play on it was a difficulty, since the camp contained more jazz and dance records than music appropriate to sentimental or ceremonial uses. But at the last minute somebody on Bahrain found a recording of Mendelssohn's "Wedding March," and rushed it over by launch.

Phil McConnell, over from Bahrain, was by this time part of the Dhahran Hundred. Wifeless and lonesome like the rest of them, he did his job by day and spent a good many night hours recording their communal life in his diary. A literate man, sensitive to the human and emotional implications of a situation, he came into the auditorium that day a little behind the crowd and had a shock that made him realize how much their morale had sagged, how much they needed such a lift as the wedding.

There they sat, every man of them, well ahead of starting time, row upon row of white collars, ties, dark suits. The raffish costume of every day was gone – not a single pair of suntan khakis with grease smudges where hands had been wiped on them, not a pair of suntans of any kind, not a pair of prospector's boots or work shoes, not a khaki or blue shirt, none of the dusty and wrinkled mixtures of American work clothes and Arab costume that they lived in the year around. This was as decorous as a church funeral;

they had scrubbed for it, and they were sober. And when the phonograph wheezed out the march and the bride came down the aisle on the arm of Dr. Alexander, followed by her two attendants – all of them wearing flowers, good Lord, with the bride in lilies of the valley – and the minister stood up in front of the two and bent his head down toward them and began to intone, some of the audience were guilty of sneaky tears.

It did them good. It did them all the good in the world, and not even the revelation that the lilies of the valley had been painfully created out of tiny jasmine blossoms sewn together with thread could undo the pleasure they took in that wedding. They might be lonesome and wifeless and marooned, they might eat like pigs and talk like ruffians and sleep in their unwashed socks, they might be completely out of touch with the world whose very recollection made them weak with homesickness, but here was an American wedding, complete with all the expected and sentimental attachments. Life had not stopped; it had only been interrupted and reduced, and enough of it remained.

As the war went on, however, life in Dhahran, once so complex and hurried, tapered off. Something like the frontier casualness returned to them. It was the conviction of C. E. (Charlie) Davis, manager of operations, that the work to be done would be better done, and everyone would better do his share of it, if there were a minimum of supervision and a maximum of personal initiative.

He could not have applied his theory of management to a more responsive crew or at a more propitious time. They all had some of Max Steineke's contempt for fussy detail; they all had some of his capacity to get things done. And as organization and discipline and supervision lapsed, their morale improved. They did their work without watching the clock, and did it better; even if they worked long hours as they often did, they seemed to have time on their hands; they compared themselves, favorably, with narrow, ingrown, rumor-riddled Bahrain. What had begun as a time of gloom and sagging spirits became a time of alertness and confidence and cooperation.

The skeleton crew of a standby operation, they tentatively tried playing tourist. Once in a while the mysterious East that they had imagined before they came out here revealed itself briefly and tantalizingly. On a trip across to Bahrain they might find themselves on a picnic with Dr. Dame, the missionary doctor, or some other old naturalized Bahraini at the Portuguese fort, a picturesque ruin on the north end of the island. Then for a few hours the scabbed desert, the raw oil camps fell away, and the Arabian Nights (which so few Saudi Arabs seemed to have ever heard of) enclosed them.

The fort was a ruin of rock and mortar 200 yards square, with a moat around it and its towered corners slotted for rifle fire, that commanded the sea to the north. Just west of it, the Shaikh of Bahrain had a large date garden which in March was a sweet wilderness of bloom – among the palms the brilliant red flowers of pomegranates, the pink clouds of apricot, the orange and lime trees with their mixture of green fruit, ripe fruit, and fragrant white blossoms, and the more exotic blooms of papaya and bitter almond. In the shade, by the purl of irrigation ditches, with rose bushes unfolding buds around the picnic blankets spread on the sand, this was hardly Arabia as they knew it.

At sunset the palms would be black against a west full of flaming clouds, and coming back in the twilight the picnickers would have shed upon them the liquid trills of dozens of bulbul birds calling through the great garden, and from a distance hear the long, monotone call of the muezzin. Arabs sitting by their donkeys before a little fire whose smoke spread among the smells of flowers and damp earth would rise then, and turn their donkeys' heads up toward the high ground, and let them go pattering away while their owners prepared themselves for prayer.

A very large number of the Americans remaining in Dhahran were from California, and some of them called themselves the

California Arabian *Stanford* Oil Company – a wisecrack which was explosively rejected by the University of California alumni among them. When Arabia gave them briefly some of the smells of home, and turned fleetingly soft and beautiful, they filled and overflowed with homesickness for the apricot orchards of the Santa Clara Valley and the spring green on the Peninsula's hills.

More often, the Arabia they knew was neither soft nor beautiful. In the winter of 1941–42 it got so cold that icicles formed on the cooling towers and great fish died of the chill and washed up on the Dammam and al-Khobar beaches. In that bitter weather they built a barge terminal at Aziziyah to increase their oil shipments to Bahrain.

The *shamals* were blowing sand into everything, through the weather stripping of windows, into food and clothes and closets, into eyes and noses and the cracks in clothing. And if it was not cold, or blowing sand, it was pouring the deadly south wind off the Gulf over them till they struggled for breath as if in a steam room. Or it was so hot and bright that their eyes ached clear to the backs of their necks.

And sometimes, too, the stern, almost Biblical justice of the Arabs ground into their soft American sensibilities until they gritted their teeth. Life in Arabia was not all bulbul birds – was very little bulbul birds. It could be bare and bitter. Traditional desert justice, with its very occasional beheading and frequent floggings, was also a part of Arabia. It kept them reminded not only of how different their own world was, but of how much constant forbearance the Saudi Arabs practiced to permit them, strangers and livers by another law, to dwell and work here.

They had plenty of uses for all the skill they had come with or learned in Arabia, for as the war dragged on and the stock of cars, trucks, tires, spare parts, and all the instrumentalities of repair were used or worn out, ingenuity sometimes reached the level of inspiration, and inspiration became desperation on the turn of a syllable.

The strain on the company was doubled by the government's distress. After 1943 especially, with the rice of India and Burma cut off and the local crops shriveled in a severe drought, the company not only had to divert many of its trucks to haul food to Riyadh, but it had to undertake the supply and distribution of hundreds of tons of staples to its Arab employees and their dependents. And when it wasn't limping through its own proper chores, or assisting the government, it found itself called upon to be the Mr. Fixit of the Gulf.

Did Lieutenant General Raymond Wheeler in India send an emergency call for tank trucks to help the war effort? The company sent down what it could — or rather couldn't — spare, and muttered angrily when the general complained that they were too rusty inside to be used for airplane gasoline. What did the General think he was drawing on — General Motors? Everything in al-Hasa, including the men, had rust in its insides.

Did Burma-Shell, also in India, send a pleading SOS for spare welding machines? The company obliged with half its creaking supply, and bore with notable meekness the insulting letter which grumbled that there were neither shields nor masks with the machines, and that the tires were in terrible condition. The ones sent were as good as the ones kept, and al-Hasa was getting by.

Did E. F. Wakefield, the Political Agent at Bahrain, request their help to pull three Hurricane fighters out of a *sabkha* near Safaniya, where they had made an emergency landing? Phil McConnell, Floyd Meeker, Charles Homewood, and Glenn Bunton took two pickups and three six-ton Marmon-Herringtons 200 miles up there, pulled out in an hour what had baffled twenty-eight men of an RAF salvage unit for nine days, and rescued the twelve-ton crane the salvage unit had bogged down in the *sabkha* beside the planes. They returned without official thanks; the lieutenant in charge of the salvage unit, who spent the afternoon shooting at tin cans while they bailed him out, neither introduced himself nor recognized their existence nor asked them to dinner.

202

That was in 1942, the summer when Rommel and Montgomery were chasing each other back and forth along the one narrow road between Tobruk and El Alamein. Dick Kerr and Bill Eltiste and Floyd Meeker and the others who had pioneered sand tires for off-road desert driving were holding their breath, for some of them had run around in the desert south of that North African road testing their equipment, and they knew that if the German general ever caught on to what any Aramco employee knew as a matter of course, he could whip around Montgomery and have him. And if Rommel whipped around Montgomery, he would have the whole Middle East; he could pick it like a plum.

Fortunately, Rommel appeared to know as little about desert transportation as the lieutenant at Safaniya, and by fall, after El Alamein, the boys breathed easier. From that time on, the behavior of the lieutenant could become a cause for laughter rather than rage; it is easy to forgive people when you know a whole lot more than they do.

The Casoc people knew plenty. In fact, they were probably the best set of teachers the Saudi Arabs could have found. And their teaching took. Don Mair, who had left Sun Yat-sen's China and gone building radio stations around the world, came over to Dhahran when he had the Jiddah-Dhahran circuit improved, and one day when out in the desert with a Saudi driver he broke a pulley in his water pump. There was no way of fixing it except with a new part. Mair sat down to wait for help, while the driver stuck the broken pulley in his pocket and went over to visit a Bedouin camp a few hundred yards away. It grew late. Eventually the driver returned. He had whittled a facsimile pulley out of the hardwood of a jack block. With a little scraping, it fitted. It worked, too. It took them into camp. That was an Arab who five years before had never looked inside a hood.

In the late war years the tinkerers and gadgeteers went to such wild extremes in an attempt to keep everything running that it got funny. Mr. Fixit or his Saudi brother, it made no difference.

Either one of them could plug a leaky radiator with old date pulp, or manufacture a part out of whatever was lying around. Phil McConnell, a great hand with a guitar and a bunkhouse song, put the whole thing into a ballad he called "Car 405."

Earlier, someone had suggested sending on camel caravans anything that could be divided into small enough parcels. It would save their cars and trucks and it would offer a few riyals to the Bedouins, who were pinched by wartime shrinkage in the economy and by severe cold and drought. They called their impromptu camel corps the Khamis Transportation Company in honor of Khamis ibn Rimthan, who acted as agent to the Bedouins. It never worked impeccably, and it cost the company at least as much, and perhaps twice as much, as automotive hauling would have, but it did make good public relations by distributing needed wages among many Arab families; and at its height it moved a considerable tonnage.

During the drilling of the al-Jauf wildcat (a dry hole) in 1944, everything except the rig and the drill pipe was sent out by camel. Some of the stuff went by dhow to what is now Safaniya, and thence by caravan; some of it went all the way in caravans of from 700 to 1,000 snarling, complaining, sneering, indefatigable, patient, and enduring beasts.

One of their first jobs, in the late summer of 1942, was the transportation of drilling mud, cement, lubricating oil, and other supplies from al-Khobar to Abqaiq, where one of their worn-out strings of tools was drilling a new well to help establish more clearly the outline and extent of the field. The plan of Cal Ross and Floyd Meeker, who had charge of the haul, was to keep about 75 camels busy on a regular schedule over the two-day route. Khamis had made arrangements, with some difficulty, for between 50 and 100 camels and their drivers. On the appointed morning, about 500 showed up.

Well, make the best of it; instead of a systematic schedule, divide the total load and send it all at once. (And what a hell of a row, said Phil McConnell, recording it in his journal, when those sacks were being loaded.) The company people, a little skeptical of the experiment, and afraid that many sacks would be broken, had to admit that in that regard the experiment was a complete success – hardly any breakage at all.

But it was sometimes like breaking a cat to harness to get a Bedouin to do the full job. He was very sharp in a deal, and good at cutting corners. At al-Khobar, Ross and Khamis had a group hauling barite from the pier to the storage yard. There was a limited amount of barite and a large number of Bedouins, and in the competition for loads, some men seemed to complete a trip and get back for another load in a remarkably short time. Khamis, a Bedouin himself, began to smell a rat. Following some of the speedsters, he and Ross discovered out among the dunes about a mile from the pier a considerable cache of barite under careful guard. The stuff was perfectly safe, and, by Bedouin reasoning, in good hands. They were just making sure that they got enough loads to make the thing worth their while, and after assuring themselves of that, they would haul the whole batch to the storage yard at their leisure.

Shortages and strains did not make any easier the task of training the Saudi Arabs in industrial techniques and an industrial attitude of mind. Sometimes the Arabs' innocent incomprehension and innocent complication of shortages drove them half wild. Jim Sutter, for instance, came during the buildup in 1944 and was first set to welding tanks at Ras Tanura. He had not been on the job more than a short time when he felt a tap on the shoulder. He raised his welding mask and looked. A smiling Arab worker stood there. It seemed he wanted a short section of four-inch pipe welded to a circular steel plate. Sutter obligingly lowered his helmet and welded the two together into a crude cup for him, and the man went away. But another came, and another, and still another, each with a section of pipe and a steel bottom plate. Sutter didn't know what the things were for, or who kept sending the men around, but he wanted to make a good impression on everybody, and to be agreeable. He was on his twenty-seventh little cup when the boss welder came around. Sutter explained that he hadn't got far with his tank welding because somebody kept sending around those pieces of pipe to be welded. What were they for, anyway? The boss welder made an examination and came back looking weary. "Son," he said, "you have spent the day making every Arab workman on the job a coffee mortar."

In the same category of exasperations was the telephone problem. All over the camp, in bunkhouses and cottages, the bells had the habit of ringing all the time, most often late at night, but when one picked up the receiver no voice would reply. One night Ohliger's patience gave out when he was called out of bed by the ringing of the telephone and found no one on the line. He hurled on his clothes and stormed down to the telephone office. Gavin Witherspoon and another outraged householder were there ahead of him. Voices of laughter came from inside, by the switchboard. Like detectives in a movie the three tiptoed in and peeked through the doorway. The switchboard operator was giving instructions to a group of his friends. Everybody was having a wonderful time pushing plugs in and out of holes. Until the irritated Americans broke it up, it was like a great punchboard or a game of tic-tac-toe.

And it was absolutely certain that after a little comic relief like the telephone incident, Ohliger would get up in the morning to discover that San Francisco wanted a new test well put down, refusing to acknowledge that every string of tools they had was worn out, and that for months they had been robbing parts off one to keep the others going. Or the Amir Ibn Madi of al-Khobar would request tires to make a trip to Riyadh. Or someone would come in to say that they were out of office supplies, typing paper, toilet paper, carbon paper, a certain size of bushings. Or the government would call and want to discuss another loan. Or a complaint would come from al-Khobar, which the company had surveyed and laid out as a model modern town, that some ambitious shopkeeper had conformed to ancient practice and set up his shop in the middle of the street.

The best time of all had been the frontier time, and the war returned the Hundred Men to the frontier. For nearly four years they went back to making do, improvising, doing without, building things out of nothing. Some things were easier than others, some were hard indeed. It was one thing to cobble industrial equipment, or even to do without it. It was another to do without fresh meat, and still another to do without mail. In both these last their low point was the winter of 1942, before improvisation had built up either sources of meat supplies or routes of communication.

For meat they could on occasion fall back upon the country, as when at Thanksgiving 1942, a providentially heavy flight of southering ducks came down on the *sabkhas* near Qatif, and John Ames, Hank Trotter, and others of the Bunyans went out and bagged enough for a Thanksgiving dinner for all hands. But for mail there was no substitute. For weeks on end no ships came in, which meant that mail could neither go nor come. With the wartime demand on the service, cables took an endless time. Men traveling to or from the States, beating their way by whatever route they could find, were sometimes on the road for as much as 110 days – nearly four months. And when Christmas drew near, and there had been no word from home for weeks, and no fresh meat for nearly as long, spirits drooped and some asked themselves what they were doing there.

Floyd Ohliger's announcement that there would be a Christmas Eve party at the club cheered them some, but not much. Same old faces, same old pretending to a cheerfulness none of them felt. Even when several carloads of hunters went out into the desert and came back with meat for Christmas dinner, their flagging enthusiasm for Arabia was not notably revived. But they went on over to the club – what else was there to do on Christmas Eve? – and there was Floyd Ohliger dressed up as Santa Claus, standing by a mock Christmas tree and trying to cheer people up by reading them phony messages and greetings from their wives and children at home.

They sat there and listened politely for quite a while before it began to seep through to them that the greetings had an intimate and authentic sound, and it was even longer before they fully accepted the truth: that Socal had rounded up all the dependents it could locate and collected their greetings and sent them on from San Francisco as a Christmas present to Dhahran. It had also sent a film, made at the suggestion of Esta Eltiste, that showed a good many of the wives and children at home. Not even the ones who had no wives and children, or whose wives and children had been missed by the camera, could resist that. There was not a dry eye in the place. They cursed Ohliger and Willie Jones, acting as his secretary, for their successful secrecy, and they would not for a thousand dollars have had Ohliger and Jones do it any other way.

One thing they had plenty of, no matter how long the war dragged on and no matter how many months passed between the freighters that brought them their long-delayed supplies and mail. Their plenty was Brussels sprouts and shredded wheat, of which Les Snyder, looking backward, insists they had a 125-year supply. They felt that, in Steve Furman's commissary, there must be whole warehouses stacked to the ceiling with cans of Brussels sprouts. They ate Brussels sprouts in every form that imagination could suggest and necessity demand, as soup, as salad, as stew, as garnishment for a dozen different things. They complained bitterly that they had been served Brussels sprouts waffles.

But of other things, especially fresh meat, they were lamentably short, and both Arabs and Americans were meat eaters. No refrigerated meat reached them from Australia or Denmark or the United States or South America; no vegetables except the pallid contents of cans passed their teeth for a long time. So, as they were forced to do in other matters, the Hundred Men decided to produce their own; in doing so they created Sewage Acres and the Animal Farm and gave Steve Furman his finest hour. The effluent from the sewage disposal plant at Dhahran ran down into low ground out toward the al-Khobar road, and had created there a patch of vivid green. It was no problem whatever to level, plow, seed, and irrigate it; it was their collective Victory Garden, the apple of their eye. They were making the desert blossom as the rose and fulfilling the buried desire of at least every western American among them. They planted onions, carrots, tomatoes, lima beans, peas, cucumbers, sweet corn, all the varieties of the weekend gardener.

Dr. Alexander gave them a little trouble – he wouldn't permit them to plant melons, for instance, because however healthful they might be inside the rind, they could be polluted in the handling. He also permitted carrots and onions only on the promise that they would always be eaten cooked, and he insisted that tomatoes, cucumbers, peas, and lima beans be supported and kept off the ground. With these limitations, they had the vegetable problem whipped within the first war year, and they kept a steady rotation of crops growing green in Sewage Acres until long after the war. Charlie Davis even tried hydroponics, and there was a night when he entertained and served proudly up to each guest, as a salad, a single air-grown leaf of lettuce.

But it was stock farming that really excited their full effort. Steve Furman, especially, was a frustrated farmer; he must have yearned all his life, without perhaps being aware of it, for the chance to run a ranch. Now, almost from the time he arrived in January 1940, he had it – and what a ranch, a ranch that made the King Ranch and the Matador and the 76 look like backyard goat pastures. He had all of Arabia to grow meat in, and he used a good bit of it. Running the Animal Farm was pure satisfaction; he was bitterly disappointed when they closed it down in 1947 and made him a wholesale grocer again.

He bought rabbits in Hofuf, chickens and pigeons in Qatif and Hofuf, local cattle, sheep, goats, and camels where he could get them, and he started building up flocks and herds like Abraham.

The stock of every sort which he got was adapted to the climate and forage conditions of Arabia, which meant that none of it was very toothsome to people brought up on the best meat in the world. So Furman began to tinker with the genetic composition of Arabian livestock. He had his henchmen gather up eggs from here and there, and he got George Vivian, the carpenter foreman, and "Goodie" Goodwin, the head electrician, to build an incubator, feeling that if he could raise up his own chickens from the shell they might have a little more meat on their bones.

The Arab farmers from al-Khobar, Qatif, and Dammam – where today there is a thriving poultry industry – seeing the eggs put in the incubator, did not believe what the Americans told them. The news spread like wildfire that the crazy Americans were building a machine to make chickens. They had accepted the idea of building machines to do men's work, but fooling around with the reproduction of life – which they understood – that was something else! It was a trick of some kind; the eggs would assuredly not hatch. When they did hatch, the farmers were astonished, but not convinced. Somebody had slipped the chickens in and the eggs out. They watched the next batch very carefully, counting the nineteen to twenty-one days that Furman said would be necessary. On the nineteenth day they were full of laughter and jeers; there lay the eggs which, carefully watched to avoid trickery, were obviously not hatchable. While they were laughing, the first chick pipped his shell. Old Habib, headman at the farm, had been at the commissary at seven in the morning on that nineteenth day, and actually sat in front of the incubator for four hours until the first egg pipped. He couldn't believe it. It was the work of jinns.

Furman was inclined to give them more miracles than that. He selected the biggest roosters and the biggest hens he could find, put them together in the chicken yard, and collected the eggs for incubation to start improving the breed. Depressed by the way Arabian sheep stored fat in their tails, as a camel does in his hump, he cut the tails off some of them to see if he couldn't make them put a little more on their ribs. He himself had to do this. The Arab helpers wouldn't have done it if he had ordered them to. The sheep, they said, would die. They didn't. They got fat. Furman had to cut the tails off perhaps 200 sheep before he was able to persuade a young Arab to learn the trick and take over the job. But probably the most dreadful thing that Furman did, in the eyes of his assistants, was to start castrating the bull calves. Cutting off sheep's tails was one thing, but taking the manhood from a male animal was something that the Saudi men, admirers of masculinity, wanted no part of.

Camels were no problem – veal camels could be bought eight or ten at a time whenever the needs of the Saudi employees' camp called for them. Sheep likewise, though with their tails cut they might make better mutton chops. The rabbits, the pigeons, and the chickens multiplied. At the peak, toward the end of the war, Furman had 2,000 pigeons, 500 rabbits, and 6,000 chickens at the Animal Farm down near Sewage Acres. Out in the desert he had flocks totaling 5,000 sheep, of which they brought in about 500 at a time to the farm feed lots for fattening and slaughtering. At that same peak period he had 1,200 cattle, part dairy and part beef. It was these that caused him the most trouble and gave him the greatest satisfaction.

Arabia is not cattle country. The Bedouins depend on camels for both milk and meat, as well as for transport, and find their fat-tailed sheep and their long-eared goats better adapted to the desert than cows. Only around the oases were there a few scrubby cattle for Furman to start with. But an old Bedouin named Mutlag, who came from somewhere down south of Riyadh, offered to bring a herd up from Yemen in the winter of 1941–42. Mutlag was an old man, desiccated and wrinkled and tough – leather on bone. For a helper he had a half-grown boy. The drive he proposed so calmly was something that would have scared a Chisholm or a Goodnight – well over a thousand miles, around the edge of the most terrible desert in the entire world and catercorner across the whole Arabian Peninsula.

It did not sound plausible that Mutlag would get any cattle through, but Furman was perfectly willing to buy them if he could. Besides, Mutlag tickled him. He was a little like the Old Man of Hisy, and he came from the same part of the country. Furman wrote up a short agreement and Tom Barger translated it into Arabic for Mutlag to sign. But when Mutlag finally realized the nature of the document, he became indignant, and perhaps he had every reason to be: after all, he was a Bedouin, and his word had been given. They never tried a contract on Mutlag again.

Mutlag started in January from the mountains of Yemen. By slow stages he and the boy brought their herd up along the Tuwaiq Mountains past Sulaiyl and Layla, moving from well to well and from patch to patch of forage where the desert lived. From the mountains, after many weeks, he broke eastward and struck the oasis at al-Kharj, watered by great flowing wells like rivers bursting from underground, and from al-Kharj he made a hard dry crossing to Haradh, and from Haradh to Hofuf. The last leg, from Hofuf up, was actually the hardest and driest part of the trip, and Mutlag's cattle, like himself, were bones held together by hide when he brought them in. Still he had brought them. He and his boy, alone and on foot, had done something that might have elicited the respect of the men who made the drives up from Texas that stocked America's northern plains.

Next year, while some of his first herd contentedly ate alfalfa and bore calves and gave milk and grew fat, and Steve Furman's farmhands tried their best to keep a few of them through that lean wartime winter as the nucleus of a breeding herd, old Mutlag and his boy went down and did it again. In 1943–44, for some reason, he did not appear – perhaps he was living on his riches down somewhere in the southern Najd. Furman had to bring in cattle from Iraq to keep his herd up to a size conforming to the size of his market.

Even if Mutlag and Iraq had been able to supply indefinite numbers of cattle, Steve Furman would have been a long way from satisfied. He had no more respect for the unmodified Arabian or Yemenite or Iraqi steer, which would run about 350 pounds on the hoof, than he had for the Arabian sheep before surgery. He set out to improve this breed also. Because every country on the Gulf had export restrictions, and because the job of explaining would have been totally impossible, he paid a dhow captain to smuggle in the biggest bull he could find in Iraq, and when the stevedores unloaded him at al-Khobar, Steve led him up to the Animal Farm and put him to work.

In the fall of 1944 Mutlag was back, ready to take on his 1,000-mile cattle drive for the third time. But that winter was very dry. No rains fell, the seeds lay unsprouted in the sand, the desert slept, many of the water holes were dry. When Mutlag, who had started from Yemen with over 200 head, struggled into al-Kharj with the hardest third of his drive still ahead of him, dozens of his cattle were dead on the road. The rest were walking skeletons.

From al-Kharj, Burt Beverly and the other engineers who were assisting the government in its big new agricultural development radioed Dhahran that if Furman wanted any live cattle he had better haul them the rest of the way by truck. He did, those of them that were still alive when the supply trucks got there to pick them up. Only twenty or thirty cattle, about one in ten, made it all the way to Dhahran, and Mutlag, betrayed like many another gambling rancher by the chances of the weather, was so broken up he didn't come in for months to collect what little he had coming for his labor. When he did, he brought Furman a small rug. Asked the reason for the gift, Mutlag replied that Furman had been very good about not talking, and had not shamed Mutlag about the failure of the expedition.

By then, early summer of 1944, Furman didn't actually need Mutlag any more. His Iraqi bull was making almost as many changes in bovine Arabia as Casoc had made in its industry.

Instead of 350-pound steers, they were beginning to get some 1,000-pound ones. They had a dairy herd of thirty-five that was supplying milk for the whole camp, and they were getting thirty-five to fifty calves a month from the breeding stock. By the time Furman had his dairy herd developed, however, they were so short of everything else that there was no glass tubing for a pasteurization unit. At first they pasteurized milk in the autoclave at the hospital; later they built a tinkerers' contraption with a stock pot, an agitator, and a thermometer, and did their pasteurizing in the mess hall kitchen.

There was evidence that the wartime mousetrap they built was appreciated. Their only regular communication with the world was by means of the flights that the Persian Gulf Command flew between Basra and Karachi. The regular landing place was Bahrain, and only special flights were supposed to bring planes to Saudi Arabia, but it was remarkable how often the pilots on those flights found it essential, for mechanical or other reasons, to come down on the makeshift landing strip at Dhahran, and when they did, how infallibly they found their way to wherever they could lay hands on a glass of cold, pasteurized milk.

Chapter Fourteen
~ *The Frontier Closes* ~

Sometimes, when the war went badly (as when Rommel took Tobruk in Libya and seemed to threaten their very gates), or when they were oppressed by loneliness, discomfort, and irritation at being asked every day to do the impossible, they wondered why they stuck. The pay was good, but not that good. Even with the bonus of 30 percent for married men, 20 percent for single men, that went into effect on January 1, 1941, it was not so good they should risk their lives for it, or leave their dependents in the States uncared for. And ingenuity could find ways of getting back home if it wanted to. On leaves or on business some of them got home around the Cape of Good Hope, or across Arabia and down the Nile to Cairo, or direct to Cairo by B.O.A.C., and from there out by ship or plane, or down to Bombay and across the Pacific. But most of them stayed with the job, though the contracts of 85 percent of them were up by the spring of 1942; and most of those who went out on leave came back again to renew their assault on the impossible.

Oil production stayed up to the maximum they could handle, and above it; their 12,000 to 15,000 barrels a day went down to al-Khobar and Aziziyah and then by Ike Smith's and Hank Trotter's barges across to the Bahrain refinery. They kept Arabian oil feeding the Allied war effort, and that was one reason for their staying. But there was another that many of them could not have articulated and that some of them would not have admitted. They were, in a way, missionaries, missionaries of what they would vaguely describe, at a time when the phrase was still hallowed, as the American way of life.

Such an economist as John Kenneth Galbraith, with whom they would not have been in general sympathy, would probably have called their way of life something like a faith in production, the belief that production in and of itself is a good from which all other goods can flow, that from production come economic security and a high standard of living, the uncomplicated conviction that old Salim, the Awamiri who had never in his life needed more than a camel, a woman, and a smooth piece of sand, would be a happier man for having learned to also like oranges, castor oil, and a Ford pickup.

For the Hundred Men it was a natural assumption – in the 1940s there was little need for a Commission on National Goals – and the Saudis certainly didn't seem to object. Already, within less than ten years, Saudi Arabia had learned to be dependent to an almost alarming extent upon the income from oil; already the nation's wants had proliferated under American example.

For every reason – enlightened self-interest, the logical desire to keep the Arab world friendly to the Allies, a shrewd forecasting of the future, even the impulse of disinterested philanthropy – the company found itself involved in welfare activities that must have astonished its stateside directors. These were largely forced upon it by circumstances and by the enthusiasm of the men who collectively were known as "the Field," but it accepted them with surprising equanimity, perhaps comforted by the fact that though they were welfare activities they were at least private enterprise, and hence more acceptable both to oilman and to Arab. Perhaps too, the experience of Arabia had helped some members of the company to look upon the modern corporation in a philosophic light, to accept the view of it that would later be formulated by Adolph Berle.

If the modern corporation was indeed, as Berle suggested in *The Twentieth Century Capitalist Revolution*, almost in the position that the church occupied when St. Augustine wrote *The City of God*, then it was not only entitled to the loyalty and dedication of its employees, but was obligated to a degree of paternal care of those it embraced in its operations. In any case, Casoc during the war years found itself devoting an increasing amount of its skill, manpower, and equipment to a sort of private Point Four program for Arabia, long before there was a Point Four program in Washington.

Tom Barger, for example, newly installed in his government relations job in the fall of 1941, found himself showered with requests: water tanks for the roof of a palace in Riyadh, electric refrigerators, truck axles, Kohler light plants, door locks, three cans of talcum powder, medicine prescribed by an Indian doctor in the interior, even facilities of all kinds for a picnic the Shaikh of Bahrain and the King were planning in al-Khobar.

Who, after all, understood these matters better than the company? Who was nearer at hand? When a Hijaz firm which had ordered 300 Fords for the government unloaded them early in the war at the al-Khobar pier, they were found to be characteristically short a number of items, including extra tires and about 200 hubcaps, and to have been in addition badly mauled by foul weather at sea. What more natural than that the company should be asked to supply the hubcaps and the tires and to repair the damages? Barger's first lessons were in all the firm ways of saying no. His next were in all the devious means of finagling, ordering, or creating out of thin air as many as possible of the things the government needed.

Repairs were always a problem. Every government car or truck that limped into Dhahran with its radiator full of alkali or its head cracked or its fan belt gone or its fuel pump conked out or sand in its carburetor or its wheel bearings grinding themselves to bits or its axles broken – and when they limped in they limped in, characteristically, not by ones but by caravans – came with touching dependence to the company shops. There nameless heroes, Arab and American, crawled in suffocating heat underneath the wrecks, and labored and twisted and dismantled and rebuilt and replaced while every fly in the Eastern Province, waiting for just that time when a man's hands were full of tools or grease and his face trickling with sweat, gathered and crawled and stuck all over lips and nose and eyelids. The mechanics might, for service above and beyond the call of duty, have received gold medals.

And there were the constant invitations to supply a government, oblivious to the fact that even production had its limits during a war, with cars or trucks or, most particularly, with tires. Those requests *had* to be evaded, for if Casoc's limited production were halted for lack of essential equipment, the company would have been finished and the government's royalties would have stopped dead. Ohliger and Barger and McConnell and the rest could not blame the government officials for asking, but they could rarely afford to grant what they asked, for tires and parts were not merely indispensable, they were priceless.

A tire, by 1942, cost 1,500 rupees on the black market – about what a secondhand car had cost before the war – and could only infrequently be had at any price. Shipments of new ones were at best improbable, at worst visionary. The few tires hoarded in the company warehouses had to be kept for absolute emergencies. Nevertheless, as things worked out, about half of them were gradually sold to the government in response to frantic pleas, and the company struggled along on half a pittance.

Their Point Four aid went far beyond these relatively minor automotive services. From the very beginning of its investment in Arabia, the company had found itself forced by continual government financial distress to act as banker. By the end of 1940 it had advanced in loans or contracted services a total of more than $5,500,000. That took some faith, but was actually entirely justified as a business gamble. More philanthropic were some other activities. Already, long before the war, Casoc men had drilled and turned over to the Saudi Arabs a number of water wells. Their missionary zeal made them fall in enthusiastically with reclamation and conservation plans, made them eager to help the Arabs save, or put to better use, the little water they had. In particular, it led them into active and continued cooperation with the al-Kharj oasis project that was a dream of Shaikh Abdullah Sulaiman.

In 1941 Tom Barger and Les Snyder made a trip out to al-Kharj, southeast of Riyadh, to inspect the great pond-like springs that burst from the ground, and to estimate the possibility of leading them by a system of canals and pumps to potential gardens of reclaimable land. Snyder wrote the first report on those possibilities, which involved not merely the engineering project itself but a considerable task of training the Arabs of the area in forms of agriculture quite new to them.

In June 1942, Karl Twitchell, who had promised the King all the help he could arrange, returned to Saudi Arabia with a two-man American agricultural mission. The Casoc people took in the wayfarers, cured their quickly caught Arabian ailments, and advised them against making the eighty-day tour across southern Arabia that their hosts were proposing; they could not have stood the hospitality, even if they had been able to withstand the mid-summer heat along the edge of the Rub' al-Khali. Casoc advised a shorter and more northerly tour, but contributed much enthusiasm to the project of examining Arabia's agricultural possibilities. Predominantly from the western United States, the Hundred Men responded to a reclamation dream as kindling responds to fire.

Thereafter, through the war and later, but especially during the years 1942–44, Casoc was virtually the Saudi Arab government's Reclamation Bureau. It assisted in getting a high wartime priority for pumps and other vital equipment, it helped the government obtain allotments of supplies from the wartime Middle East Supply Center, it helped survey the canal route, it supervised the installation of diesel pumps. Altogether it looked upon al-Kharj as one of the most valuable contributions it was making to Arabia, because this agricultural development helped make use of renewable resources, not expendable ones; this could be part of a permanently new Arabia, and to their brand of missionary spirit, this was the kind of change that counted.

Considering the welfare of the Saudi Arabs, and finding their own human compassion reinforced by enlightened self-interest, the Casoc men could not ignore the state of public health. Disease was a multiplex misery to the Arab people, and it also resulted in all sorts of inefficiency in the company's own operations. During the war years, in spite of every sort of shortage, they made their first large strides in controlling some of the worst Arab ills, and in improving the rude public health measures.

Dr. Alexander, for example, in addition to keeping the Hundred Men and all the company's Saudi Arab, Bahraini, and Indian employees healthy, and in addition to treating scores and hundreds of Arabs who had no claim upon the company's facilities beyond the fact that they were sick or hurt, worked like a mule to rid Dammam and al-Khobar of malaria. DDT, a wartime discovery which, in that pre-pollution-conscious era, was still being hailed as one of the great advances in medical history, was not to be known in civilian centers until well after the war, and would not have been available in any case.

All Alexander could do was to enlist the cooperation of the local amirs and have them order all waterpots dumped and dried once a week. Since it took eight to ten days, in the hottest weather, for development of mosquitoes from the egg, that one single act, if religiously carried out, could help a great deal. But even that one simple act involved tedious labor. Every Wednesday morning,

Plate IX

Leaning against the left-hand post, the irascible Jack Schloessin watches the spudder at work. Dhahran - 1935 ~ *FD*

An early well sputters the promise of oil, only to go dry.
Dhahran - 1937 ~ *SAW/P*

Plate X

A first-generation Saudi oil driller surrounded by drilling mud porters.
Dhahran - circa 1936 ~ *FD*

Plate XI

King Abdul Aziz ibn Saud in the desert prior to his arrival in Ras Tanura. 1939 ~ *LS*

Inspecting the oil storage facility ~ *TCB*

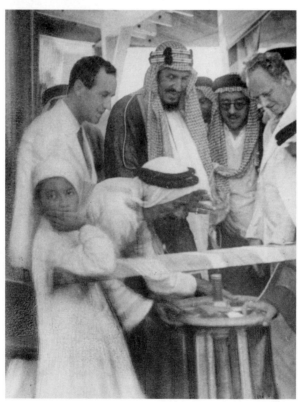

Loading of the first tanker, *D. G. Scofield*, at Ras Tanura. L-r: A.S. Russell (Standard of California), HM Ibn Saud, Mohammed Ali Reza, Floyd Oligher (Casoc). Foreground: unknown young prince, Shaikh Abdullah Sulaiman (Finance Minister). May 1, 1939 ~ *TCB*

Plate XII

July 8th, 1939, Dammam #12 explodes and a Saudi and an American perish. Within the hour the derrick will fall. These photos from rare 8-mm. movies document the struggle to extinguish the fire. ~ *TCB & LS*

Plate XIII

Discovery Well #7 to the left. Dhahran - 1939 ~ *TCB*

"Tea Kettle" refinery and oil storage tanks. Ras Tanura - 1939 ~ *FD*

In either direction it's a long way home. Dhahran - 1940 ~ *LS*

Plate XIV

Italian dinner. L-R: Esta and Bill Eltiste, Jean Corcoran, Lloyd Hamilton, Oliver Boone, Jack Ham, Frank Morrison, Babe Dreyfus.
Dhahran - 1939 ~ *FD*

Casoc housewife - 1938 ~ *FD*

Florence Steineke, Maxine and the younger Marian. 1938 ~ *TCB*

The nurse Molly Brogan, center, at a beach party. Half Moon Bay - 1939 ~*LS*

Plate XV

On October 19, 1940, the Italians bomb Dhahran; the hospital and well heads are sandbagged. By Christmas Eve most of the families have left. Johnny Thomas on accordion, Steve Furman on guitar. ~ *LS (above) & SF*

Plate XVI

The renowned desert guide Khamis bin Rimthan, at left, with two friends.
Wadi Dawasir - 1940 ~ *TCB*

Steve Furman
1942 ~ *SF*

Doc Alexander
1941 ~ *FD*

John Ames at
Abu Hadriya. 1940 ~ *SF*

To supply the drilling of the first well at Abqaiq, Khamis organized a
massive camel caravan. Dhahran - 1941 ~ *LS*

Alexander had to go and inspect a half to three-quarters of al-Khobar to see that householders had turned their waterpots upside down. Every Wednesday afternoon he went through Dammam on the same errand.

It was the merest beginning. The virtual elimination of malaria, and the partial control of bilharziasis, amoebiasis, trachoma, tuberculosis, malnutrition, smallpox, and all the intestinal parasites so common to the undeveloped areas of the world thirty years ago, would be achieved, at least in the area around Dhahran, in the years following the war.

But even the beginnings, however rudimentary and however important, were not always understood by those they benefited. Khamis ibn Rimthan, for instance, exceptional as he was, could never quite swallow the tale that malaria came from the mosquito, and if Khamis found it dubious, others would have found it completely absurd.

Without teachers except Indian male nurses up to 1938, and with only two American nurses during the war years (the later ones were Carroll Fitzpatrick and Ruby Bohlman), Alexander began to build up a corps of Saudi Arab orderlies and assistants, and through them to make a beachhead for modern medicine among a people more afflicted, probably, than any except the Egyptians, and with almost no medical lore of their own except the practice of cauterizing wounds.

These were also the years when, with the future in mind and with the shortages of the present to combat, the company made its first extended, long-term plans for the educating of Saudi Arabs for industrial jobs. On May 11, 1940, the first company school for Saudi Arabs began in al-Khobar in a boxlike, barred-window house rented from Hajji bin Jassim. The company furnished tables, benches, blackboards, chalk, lamps, and instructor, and offered to teach English to any Saudi, whether employee or townsman. It began teaching nineteen students; very shortly it was teaching fifty. That meant a second instructor, and in less than a year a new school building – a *barasti* built near the government wireless station to utilize the generator there for electric lights.

The al-Khobar school had been in operation less than two months when a second was opened, this one near the Saudi living quarters. It too was open to employees and any interested nonemployees. The first night there were 85 students, within a few weeks 165.

In January 1941, it was discovered that houseboys, waiters, telephone operators, and office boys had working schedules that prevented their attending the regular classes. A third *barasti* was built for them and called the Jabal School. It was soon instructing 110 pupils.

The dynamic statistics of growth are always heartening, but in those days they were more than that. They were explosive, for here education was being built from the absolute foundations. Unlike today, when education is rapidly closing in on illiteracy, there was not in 1941 another school in the modern sense in all of al-Hasa, not another place where Saudi Arab, child or adult, could learn anything except the folk skills of his culture. Casoc began by trying to teach only basic English, but it found that in order to teach English it had also to teach Arabic, for most of these pupils were wholly illiterate in their own tongue. Later it added arithmetic, and still later, in connection with the first-aid program, a little rudimentary anatomy.

Necessarily things went slowly, especially in the early years when trained and competent teachers were nearly impossible to find. And yet this was the germ of something momentous, for these first 300-odd pupils in the three schools near Dhahran were the first stage of a company training program that in later years expanded prodigiously and that stimulated the formation of government schools both in al-Hasa and in other parts of Arabia. Some of the boys staring at the wonderful mysteries of letters and numbers on the blackboard of a *barasti* school would end up as skilled and supervisory personnel, and a few would attend, as company scholars, the American University in Beirut. Some of them would also, by a law as inexorable as the law of falling bodies, be among the first to feel the restless pangs of people moving beyond their own culture yet not entirely part of another.

There was a new force in those eager youngsters responding to opportunity in the form of the 850 essential English words, and there was already enough occasional labor difficulty to make it clear to the Hundred Men that the force would not make the company's position in Arabia any easier. Yet no one hesitated; this was part of their missionary effort, part of the contribution Americans tended to make wherever they went, whatever the implications. They would have said, as Phil McConnell said to his journal, that they were building something new in the history of the world: not an empire made for plundering by the intruding power, but a modern nation in which American and Arab could work out fair contracts, produce in partnership, and profit mutually by their association. Gradually, McConnell wrote, Casoc was teaching some of the functions of modern man. In theory, it would sometime get repaid for its teaching, but if it did not, "the Field" at least would not complain. It could look at the wells and the reclamation projects, the roads, the schools, the improvements in public health, and feel good enough simply to have had a hand in it.

Quite outside of the intentional, deliberate training and assistance offered, there were subtler but not less significant changes. It is hard for a man who has spent ten years or so of his life drilling holes in a desert, living in a bunkhouse or a prefabricated cottage, and learning to get along with foreign people to realize the ways in which his daily actions contribute to the mighty pressures that raise or lower nations and empires and great segments of the world's people. Dropped abruptly into the heart of strangeness, he will be preoccupied by its odd look; he will be likely to look at what is near and concrete and under his nose rather than speculate on its importance to world affairs.

The average Casoc pioneer, transplanting his American practicality and his engineering know-how to a then completely unmechanized country, was geared to the performance of a particular job, and had little time to ponder his possible effect on the political and cultural balances. His cultural comments were likely to be on a level with Slim Williams' remark about Arabic script, in which some consonants are differentiated only by dots placed above or below the letters. "What a hell of an alphabet," said Slim Williams in his practical way, "for a country full of flies." Politically they were in one of two moods: in a dispute between the company and Saudi Arabia, they backed the company; in any dispute between Saudi Arabia and one of its neighbors, or between Ibn Saud and the British, they were good Saudis.

In a way, their first decade in it had made Saudi Arabia their second country. They were richer for it, as it was richer for them. While the statesmen and the generals, acutely aware of what power lay in the peoples and under the rock strata of the Middle East, struggled to steer it and couple it to their own side, and while the company pursued its commercial purposes as it could and its private Point Four as it must, and waited for the day when it would be released to go back to the simple problems of producing oil, it was the men in the field who had made the vital contacts.

So far as the Arabs of Hofuf or Dammam or al-Khobar or Jubail were concerned, any single American was America, was the West, was industrial civilization, and insofar as Arabs chose to retool themselves to fit into the industrial world, these were the models they knew. Without intending to be in any sense cultural ambassadors, the Casoc pioneers undoubtedly left reflections of themselves in Arab ways and upon Arab personalities that will persist a long while.

In more ways than oil royalties, Saudi Arabia was richer for their coming. The company had functioned, because it had to, like a whole battery of scientific and service bureaus. It had been Geological Survey, Hydrographic Survey, Corps of Engineers,

Reclamation Service, Department of Public Health, Highway Commission, Department of Education, Weather Bureau, Communications Commission, Bureau of Standards. In all of those capacities it had set patterns and established standards that were American in special ways. It had literally built America into the developing structure of Saudi Arabia's modern life, and everything from the gauges of nuts and bolts to the side of the road on which one drove was their doing.

Even the intangibles. Watch a Saudi Arab drive a car, and you perceive that he drives like the men who taught him. You can tell him from an Egyptian or a Lebanese as far as his car can be seen down the road. He drives using American-style traffic signals, he has acquired the American indisposition for a lot of useless horn-squawking, he has learned to vary his speed and stay in a lane instead of maintaining his speed and varying his lane as do the mad drivers of Lebanon, whose mentors were the French.

The concrete changes that ten years of company operations had made in Saudi Arabian life counted for much. The future was blueprinted in the maps and charts, the geological reports, the developed harbors, the hard-surfaced roads, the radio system that Don Mair enlarged and improved in 1939. It was made more secure by the water wells at Dammam, Qatif, Riyadh, Jiddah, and especially by the one they drilled at al-Hani, on the long waterless stretch between Riyadh and al-'Uqair, during the severe drought of 1943. It was enriched by the eleven-mile canal, the pumps, the irrigated acres of al-Kharj. And if the Arabs of Riyadh and al-Kharj at first looked with suspicion on carrots from the project, and fed them to their donkeys, that was both understandable and legitimate. Given time, they would learn to make use of carrots as of other modern inventions.

These things were vital, in the missionaries' eyes. And yet they had made a contribution more significant than any of the gadgets adopted by the Arabs or any of the skills and resources the Arabs had newly learned. They had begun a transformation of a state of mind. *Allah kareem*, God is kind, said the pious Bedouin when disaster struck, when his only camel died or wolves carried off his lambs, or when he dug a grave in the sand for someone of his family. He was not in the habit of trying to remodel his world closer to the heart's desire; the intense struggle for a mere subsistence in the desert left him no time or energy for more than survival.

Now, by importation and at wholesale, came not only new tools but a habit of mind new to him. God, it turned out when you studied the matter, *was* kind; but also, as the Americans said, He helped those who helped themselves.

All during the war, at erratic intervals, the world had been coming to see the Hundred Men, and they had joyfully taken time off to entertain, and pump, visitors. Their radios told them that the Gulf was a hotbed of activity, but they saw little of it. Dispensing nothing but crude oil, and that by barge, and having not even an adequate airfield, they were often bypassed. But they saw something of H.R.P. Dickson, the Political Agent at Kuwait – an old Arabian hand who flowed 10,000 barrels a day in stories and Arab lore, and who brought along a wife as rich in anecdote as he was himself.

They had visitations of other British from Bahrain and Jiddah. They entertained Ambassador Kirk from Cairo. On May 22, 1943, a Lockheed Lodestar alighted on their airstrip and the five crew members announced that General Patrick Hurley, President Roosevelt's personal representative in the Middle East, would be among them shortly. Mistrusting their airstrip, he had put his plane down on Bahrain and was coming over by launch. The Casoc boys, touched in their local pride, were somewhat pleased to find when the General got there that he and his party had taken a beating for three hours in a heavy sea.

General Hurley's visit was a high point, nevertheless. They did not get to know him at once, for immediately after his arrival Floyd Ohliger and Floyd Meeker took him off to Riyadh for an audience with Ibn Saud. His crew, left behind, were given the keys to al-Hasa, which meant principally an initiation into gogglefishing. This had been introduced to the Gulf by Charlie Davis, and the spear had been improved by the labors of at least five different engineers. In return for that pleasant excursion, the crew amiably took everybody for an airplane ride, and on one flight turned over the controls to Ibrahim, the twelve-year-old son of Shaikh Abdullah al-Fadl.

Ibrahim flew the plane from Tarut to Ras Tanura. He did not freeze to the wheel or get tangled up in his instructions. Though his feet would not touch the floor, he demonstrated how far some Saudi Arabs had already come under Casoc's tutelage, for with the sweat standing out on his face, he turned when Captain Newell told him to turn, pushed things or pulled things when he was supposed to. When they lifted him out of the plane back at Dhahran his feet still didn't touch. He walked around all the rest of the day without his feet touching.

Then when General Hurley's party had returned, and Abdullah Sulaiman gave a great dinner at Dammam, the Americans demonstrated a knack for public relations every bit as brilliant as the impression Hurley had made in Riyadh. Charlie Davis had prepared a certificate, with a pair of mother-of-pearl wings pinned on it, which said that Ibrahim was a qualified assistant copilot for the trip between Tarut and Ras Tanura when flying in a Lockheed Lodestar and accompanied by Captain Dean Newell. The entire plane crew and General Hurley signed it, and at the dinner Hurley presented it to Ibrahim in person.

It was a very American performance; it was a question who enjoyed it more, Ibrahim or the starved and isolated Hundred from Dhahran. When after dinner Hurley, who had been raised on an Oklahoma Indian reservation, demonstrated the Choctaw war whoop, and an Arab from Riyadh rose and responded with the war cry of that Najd fortress, it seemed to the dazzled Hundred that international relations could hardly be warmer.

International relations were precisely why Hurley was there. His visit was an omen and a forecast: the world was beginning to look upon their outpost with very interested eyes. With Africa secured, and with the Germans turned back in Russia, strategy could begin to contemplate massive offensives against the Japanese in Southeast Asia, and the logical source for fueling any such offensive was the Gulf. Leaving out all problems of transport, American reserves would not indefinitely stand the wartime drain of two billion barrels a year.

That was why, late in 1943, there arrived among the Hundred Men a mission from the Petroleum Reserves Corporation, which was part of the official structure built up by Harold Ickes, U.S. Secretary of the Interior, for supplying petroleum to the war effort. The mission demonstrated the seriousness of its interest by the eminence of its members, who were Everette Lee De Golyer, one of the most distinguished of the world's oil geologists; Dr. William E. Wrather, Director of the United States Geological Survey; and C. S. Snodgrass, Director of the Foreign Refining Division of the Petroleum Administration for War. The Hundred Men showed them around, and the mission went away like other missions. But within weeks this one developed portentous consequences.

It turned out that without publicizing his activities Mr. Ickes had been growing very interested indeed in the possibilities of making greater use of Middle Eastern oil. Now the United States government proposed to buy into Casoc and finance a big refinery at Ras Tanura and a more than thousand-mile pipeline to the Mediterranean, which since May 1943, when American and British forces captured Tunis and Bizerte, had become an Allied lake.

Government purchase of even a minority share in Casoc would have put the company in the position that Anglo-Iranian had occupied in Iran since 1914, when Winston Churchill concluded exactly the same sort of deal for His Majesty's government.

Commercial and political power would have been concentrated within the same corporate structure, with results for the Middle Eastern equilibrium of power that could hardly have been predicted and that would not have been likely to be good.

The Hundred Men, who had valued their purely private auspices and who had always felt that Ibn Saud's favor was conditioned by their lack of political implications, hotly debated all the news and rumor that came to them. It developed that American oil companies were protesting bitterly; a Senate investigating committee was holding hearings; a British oil mission was visiting the States. They waited, and eventually they heard: they were not to become part of a political package.

For better or worse, protest had diverted the first proposals, and the American government was not destined to come into the Middle East in the way His Majesty's government had. Instead, they heard that the pipeline notion, which would have saved the 3,300-mile haul around the peninsula and through Suez, and would have delivered oil to the eastern Mediterranean shore at approximately the cost of the per-barrel canal toll, was at least temporarily shelved. But they had approval, and a high government priority, for the construction, as a purely company operation, of a 50,000-barrel-per-day refinery at Ras Tanura.

That was the authority for a hysterical expansion; for building a Ras Tanura refinery not only meant all the boom of that construction, but entailed all the corollaries: sharply increased oil production, pipelines and stabilization plants and tank farms to handle and store it, people to perform the enlarged duties, housing to take care of the new people, people to build the housing, people to train the people who would build the housing.

Consequence bred consequence, and many of the things that had preoccupied them during their isolation would now go unnoticed. In the rush of becoming a colossus, they would hardly have time to laugh at the peculiar cultural effect of sending a certain left-handed carpenter to Ras Tanura to train a Saudi crew:

dutifully imitative, every last one of his trainees learned to saw with his left hand.

The buildup for the expansion of the Ras Tanura facilities marked the transition from Casoc's frontier period into the postwar period of enormous production and enormous growth and enormous consequences. Appropriately, it followed close upon an official change of name. After January 31, 1944, they were no longer Casoc. They were the Arabian American Oil Company, syncopated in the lingo to Aramco.

If the expansion of 1936 had struck some of them as a period of hectic confusion, this 1944 expansion struck them as bedlam. Their goal by the end of 1945, they were told from San Francisco, was 550,000 barrels a day, nearly twenty-five times what they were turning out now in their standby operation, and much more than the capacity of their existing wells. There would have to be a massive drilling program involving perhaps twenty strings of tools, and drilling that many oil wells meant developing adequate water supplies both at Abqaiq and at Qatif, where they had been instructed to put down a wildcat.

Of their three structure drills that might have been put to use for water wells, one was in Ras Tanura drilling test holes for Moore, the foundation experts looking over the refinery site. Another had been promised to Bapco for the purpose of drilling blasting holes for the foundation of its new refinery; it would be delivered as soon as the Aramco shops could rebuild its clutch. As for the new drilling machinery that in May would start coming from the States at the rate of 2,500 to 3,000 tons a month, it could not be unloaded because the big pier at Ras Tanura would not be done. The cargo would have to be lightered ashore by barge, and they had no barges. Eight were coming from the States, but of those, four would be needed for laying the pipeline to Bahrain to which they were committed. Four barges were not enough to bring the drilling equipment down to al-Khobar; the best they could do would be to unload it at Ras Tanura, where it would be in the way of the refinery construction job. So they would have to try to get barges from Basra or Abadan or from the Persian Gulf Command. And what about tugs to pull them? Well . . .

Boilers? They had five installed at Abu Hadriya and five at Abqaiq No. 5, plus nine that were available for other jobs. Two would be needed to start the small Ras Tanura refinery that had been shut down since 1941. Four would be needed at the Qatif wildcat and four at Abqaiq No. 6. That left them one short. All right, Abqaiq No. 6 would have to start on three boilers until Abqaiq No. 5 was completed and they could transfer a boiler from there. Meantime, there was the problem of firebrick for boiler settings, essential for drilling any new wells. They had not firebrick enough even for one setting, let alone all that they would require. So they would face their settings with red construction brick from India and hope for the best, and they would experiment with transit roofing, which would undoubtedly fold with the heat but which might stay in place if they gave it proper backing.

In the warehouse they had thirty truck tires left. Almost every engine they owned had a cracked cylinder head. For a year or more they had been juggling engines around, putting tractor engines in launches and compressor engines on pumps. Their gasoline was bad, and would remain bad until they could develop facilities for making a leaded product. For the influx of men expected at Ras Tanura they would need kitchens, mess halls, God knew what. In the teeth of the demands being made on them they didn't even have paper enough to issue announcements of general instructions, and their office memos were being written on the backs of old forms.

If they needed a welding machine to complete a well, they had to face a calculated choice: the machine was on the rock crusher that was preparing foundation material for houses that must be ready in less than sixty days for the advance guard of construction stiffs. But they needed to complete the well in order to increase production so as to fill the refinery tanks so that the oil line to Ras Tanura could be converted to a gas line during the drilling of the wildcat at Qatif. And if they didn't get the wildcat drilled in a hurry the refinery would run out of oil and the wildcat would be held up while the line was reconverted and 390,000 barrels of oil were pumped up to Ras Tanura.

That was the way it went. The machine shops were making spare parts of ten-dozen different kinds, most of them of such necessarily crude tolerances that breakdowns and wear were increased. They even made cylinder heads for tug diesels by welding together steel plates, with short sections of 5 9/16" drill pipe for valve cages.

On April 3, Phil McConnell, who as production manager had these problems on his hands day and night, recorded, amid pages of examples of inspired improvisation with used parts that could be recombined into working engines, the fact that they had obtained a few 13.50 x 20 tires, but that they were out of 9.00 x13s for the sedans and pickups. Their last resource was a few 9.00 x 15s, and 35 wheels to fit them, to which they could connect the cars as it became absolutely necessary. Also he noted that he was breaking up a drilling crew to provide extra men for the Ras Tanura rush, due to begin on April 20.

Three days after that entry, he recorded the arrival of Steve Bechtel and one of his construction assistants, Bob Conyes, whom Walt Miller brought over from Bahrain to talk over plans for the refinery which Bechtel McComb & Parsons (BMC) would build under contract for Aramco. That too was the beginning of something: up to now, Aramco had done its own construction work. From here on, and increasingly, it would contract out its heavy construction, generally to Bechtel; and from here on the Saudi Arab government, wanting some industrial job done, would have another string to its bow.

For the moment, all McConnell and the others felt was relief. Sreve Bechtel was obviously used to massive operations, and he was used to dealing with the agencies through which priorities and supplies must be obtained. Also he was, as McConnell noted, no "sharp pencil." He figured a job with enough margin to cover failures of supply; he talked in shiploads, not in tons, and he promised to help as he could with Aramco's own supply problems, notably that of barges for unloading freight. He also agreed with them that Aramco and Bechtel personnel should be housed and handled separately, and he promised to be guided by Aramco experience in matters of American-Arab relations. He spoke of fencing his construction stiffs into the Ras Tanura Peninsula, of permitting beer but not whiskey.

The Aramco government relations people breathed a little easier: the influx of a horde of construction workers careless of Arab sensibilities and ignorant of Arab pride and Arab culture could be rough – so rough that only the anticipated royalties from 350,000 barrels a day could justify it to the Saudi government.

As they more or less expected, nothing developed in the way it was supposed to develop. Through April and May and into June they moved heaven and earth trying to obtain barges that were lying idle in the river at Basra. They enlisted the Persian Gulf Command to help get them out of Piaforce, which controlled them. Piaforce replied that as far as it was concerned Aramco was just another civilian operation wanting favors. When it did finally release them, it released them to a Bahrain company with which Aramco had had nothing but trouble. Still, even in what the Hundred Men felt to be inept hands, they were better than no barges at all.

The first of the Americans expected for the Ras Tanura refinery job, variously estimated at 800 to 1,400, began to arrive – and began to depart again. At least one went back after taking one look: they shipped him out the morning after he arrived. Others stayed a few weeks, a few months. They did not seem to see in Arabia what the Hundred Men had seen; their complaints about housing conditions, food, lack of air conditioning, bad laundry service, and other things were frequently and generally justified. By June 13 they had assembled to the number of thirty-one. By that time too, Phil McConnell had entirely shut down the Abqaiq field after completing No. 5, and had diverted his entire drilling department to Ras Tanura. His new drillers and derrick men, recruited in the expectation of a big drilling program and a chance for advancement on the job, groused. The management people began to be seriously disturbed by sagging morale among the men. Meeting to consider speeches and announcements and instructions that might ease the period of adjustment, and to tell the newcomers something of Aramco's history and its relations with the Arabs and with the Saudi Arab government, they found themselves so short of paper that they couldn't even issue an instruction sheet. To cap it, Floyd Ohliger came back from Riyadh with the word that the King feared food riots unless some way of obtaining grains, and money, could be found in a hurry.

Then at the end of June the first ships began arriving at Ras Tanura, and with the help of three tugs that the U.S. Army sent over from Cairo, and the barges and tugs that Basra had released, they found that they could unload them at the rate of 600 to 700 tons per day. But that didn't help much, because they had only trucks enough to get about 400 tons away from the pier. The rest of it stacked up in their way, still desperately and tantalizingly needed, yet almost as unavailable as if it had been on the other side of the world.

In August, at a grand conclave to discuss their troubles, they made the sort of decision that gave them their peculiar capacity to get things done. The bunkhouse building was sixty days behind schedule, worse off than anything else, and basic to most of their effort. So the refinery closed down, the crews rigging up for new wells were transferred, the Bechtel men on the pier construction job were pulled off it, and they all tore into the building of bunkhouses.

By August 19 they were moving into the second completed bunkhouse, and the mess hall was open. Also they were beginning to get some trucks — not necessarily the right kind of trucks, or the most efficient for desert work, but welcome nevertheless. And they got new men in erratic bunches — sixty-nine of them on August 14. By that time the Bechtel men were sleeping eight or more to a bunkhouse room.

On the night of August 31 occurred the first of the kind of incidents the Aramco people had all been fearing: two Bechtel men, drunk enough to be adventurous, took a car and went into Dammam in the middle of the night to see what they could find in the way of entertainment. An Arab policeman found them touring the dark streets followed by a crowd of boys, and told them to go home. Surprisingly, they did. Next morning the company told them the same thing, and put visas into their hands.

On September 4 the camp received word that their ship No. 8 had been torpedoed and sunk. Immediately it began to seem that everything crucial, everything that had been totally and absolutely and excruciatingly necessary, had been on that boat. They were missing the oxygen plant, essential for welding, plus eighty-eight tons of kitchen equipment for the Arab mess hall. They were missing plywood, nine dump trucks with sand tires, large supplies of sodium hexamate phosphate.

More new men, and more going out almost as fast as they arrived. On September 21, Les Snyder estimated that 20 percent of those who had come in had already left. He knew of 255 altogether who were no longer with them. Those who remained had wretched conditions and inadequate food and practically no recreational facilities at all and incessant frustrations on the job.

The jukebox was busted, the ice cream machine didn't work, the management people complained that they were getting the dregs of the U.S. labor market, and the laborers complained that they had been sold down the river. Four crane operators quit in a single week and stopped all unloading on the Ras Tanura pier. There were all-day executive meetings. There were attempts to enlist a labor force from India, from Iraq. Workers from both places came in before there were facilities to care for them, and added their bit to the bedlam and their complaints to the sleepless nights of Aramco and Bechtel bosses. Several hundred Americans were waiting expensively in Cairo for transportation to bring them to Arabia.

On October 19, under Navy guard, Bill Burleigh supervised the unloading at Ras Tanura of 2,000,000 silver riyals, symbols of the growing needs of Saudi Arab life, from Boat No. 10. In November there came and went, almost unnoticed in the uproar, a pipeline mission interested in examining the route for a proposed Gulf-Mediterranean pipeline, now renewed as a company project without government participation. That, when it came to pass a few years later, would be the Trans-Arabian Pipe Line, known as Tapline, a subsidiary operation that would dwarf many whole industries. The day after that group, which included Lenahan and Hamilton, left Dhahran, Vic Stapleton came back from a visit to Eritrea with an optimistic report on the possibility of using interned Italian colonists as a short-term labor force.

Gradually, no one knew precisely how, things improved. Indians who had been striking because of the food situation settled down; the Iraqis proved to be good craftsmen; bunkhouses got built and cargo unloaded; new men came in and the discontented went out again and the others settled down to the jobs they had come to do. Someone fixed the jukebox and the ice cream machine. Outdoor movies flickered in the Ras Tanura evenings. McConnell's drilling department finally managed to spud in Qatif No. 1 and Abqaiq No. 6 by the middle of December.

They had upped their delivery of crude to the Bahrain refinery to 32,000 barrels a day. Their own teakettle refinery was running. Several miles of the Arabia-Bahrain pipeline had been laid, and with good weather they could push that ahead at the rate of 1,000 feet a day. At the end of the year their total strength was over 900 Americans, of whom somewhat more than 500 were Aramco, the rest BMC.

And in mid-December had arrived the first 88 Italians from Eritrea, hastily assembled and flown over to prepare a camp for 1,100 more. They were welcomed by the Saudi Arab government only because it had been assured that no qualified Saudis were available, and that Italians would be given no preference in any way over Saudi workers. That promise could be kept: the first Italians arrived during a rare rain storm in a camp that was bursting with a hundred other preoccupations and that had not been warned of their arrival. It was weeks before they had anything even primitively adequate in the way of shelter or mess halls.

Sometime during all this Dr. Alexander was upset to discover amoebic dysentery bugs in the stools – compulsorily supplied – of fifteen houseboys. Shortly thereafter he lost his first perturbation. One of the houseboys, for a slight fee, had been saving the others all that bother, and had been supplying sample stools for them all. The harried Hundred Men, swamped and overrun, made the most of that bit of comic relief.

They had been like the island outpost of an army – cut off, isolated, out of touch, holding out as they could and starved for word of how the war went elsewhere. But by the fall of 1944 there was no longer any doubt which way it was going; there was only doubt about how long it would take. Dhahran no longer felt like the end of the world. It saw increasing numbers of ships and planes, it got supplies and a flow of new people that grew rapidly to a flood, it received mail, it was in communication. And it began to be very impatient to see its wives, exiled to safety in the United States since 1941.

Floyd Ohliger, as general manager, was the appropriate man to make the suggestion that they start coming back. He had been in a position of great power and responsibility during all the war years, and had grown in it: he was a long way from the freckle-nosed boy who had landed at al-Khobar at the end of 1934, or the young husband, baffled by his first turkey-carving, that Phil McConnell had described in 1938. He had become a friend of kings and princes; indeed, Ibn Saud had often kidded Ohliger that he was going to find him a nice Bedouin girl for a second wife, and that he was sure Dorothy would not mind. Ohliger had also become a companion of generals, a consultant of governments, besides holding virtually single responsibility for emergency company action. So when he suggested to San Francisco that it was time the wives returned, or at least the wives of the people with the highest seniority, San Francisco listened, and agreed, and looked around to see what it could do.

In November 1944, seven Aramco wives in different parts of the United States got telephone calls asking if they could be ready to leave for Arabia within a week. They said no, of course not, but they were all in Philadelphia for Thanksgiving, just the same, and next day they were all at the dock for the sailing of the Portuguese ship that was to take them. They were Dorothy Ohliger, Esta Eltiste, Kathleen Barger, Gertrude McConnell, Roberta Scribner, Maye Beckley, and Marie Ross. Not all of them were "management" wives – Marie Ross and "Scribby" Scribner were the wives of foremen – but they were all wives of men with long service, and anyway the kind of thinking that would have made a distinction among them on the grounds of job or status had never applied on the Arabian frontier. Kathleen Barger and Maye Beckley, the only two of the seven with young children, had to leave them in the United States.

Their plan was simple and direct. This neutral ship would take them to Lisbon, where they would transfer to another Portuguese vessel bound for Haifa. From Haifa they would make their way, by air if possible, by land and sea if necessary, to Basra and Bahrain and thence "home." So self-confident were they that they dared Providence in the matter of luggage: Gertrude McConnell, for one, asked how much luggage she was allowed and was told she could take what she needed. She took not only her suitcase but a good large steamer trunk, its whole bottom full of her flat silver.

They went with lights blazing and the Portuguese flag prominently displayed to mark their neutrality, but they neither feared nor should have feared submarines at that stage of the war. Across the South Atlantic they were like seven schoolteachers on a cruise. They did not begrudge Kath Barger, the youngest and prettiest, the admiration she obviously inspired in a handsome young Spaniard; and if the sea roughened, or shipboard life began to grow tedious, they could always be roused into hilarity by one of Maye Beckley's lectures on what "we ladies" might or should or should not do.

Then at Lisbon fell a blow: the ship they had hoped would carry them to Haifa had gone somewhere else. They were like a truck in a *sabkha* – their wheels spun, they settled, there they were, embedded in Portugal. Gertrude McConnell put her trunk in bond at the customs house and they came ashore. In Estoril they lived in appalling luxury at the Palacio while they waited for someone to find them a ride to Arabia. The messages they sent to their husbands might or might not reach them (they didn't), but in the meantime the ladies might as well enjoy themselves. Enjoyment was made easier by the courtly attentions of another Spaniard, the uncle of the young man on the ship, who like his nephew fell hopelessly and gallantly in love with Kath Barger. He turned out to be the manager of a famous winery in Spain; their table was impeccable.

They had arrived early in December. Around their little neutral country the nations were locked in war, and though beyond the eastern end of the Mediterranean was an aura of relative peace toward which they were bound, there was no way to get across to it. On Christmas Eve, however, they had a flurry, and had their bags half packed, ready for instant departure: Dorothy Ohliger and Gertrude McConnell had a promise that they could hitchhike to Alexandria aboard a British military plane. From Alexandria it should be possible to get down to Jiddah, or to catch a plane across to the Gulf. But that hope too went glimmering: two wayfarers named Churchill and Eden came through on their way to try to settle the Greek civil war, and the plane that was to have taken the seven ladies flew away on sterner business.

They had been in Portugal nearly six weeks, and they as well as all associated with them were beginning to feel fairly desperate, when it appeared that the British government, which meant in these parts a set of very decent and lonesome British officers, would arrange to get the seven from Gibraltar to Alexandria if Thomas Cook & Son could get them to Gibraltar.

It was actually rather dangerous, but they said they did not care how dangerous it was, they wanted to get on to Arabia. Gertrude McConnell had already had to get her trunk out of bond, because six weeks in a luxury hotel had put a strain on her wardrobe. Now she bundled it aboard the train with the rest of their luggage and they went down to the southern tip of Portugal, under orders not to talk about where they were going. Feeling like smugglers or international spies, or perhaps like contraband, which is essentially what they were, they transferred secretly to a converted yacht, and that night they ran blacked-out and tense through what remained of the submarine blockade in the Straits and arrived in the morning safe inside the nets of Gibraltar.

The intention of the officers who had engineered their hegira from Portugal had been to put them aboard a French vessel commandeered by the British at Madagascar and now used as a troopship. This was to take them to Alexandria. But their troopship arrived at Gibraltar with her stern blown off by a torpedo. The ladies settled down for another wait.

British gallantry was put to the test and met it like the Scots Greys at Waterloo, or the Light Brigade at Balaklava. Making their quarters on the torpedoed troopship while she was being repaired, the ladies spent ten days being squired around and smothered with attentions and acquiring information on the fortifications of Gibraltar that would have made their fortunes in any Axis country. Military security melted away before them like

wax. Whatever they expressed a desire to see, they saw. If the
sentiments of the garrison could have been expressed without
hindrance, the seven wandering wives would have had a salute of
a hundred and one guns when their patched-up ship pulled out
for Alexandria, with Gertrude McConnell's steamer trunk of
silverware battered but intact in her hold.

Alexandria did not hold them. Trailing a taxi-load of suitcases
and the albatross-like trunk, they took the train to Cairo. And
Cairo was practically home. It had the proper smells, the proper
snarling uproar of camels, donkeys, and automobile horns, the
proper Arabic signs and dress and the sound of the Arabic tongue.
Most important, in Cairo there was an Aramco office. From here
on they were in company hands.

The company's hands turned out to belong to Willie Jones, he
who had helped Floyd Ohliger engineer the Christmas greetings
from home. The seven put themselves helplessly at his disposal.
Gertrude McConnell's trunk was in bond again. They settled in
Shepheard's Hotel, and sat on the terrace having a cool drink and
watching the incomparable traffic of Cairo howl and catapult and
lope past, and waited for Willie Jones to find them transportation
to Dhahran. That was not easy for Willie to do. At one time he
had had as many as 200 prospective construction men bound for
the Ras Tanura project stacked up on his Cairo doorstep waiting,
sometimes for weeks, for that same thing.

Fortunately, in deference to the company's importance for the
prosecution of the Pacific war, Floyd Ohliger had been able to
squeeze out of the United States government the rental of a C-47
from the U.S. Air Force for essential company business. This plane,
though subject to military orders and even to diversion to other
purposes in emergencies, could be used to transport essential
personnel and supplies between Cairo and Dhahran or Bahrain.
The military authorities on the scene, with lamentable myopia,
decided that the seven ladies were not essential; but, since the
aircraft was going to Dhahran anyhow, and didn't have a full load,

Willie Jones persuaded the brass that no great harm would result if the girls went along, trunk and all.

And now Gertrude McConnell, after dragging her trunkful of silver by train and freighter and train and converted yacht and troopship and train again from California to the shadow of the sphinx, was brought by it to a difficult moral choice, what social psychologists call a crisis situation involving conflicting value systems. At the last moment there showed up a young Aramco employee hitching his way out to Dhahran, one of the influx scheduled to build up the Ras Tanura refinery and win the war. He had applied for passage and found that the C-47 was loaded to its very limit, but that there was a trunk. He came politely to Gertrude McConnell to ask if she would mind dumping the trunk to make room for him.

She looked at him and breathed deeply and weighed his importance to the war effort against all the trouble she had been to about that trunk through more than two months of very erratic travel, and she pondered all that could happen to it, stored in Cairo while it waited for another chance that might never come, and thought of the months that might elapse before she could set her table in Dhahran with the things she had wanted there. Then she looked at the young man, who was polite and anxious, and took a deep breath and said no. Not for Eden, not for Churchill, not for the President of the United States. She was sorry, but that was the way she felt.

They emplaned, the motors whirred and caught, the plane shuddered through its warming-up and the bumps of taxiing down the strip. They fastened their belts and took off into the pale sky and saw Cairo fall away beneath them, and the palm-fringed river, and the desert pale and splotched with shadows. In an hour they crossed Suez, a thin inked line seen between puffs of cloud, and after a while, away up northward, they saw stretching away the fantastic canyons of the Sinai Desert half-filled with sand, cliffs, and mesas and sheer surrealist rims reaching backward into the haze. In another hour or two they would be in Basra, in a few hours more in Bahrain. And then home.

At about that time word dribbled back from the crew's compartment in the nose that they had military orders to stop at Abadan and pick up passengers. The ladies looked at one another and there was sympathy in every face and defeat in Gertie McConnell's. There went the trunk. There, maybe, went some or all of themselves.

But there was only one passenger at Abadan, and when she saw who it was, Dorothy Ohliger screeched and could hardly get off fast enough. It was Floyd Ohliger, as startled as they were. The last word he had had was that the seven were somewhere in Spain or Portugal, safe, but hardly imminent. Of all the passengers they might have been asked to pick up in Abadan, there was none more likely to show sympathy with Mrs. McConnell's trunk problem. He got both it and himself aboard; they thought it best not to inquire too closely how. They were too anxious to get home to question anything; they had been out since the day after Thanksgiving, and it was now nearly St. Valentine's Day.

In Dhahran, when the word came through that they were coming, work utterly stopped. The radio said they would arrive around four o'clock. The men had oiled the landing strip a day or two before, in general and hopeful preparation, and there was nothing to do down at the airfield, but by lunchtime on arrival day Cal Ross and Bill Scribner were both down there, wearing neckties. A little later Phil McConnell and Bill Eltiste showed up. Eltiste, slouching along the strip and ruminating problems, suggested that they ought to make some preparations for a night landing in case there was any delay. It was his particular genius to foresee and forestall problems, or solve them when they arose. So he got together a batch of five-gallon oil tins and a barrel of mixed kerosene and crude oil, rigged each tin with a wick, and had the boys outline the landing strip with them. By that time it was nearly four o'clock, and the whole camp was down there.

Then delays — word from here and there, rumors, explanations. Four o'clock passed, and five, and no plane. Six o'clock, and it began to grow dusky. They lighted the flares and outlined the strip with smoky, flickering red. Still no plane, no sound of motors, no wing lights in the pure cooling sky over the Bahrain channel. The stars began to appear, and here and there men had hallucinations, seeing what they hoped to see: "There she is! There she comes!" But it was always Canopus, or Arcturus, or Polaris, or Deneb, or the rainy Hyades.

Darkness, and still they didn't come. And then finally the plane was coming in truth, they all heard her at once, and saw her lights sure, and no star. She circled the flare-marked field, went away and came back, turned and headed in. The moment she hit the runway the pilot slammed on his brakes and all but stood her on her nose. She skidded, and shuddered, and swung sideways, and finally stopped.

Later, when the first clamor of welcome had subsided, they found out the cause of that abrupt landing. The pilot, who had never seen the field, had been all for stopping in Bahrain. He had no wish to set down a plane as big as a C-47 on an unmarked, unlighted airstrip with no control tower or ground-to-air communications. The ladies pleaded with him. Ohliger was sure he could guide him in. Esta Eltiste was positive that the boys — meaning Bill — would have made some sort of preparations for an after-dark landing. The pilot yielded, but he was skeptical until the last second. As soon as his wheels touched the oil he hit the brakes, afraid he would run her off into the Gulf or into the side of a *jabal* or flip her in deep sand.

But all he did run into was the lonesomest and happiest crowd of men in the Middle East. And with the marks of his skidding wheels he drew a line between the Time of the Hundred Men, as Phil McConnell had called it, and the later time, nameless, busier, more crowded, and less worth a man's devotion. Within a few months another plane brought Muriel Davis, Anita Burleigh,

Virginia Hattrup, Leda Mair, and some others, who had experienced their own odyssey and who had been hung up a long time in Casablanca. And within a few months construction was going full blast, the place was swamped with newcomers who knew nothing about Arabia and (old-timers thought) cared less. The solidarity of the Hundred was broken, the Animal Farm was gone, Sewage Acres was a memory, married were separated from single, the golden age of bunkhouse solidarity was gone by.

Though they didn't know it yet, the best time of many lives was over. The pioneer time of exploration and excitement and newness and adventure was already giving way to the time of full production, mighty growth, great profits, great world importance, enormous responsibilities, and the growth of corporate as distinguished from personal relations. Many of their greatest accomplishments were still ahead of them, and the American involvement in Middle Eastern economic, cultural, and political life that Lloyd Hamilton had begun at Jiddah in 1933 would grow deeper, more complicated, and more sobering. Not inconceivably, the thing they all thought of as "progress" and "development" would blow them all up, and their world with it. But that is another story. This one is purely and simply the story of a frontier, and the return of the seven war-exiled wives to Dhahran's makeshift airstrip in February 1945 is as good a date as any to mark its passing.

The End

Glossary

Aba (abaya) - The black overgarment worn by Saudi women.

Agaal - The woven head rope that holds the *ghutra* or head scarf in place.

'Ain - A well or spring of palatable water.

Amir (emir) - A prince or a leader of a tribe, city, or group.

Barasti - A building made of woven palm fronds.

Bisht - A woven wool cloak worn over the *thaub*.

Bismallah - "In the name of God."

Dabb - A large, desert lizard. Its tail is considered to be a delicacy.

Dahl - A cave or limestone sinkhole ranging in size from a narrow tunnel to a cavern.

Dhalul - A racing camel.

Dibdiba - A flat, gravel plain.

Dikaka - Sand plains covered with knee-high hillocks that drift behind woody shrubs.

Ghurba - A water bag made from a goat hide.

Ghutra - The head scarf held in place by an *agaal*.

Gufiya - A skullcap worn by males.

Faroush - Slabs of coral used for construction material on both coasts of Arabia.

Jabal - A hill or promontory.

Jalbout - A fast, open-hulled sailing sloop.

Khuwiya - Bedouin soldiers, often the armed retinue of a specific amir.

Majlis - An official reception room for visitors.

Mubty - Ancient.

Muhendis - An engineer or mechanic.

Mukhtal - Crazy. In the Al-Murrah dialect it means "hungry."

Mukur - A generic term for a well.

Qadi - The judge of an Islamic court.

Qahwa - Coffee.

Rababah - A Bedouin one-stringed instrument with a rectangular sound box. Often homemade.

Ra'is al-baladiyah - The boss of the city, i.e. the mayor.

Sabkha - A salt flat covered with a crust of dried mud.

Shamal - An annual sand storm caused by north winds in the late spring.

Suq - A bazaar or marketplace.

Taht - Under, or the command to drop something.

Thaub (thobe) - The white cotton robe worn by males.

Wadi - A valley, usually a large dry watercourse.

Wudayhi - The oryx, an antelope with straight, tapering horns. The *wudayhi* can weigh up to 200 pounds.

Bibliography

Ajami, Fouad. *The Arab Predicament: Arab Political Thought and Practice Since 1967*. Cambridge, U.K.: Cambridge University Press, 1981.

Antonius, George. *The Arab Awakening*. New York: Lippincott, 1939.

Armstrong, H. C. *Lord of Arabia*. Beirut: Khayyat, 1954.

Atiyah, Edward. *The Arabs*. New York: Pelican Books, 1955. Various editions.

Barger, Thomas C. *Out in the Blue: Letters from Arabia 1937-1940*. Vista, CA: Selwa Press, 2000.

Belgrave, Sir Charles D. *Personal Column*. London: Hutchinson, 1960.

Berle, Adolf A., Jr. *The Twentieth Century Capitalist Revolution*. New York: Harcourt, Brace and Company, 1954.

Brockelmann, Carl. *History of the Islamic Peoples*. New York: Putnam's, 1947.

Bronson, Rachel. *Thicker than Oil: America's Uneasy Partnership with Saudi Arabia*. New York: Oxford University Press, 2006.

Brown, Anthony Cave. *Oil, God and Gold: The Story of Aramco and the Saudi Kings*. Boston: Houghton Mifflin, 1999.

Bullard, Sir Reader. *The Camels Must Go*. London: Faber and Faber, 1961.

Burton, Sir Richard F. *Personal Narrative of a Pilgrimage to Al-Madinah and Meccah*. London: Bell, 1898, and other editions.

Cheesman, R. E. *In Unknown Arabia*. London: Macmillan, 1926.

Cheyney, Michael Sheldon. *Big Oil Man from Arabia*. New York: Ballantine Books, 1958.

De Gaury, Gerald. *Arabia Phoenix*. London: Harrap, 1946.

Dickson, H.R.P. *Kuwait and Her Neighbors*. London: Allen & Unwin, 1949.

...... *The Arab of the Desert*. London: Hodder and Stoughton, 1957.

Dickson, Violet. *Wild Flowers of Kuwait and Bahrain*. London: Allen & Unwin, 1955.

Doughty, C. M. *Travels in Arabia Deserta*. 2 vols. London, 1921. New York: Random House, 1946.

Eddy, William A. *F.D.R. Meets Ibn Saud*. New York: American Friends of the Middle East, 1954.

Facey, William. *The Story of the Eastern Province of Saudi Arabia*. London: Stacey International,1994.

Glubb, Sir John Bagot. *A Soldier with the Arabs*. London: Hodder and Stoughton, 1957.

Hart, Parker T. *Saudi Arabia and the United States*. Bloomington, IN: Indiana University Press, 1998.

Hitti, P. K. *The Arabs, a Short History*. Princeton, NJ: Princeton University Press, 1949.

..... *History of the Arabs*. 10th edition. Boston, 1970.

Hogarth, D. G. *The Penetration of Arabia*. New York: F. A. Stokes, 1904.

Howarth, David. *The Desert King*. London: Collins, 1964.

Ibn Khaldun. *The Maqaddimah: An Introduction to History*. New York, 1958.

Kaplan, Robert D. *The Arabists*. New York: Simon & Schuster, 1993.

Kelly, J. B. *Arabia, the Gulf and the West*. London: Weidenfeld & Nicolson, 1980.

Lacey, Robert. *The Kingdom*. New York: Harcourt Brace, 1982.

Lawrence, T. E. *Seven Pillars of Wisdom*. Garden City: Doubleday, 1935.

...... *Revolt in the Desert*. London: J. Murray, 1957.

Lippman, Thomas W. *Understanding Islam: An Introduction to the Muslim World*, 3rd ed. New York: Plume, 2002.

...... *Inside The Mirage: America's Fragile Partnership with Saudi Arabia*, Boulder, CO: Westview Press, 2004.

Long, David E. *The Kingdom of Saudi Arabia*. Gainsville, FL: University Press of Florida, 1997.

Longhurst, Henry. *Adventure in Oil: The Story of British Petroleum*. London: Sidgwick and Jackson, 1959.

Longrigg, Stephen Hemsley. *Oil in the Middle East: Its Discovery and Development*, 3rd. ed. New York: Oxford University Press, 1968.

Longhurst, Henry. *Adventure in Oil: The Story of British Petroleum*. London: Sidgwick and Jackson, 1959.

McConnell, Philip C. *The Hundred Men*. Petersborough, NH: Currier Press, 1985.

Meinertzhagen, Richard. *The Birds of Arabia*. Edinburgh: Oliver & Boyd, 1954.

Meulen, D. van der. *Aden to the Hadramaut, a Journey in South Arabia*. London: Murray, 1947.

. . . . . . *The Wells of Ibn Saud*. London: J. Murray, 1957.

Mountfort, Guy. *Portrait of a Desert*. London: Collins, 1965.

Musil, Alois. *The Northern Hejaz*. New York: American Geographical Society, 1926.

. . . . . . *Arabia Deserta*. New York: American Geographical Society, 1927.

. . . . . . *In the Arabian Desert*. Ed. K. M. Wright. New York: Liveright, 1930.

Nance, Paul. *The Nance Museum*. Lone Jack, MO: Nance Museum, 1999.

Nawab, Ismail I., Peter C. Speers and Paul F. Hoye, (eds.) *Saudi Aramco and Its World*. Houston: Aramco Services Company, 1995.

Philby, H. St. John B. *The Heart of Arabia*. London: Constable, 1922.

. . . . . . *Arabia of the Wahhabis*. London: Constable, 1928.

. . . . . . *The Empty Quarter*. New York: Henry Holt, 1933.

. . . . . . *Arabian Days*. London: Robert Hale, 1948.

. . . . . . *Arabian Jubilee*. London: Robert Hale, 1952.

. . . . . . *Forty Years in the Wilderness*. London: Benn, 1957.

St. Augustine. *The City of God*. Cambridge Texts in the History of Political Thought. Translated by Robert Dyson, edited by Raymond Geuss and Quentin Skinner. Cambridge: Cambridge University Press, 1998.

Sander, Nestor. *Ibn Saud: King by Conquest*. Tuscon, AZ: Hats Off Books, 2001.

Schwadran, Benjamin. *The Middle East, Oil, and the Great Powers*. New York: Praeger, 1955.

Stegner, Wallace. *Big Rock Candy Mountain*. New York: Duell, Sloan and Pearce,1943.

. . . . . . *Angle of Repose*. New York: Doubleday, 1971.

. . . . . . *Crossing to Safety*. New York: Random House, 1987.

Thesiger, Wilfred. *Arabian Sands*. New York: Dutton, 1959.

. . . . . . *The Last Nomad*. New York: Dutton, 1980.

Thomas, Bertram. *Alarms and Excursions in Arabia*. New York: Bobbs-Merrill, 1931.

. . . . . . *Arabia Felix*. New York: Scribner's, 1932.

. . . . . . *The Arabs*. London: Butterworth, 1937.

Twitchell, K. S. *Saudi Arabia*. 3rd ed. Princeton, N.J.: Princeton University Press, 1958.

Van Der Meulen, D. *Aden to the Hadramaut, a Journey in South Arabia*. London: Murray, 1947.

. . . . . . *The Wells of Ibn Saud*. London: J. Murray, 1957.

Vidal, F. S. *The Oasis of al-Hasa*. Dhahran: Arabian American Oil Company, 1955.

Wahba, Hafiz. *Arabian Days*. London: Arthur Barker, 1964.

Williams, Kenneth. *Ibn Sa'ud*. London: Cape, 1933.

Wilson, Sir Arnold T. *The Persian Gulf*. London: George Allen and Unwin, 1928.

Winder, R. Bayly. *Saudi Arabia in the Nineteenth Century*. New York: St. Martin's Press, 1965.

Winnet, F. V., and Reed, W. L. *Ancient Records from North Arabia*. Toronto: University of Toronto Press, 1970.

Yergin, Daniel. *The Prize: The Epic Quest for Oil, Money and Power*. New York: Simon & Schuster, 1991.

Index

Index

Acknowledgments

Photographs courtesy of:
> The T.C. Barger Collection
> Chevron Corporate Archives
> The Felix Dreyfus Collection
> The Steve Furman Collection
> Saudi Aramco World/Padia
> The Les Snyder Collection
> The Stegner Collection, J. Willard Marriott Library,
>> University of Utah

Front cover:
> Oil Well - Saudi Aramco World/Padia
> Field Party - T.C. Barger Collection
> Background Element - Saudi Aramco World/Herring Design

Back cover:
> T.C. Barger Collection

Front flap:
> Man on Camel, photo by J. W. "Soak" Hoover,
> Saudi Aramco World/Padia

Back flap:
> Photo of Wallace Stegner by Chuck Painter,
> Stanford News Service

Cartographic design:
> Bodie Shaw

Copy editing and proofreading:
> Carolyn Fox, Proof or Consequences

Cover design:
> Ellen Goodwin Graphics

Editorial coordinator:
> Karla Olson, BookStudio

Endpaper maps:
> Courtesy of the American Map Company

In Appreciation

Our special gratitude to Steve Furman, Miles Snyder, and the late Tom Dreyfus for preserving and contributing the photographs taken by their fathers.

Felix Dreyfus, one of the first dozen Americans to land in Jubail, captured many priceless moments from a distant era. His rare photographs will not soon be forgotten, nor will Tom's generosity in sharing them.

Colophon

Printed in 13 point Fournier type. This light, clean-looking font is based upon "St. Augustin Ordinaire," designed by Pierre Simon Fournier in 1742. Nearly two hundred years later in 1924, the Monotype company distilled this font into modern Fournier. Colonel H. R. P. Dickson employed this same typeface in his classic work on traditional Bedouin life, *The Arab of the Desert*, published in 1949.

Study Guide

For classroom and book club discussion groups, a study guide about life in early Saudi Arabia, Wallace Stegner and *Discovery!* is available as a freely downloadable PDF document at *www.SelwaPress.com/Discovery Guide.htm.*

Rare movies depicting the people, places and events mentioned in this book are displayed at *www.SelwaVideo.com.*

For students and groups interested in purchasing multiple copies of *Discovery!*, IPG (Independent Publishers Group) offers an educator's discount at *www.ipgbook.com.*